CW00971746

BORN IN A SMALL TOWN JOHN MELLENCAMP

THE STORY by HEATHER JOHNSON

OMNIBUS PRESS
LONDON · NEW YORK · SYDNEY

Omnibus Press
A Division of Music Sales Corporation, New York

Every effort has been made to trace the copyright holders of the photographs
in this book but one or two were unreachable. We would be grateful
if the photographers concerned would contact us.

Exclusive Distributors:
Music Sales Corporation
257 Park Avenue South, New York, NY 10010 USA
Music Sales Limited
14 - 15 Berners Street, London W1T 3LJ England
Music Sales Pty. Limited
120 Rothschild Street, Rosebery, Sydney, NSW 2018, Australia

Order No. OP51403
International Standard Book Number: 978.0.8256.7336.8

Printed in the United States of America

Visit Omnibus Press on the web at www.omnibuspress.com

Library of Congress Cataloging-in-Publication Data

Johnson, Heather, 1971-
 Born in a small town: the John Mellencamp story / by Heather Johnson.
    p. cm.
 ISBN 978-0-8256-7336-8 (hardcover : alk. paper)
1. Mellencamp, John, 1951- 2. Rock musicians--United States--Biography. I. Title. II. Title: John
Mellencamp story.

ML420.M357J64 2006
782.42166092--dc22
 [B]
                                    2007005088

TABLE OF CONTENTS

INTRODUCTION V

CHAPTER ONE
YOU'RE A MELLENCAMP: YOU TRY HARDER 1

CHAPTER TWO
THAT'S WHAT AH SAID—A MELLENCAMP RESCUED BY
    BUNNY BREAD 15

CHAPTER THREE
I NEED A DRUMMER WHO WON'T DRIVE ME CRAZY 33

CHAPTER FOUR
NOTHIN' MATTERS TO AN AMERICAN FOOL 43

CHAPTER FIVE
FIRST IMPRESSION SESSIONS 61

CHAPTER SIX
WOODEN CROSSES, LONELY NIGHTS 77

CHAPTER SEVEN
WHO'S YOUR BIG DADDY NOW 97

CHAPTER EIGHT
WHATEVER, WHENEVER .111

CHAPTER NINE
HAPPY LITTLE BASTARD 131

CHAPTER TEN
MERCURY BLUES 141

CHAPTER ELEVEN
VISION AND CONNECTION 153

CHAPTER TWELVE
SAYING GOODBYE 167

CHAPTER THIRTEEN
THE CAMPAIGN TRAIL TOWARD FREEDOM'S ROAD 175

SELECTED DISCOGRAPHY 187

BIBLIOGRAPHY 193

ACKNOWLEDGEMENTS 199

ABOUT THE AUTHOR 201

INDEX 203

INTRODUCTION

R ichard and Marilyn Mellencamp rose before dawn one warm Sunday morning in September 2003. They put on nice, comfortable clothes—not the usual stiff suits and toe-pinching heels that one normally endures this day of the week. Today, they could wear tennis shoes if they really wanted to, because instead of attending Sunday service, they were going on a road trip.

Marilyn smoothed her hair and checked her lipstick in the mirror one last time before she and Richard got in their car, pulled out of the driveway of their large white house with black shutters and settled in for a three-and-a-half-hour drive from Seymour, Indiana, to Columbus, Ohio. They had tickets and VIP backstage passes to see their son play the 16th annual Farm Aid concert at Germain Amphitheater that night, and he invited them to be his special guests. The concert had sold out in two weeks and was being taped for PBS and an eventual DVD release. With minimal pit stops, they arrived at the venue, parked the car and made their way to their seats up close to the stage. The sun had set and acts such as Sheryl Crow, Hootie & the Blowfish and Los Lonely Boys had already played by the time their son, John Mellencamp, took the stage with his band. The lights beamed hot white and blue as they assumed their positions around the frontman. The crowd roared. Richard and Marilyn Mellencamp must have puffed up with pride as they watched their middle son launch into his near-flawless performance. It didn't seem that long ago that he was playing at an old geezer bar in Seymour, barely out of high school, with a wife and young child. They kept wondering when he'd pack it in and get a real job, but he never did and it sure worked out well for him. John started to play a new song he had worked up with the band, "Stones in My Passway," but before guitarist Andy York uttered the first note on the slide guitar, the mood shifted from sunny enthusiasm to stormy anger and protest. Just moments before walking on stage, John learned that President George W. Bush had just asked Congress for $87 billion for the war in Iraq. John relayed this fact to the 20,000 people in the audience. "Think about what that money could do for the family farmer," he continued. Thousands of people booed and yelled back at the artist. A few brave souls cheered. Richard and Marilyn Mellencamp were stunned by what they saw and heard. Their son had helped found the organization that brought them this concert in the first place, and many of them owned his records. And now they want to boo him off the stage? They had seen their son perform hundreds of times, but never had they heard such jeers.

For John and his longtime guitarist/co-producer Mike Wanchic, this was nothing. They both developed a pretty thick skin over the past 25-plus years, so a few hecklers wouldn't ruin their day. They had dodged whiskey bottles, spit bombs and any number of flying objects from their audience. They had played in dive bars to no one but the bartender. Their friends, family and people in the music industry repeatedly told them that they would not make it, they were not good enough and their records were terrible. Even John agrees that, yes, some of them were terrible. John wasn't a good songwriter when he launched his career in the mid-'70s, and his bandmates weren't very good musicians. Heck, it took them three albums before they learned key changes!

After years of criticism and costly mistakes, a weaker man would have either given up or continued a mediocre career singing cover songs in bars. But weakness and surrender are not part of the Mellencamp vocabulary, and they don't settle for mediocrity. The Mellencamps do not give up; they fight, both physically and mentally. John Mellencamp had big dreams that seemed impossible to almost everyone at first, even himself. But over time, he inched his way closer to those goals. His songs got better. His band got better. They shut out the negative voices of the record labels, the record producers, the press and everyone else around them. They ignored whatever trends dictated popular music at the time, and they pressed on. By staying true to himself, John Mellencamp created his own genre, culled from the sights, sounds and the people that lived in his own back yard. What he heard in his head evolved over time, from the raw, in-your-face garage rock with singable choruses, to acoustic-based Americana with a conscience, to a melding of the two with loops and samples. An old saying goes, "when you get mad enough to swear, it's time to invent something." John Mellencamp swears liberally; likewise, he's invented and re-invented himself many times.

The only voice John listened to was his own, and he held steadfast to that vision no matter how many times life side-swiped him with obstacles. He sets high expectations for himself and those who work for him, and the hard work and bullheadedness he logged in through the years resulted in a recording career that has sustained over three decades—about three decades longer than most people thought he would last.

One lesser recognized reason that John Mellencamp has excelled in creating what he calls "R&B-flavored folk music with a rock beat"—music that's not necessarily hip to like but usually quite likeable nonetheless—stems from the small assemblage of musicians that have backed him through the years. Because just as John has had to remain fully committed to his vision, his bandmates had to commit themselves just as thoroughly to that vision. To lose focus was to face the wrath of a five-foot-seven taskmaster who doesn't generally censor his words. Early on, a group consisting of Mike Wanchic, Larry Crane, Toby Myers and Kenny Aronoff set a goal in their minds to be the America's best band, and particularly during the peak years of *Scarecrow* and *The Lonesome Jubilee,* they hit the mark. These supporting roles in John's personal drama have changed hands through the years, but all have played pivotal parts in his success. The chapters that follow tell his band's story as much as John Mellencamp's. And after 56 years, that tale contains elements of dark comedy, tragedy, drama and suspense, with enough ups and downs to cause motion sickness in those weak in the knees. But then again, the weak don't last long in John Mellencamp's circle. Only the strong survive.

CHAPTER ONE

YOU'RE A MELLENCAMP:

YOU TRY HARDER

It was around 10 P.M. one Saturday night in Seymour, Indiana, circa 1957. Marilyn Mellencamp had long put her boys, Ted, John and Joe, and two girls, Laura and Janet, to bed. The restless six-year-old middle son stayed awake some nights listening to the thwack-thwack coming from the other room. Richard and four of his friends carried on like the kids they still were, laughing, talking and listening to old blues records during their regular bongo parties. At only 26 years old, Richard was finishing a four-year stint at electrical school, supporting a wife and kids and throwing some wicked parties. He and his friends listened to everything from Odetta to Julie London, the muffled tones migrating through walls to John's bedroom. When his parents weren't around, John would stare at the album covers; mainly, at London's breasts.

Considering his propensity for skirt chasing later in life, it's fitting that John's earliest musical memories would involve ogling the female form. But at this young age, football, antagonizing his school-age neighbors and beating up on his siblings interested him more. And really, in a town such as Seymour, there really wasn't much else to do. The nearest big town, Bloomington, was more than an hour away and his own small community's populace led generally conservative lives book-ended with church on Sunday, back to work on Monday, grill out in the back yard if it's nice out. The Mellencamps abided by one of the strictest organized religions—the Nazarene Church, a requirement enforced by John's devout grandmother, Laura. Every Sunday, the Mellencamps attended First Church of the Nazarene's 8:15 A.M. service, and sometimes the 6 P.M. service, too. This

"Right Wing of the Holiness Movement," as one historian calls this extreme group, traditionally required women to wear dresses only, with their long, unstyled hair tied up in a bun on top of their head. No shorts or slacks, jewelry, cosmetics or make-up were allowed for women, and no short sleeves, wrist watches or wedding rings for the men: only pressed, white shirts and slacks. The fundamentalist church forbade the use of alcohol, tobacco, social dancing, movies and card playing. As much as he loved his grandma (she spoiled him rotten), he hated going to church. But if the kids didn't go, they got beat. So every Sunday, he begrudgingly spent his Sundays at the holy address of 311 Myer Street, until he was old enough at 13 to say, "I ain't going to church or staying home and cutting the grass," he recalled. As much as he rejected the church's strict rules, its repeated inferences of sin still managed to seep its way into his young consciousness.

Situated along Interstate 65 and three state highways in south central Indiana, the Seymour that John knew as a kid had all the antique shops and country stores an old person could want and enough bars to keep them sedated, but not much to appeal to the youngsters. The Muscatatuck Natural Wildlife Refuge, Jackson/Washington State Forest and Starve Hollow State Recreational Area all reside within 15 minutes of the city center, and about 40 minutes in a car will get you to the Lake Monroe area. Youth sports included soccer, baseball and softball (if your parents signed you up for a league), but beyond that, the kids pretty much had to fend for themselves. This could mean anything from traipsing through the woods to pick-up games in the back yard, or, well, mischief on a multitude of levels.

When he was only four years old, the Seymour High School football team named John Mellencamp their mascot. He started showing up when the big kids practiced. Soon, he got up the nerve to join them when they ran 40-yard wind sprints at the beginning of practice. Then he showed up wearing a football jersey, knee-length pants and a helmet, just like the big kids. Brazen since birth, he probably didn't even realize that he was some 14 years younger than his "teammates." Over time, the high school kids adopted him as one of the guys.

He didn't want to lose his esteemed position with those tough football players by mouthing off to them, so he directed his attacks toward kids his own age. He wasn't even old enough for kindergarten, but would throw rocks at the 11- and 12-year-old neighbors as they rushed to the school bus. Gary Boebinger, who later befriended their mean-spirited neighbor, has said it was like entering combat every Monday through Friday.

When he started school himself, he turned his little boy rage toward the crossing guard, whom he frequently whacked in the knees with sticks; the teachers who scolded him for such behavior; and his classmates, whom he'd either antagonize or rile up by saying those strongly forbidden four-letter words. "John used to beat up on all the kids when he started grade school," his father, Richard Mellencamp told *Performing Songwriter*. "He was bigger than most of the kids. Then one year, all of the other kids grew and John didn't— only his *mouth* never stopped growing."

Richard heard about John's antics, as well as the activities of his other four kids, but wasn't around much to do anything about it. After finishing his four-year stint at electrical school, he took an entry-level job at Robbins Electric. He worked double shifts six or seven days a week as he worked his way up the company ladder, and didn't slow down as the company promoted him to department supervisor, then moved him into the office to work as an estimator. Over time, he reached one of the top rungs as an executive VP and member of the company's board of directors. In his upper management role, he supervised projects ranging from a large nuclear power plant to the Louisiana Superdome. He missed much of his children's upbringing though, and left a harried Marilyn to raise five ornery kids by herself.

Richard Mellencamp's tenacity runs so thickly in his blood, he almost had no choice but to succeed. His father, Harry Perry Mellencamp (aka "Speck") grew up among five siblings (two brothers, three sisters) in Jackson County, Indiana, and became a working-class citizen before he reached the third grade. Speck's father, Johann Herman Louis Mollenkamp—anglicized as John Henry Mellencamp—died in 1916 of a gall bladder attack. The family didn't have the money for the operation he needed and John Henry's pride wouldn't let him borrow it, so they had to let him die. Speck quit school in the third grade and went to work as a cabinetmaker and carpenter. When John Henry died, the 120 acres of corn and wheat fields he owned and farmed for a living were divided among his survivors, but the tragedy of his death left most of the family embittered and impoverished, so most of them sought other vocations.

In 1924, "Speck" married Laura Noblitt, another Indiana native, and the two of them moved to a home in Seymour. John may have gotten some of his musical inclinations from the Noblitt clan. Laura's brothers and sisters played banjos, violins, guitars, harmonica or the family pump organ while their Dad kept time by playing the cow bones (two ribs, polished, balanced between one's fingers and swung side to side to produce a fast clicking sound). He taught Laura traditional folk songs when she was about eight years old, and she often sang them while her family played behind her. She would sing one of these songs, "The Baggage Coach," with her grandson several decades later.

During the Depression, Speck needed work so badly that he broke down and worked as a farmhand on Seymour's rich soil and hunted mink and raccoons for hides. Despite his best efforts, he and Laura lost their house. Times were tough, but no matter how lean the bank account or desperate the situation, he refused to accept charity of any sort. He refused to borrow money, from friends, family, or the government. By the time the Depression lifted, he and Laura had six children to raise—four boys (James, Jerry, Joe and Richard) and two girls (Toots and Mary). A drunk driver killed their first son, 15-year-old James Archie, when he ran into the child as he was riding his bicycle down Highway 31. The family struggled until the late 1940s, when Speck saw an excellent opportunity to put his carpentry skills to use. World War II's conclusion led to a period of prosperity in the U.S. and Canada that spawned both a baby boom and a building boom. Speck took note of the need for more housing for returning troops and aimed to fill the void by founding the Harry P. Mellencamp Building & Construction Company. His new enterprise built—with the help of Richard, Jerry and Joe, of course—roughly 40 houses for troops returning from World War II. Finally, he could provide well for his family.

The large Mellencamp family was a close-knit bunch—collectively independent, proud and physical. Speck was known to express anger with his fists—no talking over feelings for this guy—and his kids picked up that trait in varying degrees. Joe would earn a reputation as a formidable boxer and star running back at Seymour High and Indiana State University, then go on to start his own concrete company. Richard had a competitive streak, and Toots was the tomboy. Collectively, they developed a reputation as a rough bunch with a bad attitude, and the other townspeople kept their distance.

In fact, the first time Richard Mellencamp laid eyes on a stunning brunette named Marilyn Joyce Lowe, he and brother Joe had just gotten into a fight, but were pulled apart under a police car's flashing blue lights. The cops hauled Joe Mellencamp to jail, but Richard managed to sweet-talk himself out of the situation, which allowed him some precious few minutes to flirt with Marilyn Lowe. At the time, she was recently divorced from a six-month marriage to her high school sweetheart and had a young son; coincidentally, also named Joe. Richard had every reason to fall for Lowe. Her brains, poise and beauty had earned her a crown at the Scott County Fair in the mid-'40s and a runner-up slot in the 1946 Miss Indiana pageant.

In some ways, Lowe was a big-town girl trapped in a small town life. When she left town to attend the School of Elementary Education at Indiana University, she didn't tell anyone she was from tiny Austin, Indiana and she sure didn't talk about her family. Her father, Joe Lowe, owned and operated a combination restaurant/poolroom/gambling parlor and speakeasy in Austin, and had a reputation as something of a conman. He fared quite well at his chosen profession, however, and his daughter Marilyn Lowe grew up with a strong desire for exquisite things and a need to keep up a high society image. When she met then-20-year-old Richard Mellencamp, he certainly wasn't rich or successful, but she fell for his ambition, honesty and intelligence and knew he would make a wonderful provider for the son she already had and the family they would have together. They married within six months.

Turns out Marilyn's instincts served her well, as the succession of promotions at Robbins Electric naturally led to a higher salary for Richard Mellencamp. For the first time probably ever, he didn't have to worry about money and he could give his family a comfortable life. He once decided to buy a new car—a Cadillac, the best of the best. When he pulled into the Cadillac dealership in nearby Vincennes, the salesman turned up his nose, stating, "You can't afford one of these cars." As his son, Ted Mellencamp, recalled in John's 1986 biography, "I guess their attitude was, hell, the Mellencamps are just a bunch of poor people from outside Woodstock, the poor part of town." Richard Mellencamp ultimately bought two Cadillacs—in Indianapolis.

The locals snubbed him again when he began hunting for a home larger than their brick house on West Fifth Street in Seymour. He and Marilyn found a place that would suit their needs, but the bank wouldn't let them bid on it; again, making assumptions based on family history. Richard Mellencamp's tenacity kicked in. He'd show them, he figured, and bought the biggest house in town at the time—a large, white two-story with a circular drive and several acres of land in nearby Rockford. It needed work, but he proved his point: You didn't have to like the Mellencamps, but you had to respect them.

The Mellencamp's Indiana lineage dates back to 1851 when Johann Heinrich Mollenkamp, who worked as a plowman, and wife Anna Marie migrated from Hamburg, Germany to settlements in southern Indiana. Along the way, they stopped in Philadelphia while Anna Marie delivered their first child, Mary. The aforementioned Johann Herman (John Henry) was born in 1855. The family's rough-hewn, independent streak came through in both father and son. Dad sought adventure by traveling to the New World and continuing his work in the fields, and the son spent his adult life as organizer of the White Creek Lutheran Church in Hamilton Township, later married Carrie Mackey and raised his six-child family. Two more generations would take on their tough exterior, up through the John Mellencamp that we know, born October 7, 1951, and his extended family.

John had yet to reach puberty when his family moved from their modest Seymour home to their spacious Rockford "estate." By this time, John and his energetic brothers had gotten into plenty of trouble for such rowdy activities as throwing walnuts at windows, which eventually earned them a visit to the police station.

In their new locale, however, Richard Mellencamp worked them too hard for them to cause trouble. After school and on weekends, the trio sanded walls, hauled lumber and worked in the yard. If friends came over, Richard put them to work, too. "I always seemed to get invited over when Richard had a project for John, Joe and Ted to do around the house," said Mark Ripley, a friend of John's who lived down the street from the Mellencamps. "I have to give credit to Richard though. He'd say, 'Well if you're here, grab a shovel.' I'd go over there thinking John and I were going to pal around, get in trouble, stir up some meanness. Instead we'd get put on a project! It got to the point where I'd say to John, 'Naw man, I'm not coming over because I know Richard's got something going on.' His thinking was the more hands you had, the quicker the job got done."

Richard Mellencamp kept his child laborers motivated by bringing out their own competitive sides. In between jobs, he'd put them in footraces, chin-up and push-up contests and boxing matches. He wanted his sons to be macho. "He was a jock in high school and he pushed us real hard," John recalled. His motto was "You're a *Mellencamp*. You try harder."

Sometimes, they'd push Richard Mellencamp himself. "You don't speak to the enemy about your doubts and weaknesses," John said in one of his album's liner notes. "So I pushed up against him, found out I couldn't win, got tired of getting my ass kicked and [we] stopped communicating altogether for a good while."

In the summertime, Richard sent the boys to Uncle Joe's for more grunt work at his concrete company. Their 220-pound uncle thought his nephews should toughen up for football season. His version of summer training included pouring concrete, and, in John's case, running with a wheelbarrow full of heavy rocks.

Mark Ripley and John met as members of the football team that John trained so hard for. Tim Elsner, who attended a nearby Catholic School, was on the same team. They didn't like each other as teammates, but warmed up to each other a few years later.

John's interest in sports paralleled his fascination with music. His first record purchase was Chubby Checker's 1960 hit, "The Twist." That inaugural find led to an early fascination with soul music, unusual for a white Midwestern kid. Almost every night after dinner, he lost himself in the music coming through AM radio stations out of Detroit, Chicago and nearby Louisville: Sam and Dave, The Temptations, James Brown, the Four Tops. He picked up the guitar at age 13 after watching a band called the Tikis play surf-guitar music at a local dance. Not only were they high school guys, which was cool enough, but high school *musician* guys. Whoa.

In the seventh grade, he and classmate Sam Abbott performed the song "Abilene" for a student convocation. Abbott played guitar, John sang and another kid played congas. "It was horrible," John recalled, but a step up from taping black magic-marker sideburns onto his cheeks and singing Elvis songs on his front porch (his first "onstage" performance), or watching his older kid neighbor play "Peter Gunn" on his electric guitar, which he did when he was eight or nine years old.

In 1965 at the tender age of 14, he formed his first "real" band, Crepe Soul, with his 17-year-old friend, Fred Booker. Their bandmates consisted of Dennis Blair, Rod Chavez, Steve Fletcher, J. "Art" Johnson and Duane Zimmerman. As one of the few black kids in Seymour, Booker already stood out from the crowd. When he teamed with some skinny white troublemaker to sing James Brown and Wayne Cochran covers, complete with copied dance moves, they became Seymour's musical odd couple. They donned jackets with Nehru collars, tight pants and English riding boots and pretended that they were rock stars. They played frat hops and landed a gig at Uncle Joe's Rok-Sey Roller Rink for $30 a weekend. Their career came to a halt when they played a bar in Salem, Indiana, the unofficial watering hole of the Salem Speedway. A fight broke out on the dance floor between a black and white man, one of them got knifed, and the young house band packed up for home. After a year and a half, John dismantled Crepe Soul. He got tired of the rehearsals (practicing was lame), and their democratic decision-making process didn't work, because ultimately nothing got done. He'd rather go it alone, even if that meant playing on his front porch again.

He fiddled with music through high school, though his guitar became more of a tool to pick up girls than an instrument of study. At 15, he enlisted the Donovan jukebox. He learned a bunch of his songs, and in the summertime, either on his front porch or in the sun at nearby Star Hollow Beach, he would turn on his secret weapon. It took him about two Donovan songs to get a girl into his arms. He then joined a band called Snakepit Banana Barn. They played a few gigs at his brother Joe's frat house before John got kicked out of the band because he couldn't sing. Yes, this band stuff was just too much work.

Back at home, his parents worried about their son, who careened dangerously on the wrong side of the tracks. He grew his hair long, lost his virginity and started smoking all before he was old enough to drive. His fascination with Stax-Volt soul had expanded to include folk, and within a short time, the raw sounds of early rock 'n' roll. He secluded himself in his room listening to, and in some cases, learning to play, Bob Dylan, Woody Guthrie, Donovan, Paul Revere and The Raiders, The Animals, Cream or the West Coast psychedelia that was starting to infiltrate the rest of the U.S. He whiled away the rest of his hours with buddies Mark Ripley and/or Gary Boebinger cruising the streets of Seymour and Bloomington and picking up girls. Like most teenagers, he tried to hide his carousing from his parents, but he really did want them to understand his passion for music. He even told them he wrote the anti-war song "The Universal Soldier," which he had heard

Donovan sing. His parents believed that the long hairs and hippies were "ruining American society," and John thought that if they could just hear how good this music was, they'd change their minds. Of course, Marilyn Mellencamp, believing her son a talented writer, loved "The Universal Soldier." Had she known that one of those folkies wrote it, she might have responded the same way as when John played Dylan's "The Times They Are A-Changin'" for her—a cold, blank stare.

John's times a-changed radically during his junior year of high school. One night, he and his friends snuck out of the house after curfew to crash a party in town. A mix of older kids and teenagers mingled inside and outside of the house, drinking and carrying on as most young adults do. Pricilla Esterline, or 'Cil for short, a pretty young woman with light brown hair and a warm smile, stood chatting with friends, but got distracted by the loud voice of a boisterous guy in another room. She wasn't impressed with John's extroverted behavior, but he sure was cute, which intrigued her enough to strike up conversation. Esterline had the ideal good-girl/bad-girl mix that easily endeared a rebellious young John. His parents didn't like her at all, which made John love her even more. She was three years older, had a job, an apartment and the gumption to join her new boyfriend for a toke, an LSD trip or a ride on his motorcycle. On the other hand, her easygoing nature put John at ease, and he could open up to her in ways he couldn't with other girlfriends. Within two months they became best friends and lovers and she nurtured John in ways that even tough guys crave, though they'll never admit it. "She worked for the phone company, and she'd bring John's lunch to school," recalls Mark Ripley. "We'd spend our lunch hour smoking cigarettes and drinking cans of Big Red."

During their courtship, John continued to cause trouble in and out of the classroom. As the first guy in his class to grow his hair long, he refused to cut it, much to the dismay of teachers and parents. He and his friends experimented a little with alcohol, pot, LSD and amphetamines, but never any hard drugs. Typical high school. Ripley got busted their senior year for carrying speed, which he was using partly to lose weight. He gave some to John, who ended up staying up all night, sweating and shaking in his bed. When he showed up at school the next morning still tweaked, the principal called the police, who only made the teens call their parents. Richard Mellencamp flipped. Furious, he dragged his son home and forced him to cut his hair and wear respectable clothes. When he returned to class, he looked more conservative, save for the sign he hung around his neck that read, "I am the product of my father!"

Ripley thinks that people blew John's "bad kid" rap out of proportion. "He had his moments, but who of us haven't?" he says. "Sometimes the worst thing that happened to John was not that he did anything worse than anybody else, but that he got caught."

Richard and Marilyn Mellencamp used every trick in the book to straighten out their son, to no avail. They threw up their hands when, at age 17, they found out that his girlfriend was pregnant. John wanted to do the right thing by marrying Esterline, but he shuddered at the thought of telling his parents. Esterline tried to break the news to Marilyn herself one afternoon. "Don't even talk about it because John is not going to marry you," she raged. "I would never consent to it. He's not prepared to get married for a long time—he's still a kid. And you're not the girl he should marry anyway." Esterline hadn't even gotten to the part about the baby before leaving the room in tears.

After that stormy forecast, Esterline picked up John after school and the two of them drove to Louisville, Kentucky, to get married before a Justice of the Peace. Kentucky had no age of consent at the time. They didn't think anyone would find out, but they forgot that the *Louisville Courier-Journal* prints marriage announcements, and Richard Mellencamp's office subscribed to the paper. Oops. They had to say something now, but they knew that John might not live through the experience. To soften the blow (no pun intended), they decided to break the news at Grandma Laura Mellencamp's house. She fed her grandson and granddaughter-in-law breakfast, then called up her son Richard. "We've got a little surprise for you," she told him on the phone. "So come on over, but don't bring Marilyn."

Marilyn Mellencamp stewed in the car, while Richard entered his parents' house, where a sheepish trio announced both the marriage and the baby. Quietly, inner rage roaring, he asked to see the certificate. He promptly kicked his son out of his house and left. A scorned Marilyn Mellencamp insisted they have the marriage annulled. She eventually backed down, but the damage was done. "Didn't speak to me for years," John said of his parents. "No, actually once I was standing around downtown and my mom came by in a car and rolled down the window. She goes, 'You taking drugs, John?' I said, 'Yup.' And she rolled up the window and drove away."

John graduated from Seymour High School in June 1970 as a married man. His daughter Michelle was born six months later on December 4, 1970. By this time, he and 'Cil lived with the Esterlines, having tried unsuccessfully to live on their own. They had lived with Gary Boebinger and his wife, Donna, then moved to a dump of a trailer park in Vallonia with no running water. From there, they moved to an apartment behind Mark Ripley's grandmother's house, but she gave them the boot after getting sick of having her yard and porch littered with John's cigarette butts.

The Esterlines took good care of their responsible daughter, new baby granddaughter and freeloading son-in-law. After a short maternity leave, Mrs.

Mellencamp returned to her job at the phone company and John stayed real busy doing nothing. He protested the Vietnam War, met up with his friends, and collected unemployment. "Those were the days," John recalled in an interview with *Musician*. "I'd get up at the crack of noon and Pricilla's mother would fix breakfast for her brother and me. Then we'd throw around the Frisbee, smoke pot, go into town and look for girls—with, you know, the brother of my wife. At night we'd get money to go to the movies and have a drink. What a great life."

In 1971, he had the motivation to write a letter to the *Seymour Daily Tribune* about Ordinance 1580, an initiative that presumably took issue with people standing on street corners. "I suppose this ordinance does concern me since I am considered one of the hippies that stand uptown," he writes. "I believe the people of Seymour should open their eyes and minds to the world around them and forget about such trivial matters as longhairs standing on the corners. There are people dying overseas, but this is nothing compared to long hair—or is it?"

Seriously into music but not serious enough to become a musician (yet), John applied to Vincennes University, a two-year college nearby and one of the few institutions that would take a guy with a D average. The Vietnam War still raged, but while many of his peers disappeared into the armed forces, he managed to avoid the draft due to an operation he had as an infant. John came into the world with a form of spina bifida, a neural tube defect that happens in the first month of pregnancy when the spinal column doesn't close completely. In the worst cases, fluid forms on the brain and the child must have a "shunt" inserted to help drain the fluid, which stays in place for the child's lifetime. Other cases can lead to full or partial paralysis and other special challenges.

John came into the world with a sack-like growth fused to his spine about the size of a man's fist that stretched from his back to the base of his skull. He underwent surgery at Indiana University Medical Center when he was six weeks old. One of the lucky ones, the operation was a complete success and John had no lasting physical effects, despite losing two vertebrae from his spine. Eighteen years later, this condition exempted him from serving in the war.

Instead, he enrolled in Vincennes' broadcasting program, figuring he would work as a disc jockey after graduation. He liked listening to records at home, so listening to records for money seemed like the dream job. In his ample free time, he hung around with Tim Elsner, who, like Mark Ripley, played on John's junior high football team. They didn't know each other back then, but when Elsner returned home from a semester at Purdue, they became friends. "I quit Purdue after a semester and came home, but a lot of other people were still in school, so me and John kind of got thrown together," he recalls.

John soon moved into an apartment with Elsner, wife Pricilla and daughter

Michelle in tow. While Elsner studied and later completed his degree at Indiana University, John skated through college, studying just enough to eke out a passing grade. When it came time for him to get some on-air experience through the school's WVTU radio station, it became painfully clear that he would *not* become the next Alan Freed. He dug playing new music, but he had a difficult time pronouncing the Vietnamese names in wire reports on the war in Southeast Asia. When he got flustered, he stuttered and let loose a long string of expletives. On air.

As a community college student in the early '70s, John had a toddler-age daughter; a patient, hard-working wife; and gaggle of friends and family asking him when he was going to get a real job and admit some responsibility for once. He wasn't inherently lazy, but he did lack direction.

"John was as confused as everybody else at that age as far as what he wanted to do when he grew up," says Elsner. "He knew he wanted to do something in music but at 18 or 19 years old, how in the world do you know how to go about that? And certainly everybody you know is telling you to stop dreaming and that's never going to happen. You would expect people to say that, and 99.9 percent of the time they'd be right. But they weren't in this case."

After years of dipping his toe in the music world, he got the gumption to sink in a little deeper. He moved his family back to Seymour to a rented farmhouse on the outskirts of town and put together a band called Trash. He recruited Pricilla's brother, Dennis Esterline, and buddy Kevin Wissing for the rhythm section and snatched up Larry Crane, a local guitarist who, at only 16 years old, was already gaining attention around town for his six-string chops. In Seymour, that's not hard to do, but nevertheless, he could play by ear most of the songs on the radio, which was far better than what his new bandmates could accomplish. John's brother Ted signed on as "road manager," which meant he didn't get much work out of Trash.

In the early '70s, groups such as Crosby, Stills, Nash and Young; the Allman Brothers; and Creedence Clearwater Revival were the hot acts of the time, but John wasn't into what they would now call "classic rock." During his tenure in college, he had gravitated toward the more "urban" sounds of David Bowie, the New York Dolls, Lou Reed and Iggy Pop and The Stooges. "He was such a small town hillbilly," Crane said earlier of the Trash frontman. "Anything that was remotely urban, he loved. When John was younger, all the young white kids with their Bass Weejuns were listening to James Brown. John liked anything urban, anything that was just the opposite of Seymour, Indiana." One of their first set lists included Free's "Walkin' My Shadow," Iggy Pop's "I Wanna Be Your Dog," David Bowie's "Suffragette City" and "Ziggy" and John's first original song, "Loser." During one of their first shows, they got pegged with a liquor bottle. Loser, indeed.

Their attempt to look cool didn't go over well with the locals, either. Going for the "glam" look, they donned little wisps of hair under their lips, heavy eyeliner, and hair dyed blue and green. They wore high-heeled boots and leather, tight shirts that revealed sprigs of chest hair and belly buttons. But since they didn't fully cross over into Bowie's more androgynous "space odyssey" look, they came across looking more "greasy, more Mexican," as John described to author Martin Torgoff. Considering they couldn't play too well and they looked just plain weird to the Seymour folks, they didn't land too many shows. They did get a potentially plum gig in Indianapolis, though. "Some promoter had booked Kiss into a little theater in downtown Indy," Crane recalled earlier. "Still showing movies there. They were going to show the movie *Woodstock* and then Kiss would come play. A weird combination. In between the booking and the date, Kiss had been on *Midnight Special* and it had launched them. So they were canceling all their little dates, so the promoter is stuck with the date, tickets sold and he's looking for a band that wears makeup: We're it, in about a five-state area. All these people are hyped up to see Kiss, the promoter hadn't bothered to tell them that Kiss wasn't gonna be there. Out we walk with our little guitars and makeup; the crowd wasn't very happy."

Trash lasted almost two years—the longest any of John's bands had held together. While John messed around with school, a band and a feeble attempt in the radio business, Pricilla Mellencamp worked to pay the bills and put food on the table. She didn't like being the sole breadwinner, but what choice did she have? Faced with a dire financial future, John buckled after graduation and got a job installing telephones for Indiana Bell. Crane finished high school and Ted Mellencamp continued his job at a grocery store.

John never really enjoyed his job at the phone company, but he enjoyed the money he earned, which allowed him to buy more records, pay for his Gibson Hummingbird guitar and later buy a Gibson Dove. Oh, and he pitched in a little for rent and bills, too. He spent much of his free time playing those guitars and trying to write his own songs. He had the will, but not the focus. But one of his old classmates, George Green, did have the focus, as well as the gift of rhyme and meter. Even early on, they made a great team. They forged a friendship and a songwriting partnership that would endure for more than 25 years.

In time, John got a regular gig playing at a local bar called The Chatterbox, a neighborhood dive inhabited by the veteran Seymour barflies. His friends came out for the cheap beer and entertainment, and as he played his songs to sparse, drunk crowds, he discovered his gift of showmanship, as well as a deeper thirst for playing music. The bar built him a small stage, and he would sit up there for hours, indulging himself and whoever sat long enough to listen. During his four appearances at the bar, underneath some Christmas lights strung up by Ted Mellencamp, John played anything from David Bowie, Bob Dylan and Rolling Stones tunes, to recently made-up songs that often painfully displayed his inexperience. He and Green put together a song called "Loser" that included some nasty jabs toward Lou Reed. It was, as the title suggests, a loser of a song.

Playing music as a hobby seemed an acceptable side venture for John's friends, spouse and family, but not for him. As his desire to be a *full-time* rock star welled inside of him, he became more and more frustrated and resentful of his day job at the phone company. He wanted more, he deserved more and knew he could become more than any nine-to-five Seymour job could ever bring him. It wasn't clear yet, but he wanted something big for his life, and his yearning to pursue that vision consumed him.

Just short of his one-year anniversary, Indiana Bell fired lineman John Mellencamp. They had received complaints from housewives about an employee who would enter their home to work on a line, screw it up, then proceed to yell, curse and slam phones in frustration. He botched a few other jobs at the waystation, but the kicker came when he inadvertently disconnected all of the phone service in Freetown, Indiana. He could turn in his hardhat and go. John was ecstatic. Finally, he had the freedom to play music full time! Earning an income to feed his family, well, he'd figure that out later. His friends and family asked what he would do now: Get another job, perhaps? No, he informed them. He would go to New York to become a songwriter and entertainer. He had put his family's needs ahead of his own for a whole year; now it was time to think of himself. Again.

His obsession with becoming a rock star didn't stem entirely from selfishness, really. His fierce independent streak put him in line with James Dean (whom people frequently compared him to); Marlon Brando's character, Johnny, in *The Wild One*; and Paul Newman's *Cool Hand Luke*. He identified with these bad boys, but couldn't relate to the family man. He absolutely would not settle for a staid life of mediocrity, silently suffering working the day shift at a factory while his heart yearned to be pressed against a guitar. Combine that desire with a dash of stubborn and you've got a young man who would, yes, go to New York to make himself a star. The more people told him "you can't," the more he said, "I will," and get the hell out of my way before I run you down!

The first step in his semi-planned mission: a crude cassette tape of himself singing two songs, sent to virtually every record company in Manhattan. He followed up the mass mailing with enough phone calls to yield hundreds of dollars in long distance charges. Replies trickled in—rejection, in the form of politely composed form letters from A&R departments throughout greater New York. He and his family had moved out of the farmhouse and now lived in a dumpy apartment above the garage of his aunt's home. He gradually papered an entire room with rejections on record company letterhead. Wall space and unemployment benefits dwindled, yet he ignored the harsh reality of the bank account and planned a trip to New York to bang on some doors in person. He had no idea what he would say or do when those pearly gates opened, but a face-to-face meeting had to be better than sitting around in Indiana waiting by the phone. He gathered his wife and daughter and drove 18 hours to the Big Apple, rented a room at a Holiday Inn and hoped for a stroke of luck.

Not a man known for his tact, John canvassed the city, knocking on the doors of any music company or record label he could find, sometimes letting himself in and promptly harassing secretaries and cornering any record label employee he could find. Those graced with his presence gave the small-town hick a universally chilly "We'll cawl you." Right. After two weeks of blow-offs and cold shoulders, his savings were all but depleted and he had not even a nibble of interest from anyone. The day before he planned to check out of the Holiday Inn, he walked into Sunshine Records, an independent not necessarily known for a strong roster of rock acts. He strolled through the office when the receptionist had conveniently left for lunch and encountered what he believed to be an A&R man. The man listened to his homespun cassette (the most attention he'd received in two weeks!) and gave him some feedback: The tape stinks, but if you can come back with $2,000, I'll kick in another two grand and we'll cut a proper demo. With that new demo, he promised John a record deal.

Hallelujah! A break! They parted on a handshake, and John darted back to his wife and child, wondering how the heck he would come up with $2,000. He asked Richard first for a loan. He refused, advising his son that the deal sounded "too dicey." But he's a Mellencamp. They don't give up, they just try harder.

CHAPTER TWO

THAT'S WHAT AH SAID—
A MELLENCAMP RESCUED BY BUNNY BREAD

John's lyricist friend George Green has one of those rare, brilliant minds that's equally left- and right-brained. Not only can he write clever song lyrics, he also excels in statistics. To pay the bills, he delivered Bunny Bread to all of the local supermarkets, a job that would yield rewards far beyond his weekly paycheck. Bunny Bread had launched a new promotion where customers could pick up a scratch-off card at their local supermarket for a chance to win a $1,000 grand prize. "If you scratched off four or five spots, and if you got a certain pattern, then you won," recalls friend Tim Elsner. "George, a pretty sharp guy, would go to these stores, talk to people at the counter and either ask for some of these tickets, or he'd grab a handful as he walked by. So he had a bunch of tickets. He went home, scratched off every space, and started seeing recurring patterns. He saw that they only made about 50 different cards. So he basically cracked the code and finally got a $1,000 winner. But George couldn't turn it in because he worked for Bunny Bread." He talked a friend into turning in the first winning card and continued scratching until he uncovered a second grand prize. "After the second one, the store got suspicious—the odds of having two winners from the same area were astronomical. Three days later they shut down the contest! I'm sure the people at Bunny Bread went to their graves wondering how the heck that happened."

While the Bunny Bread executives ran the numbers on their promotion, Green called up his friend John. "You are about to receive $2,000," he told him. If John was the praying kind, his plea for demo money would have been answered thanks to Bunny Bread.

After collecting the winnings, John dashed back to New York to visit the "A&R man" (he was nothing of the sort—just a shady lawyer who happened to be in the office) from Sunshine Records. They cut a one-song demo of Paul Revere and The Raiders' "Kicks" at a nearby studio. The lawyer promised to call John in a few weeks when he had a deal put together. John, Pricilla and Michelle headed for home where the rock star-to-be hovered over the phone, waiting for his call from Mr. Sunshine. The lawyer had no intention of getting him a deal. He took John's money and dropped out of sight.

Getting the shaft caused John to sink into a months-long depression. Still, he wasn't ready to give up, even though his friends and family urged him otherwise. Why don't you just get a day job and play music on the side, Mark Ripley advised. Pricilla Mellencamp, who had supported him financially and emotionally all this time, went through her own waves of doubt. She knew he was working hard to make something happen for himself, and she consented to being the sole breadwinner while he chased his dream. But come on, she wondered. They had to decide how long he was going to give it, because if he continued to chase his rock star ambitions without success for much longer, she might not be around when he got back.

Rather than throw in the towel, he decided to make one more trip to NYC to shop his demo. But this time, he zeroed in on the management companies; specifically, MainMan Ltd., the company run by Brit music mogul Tony DeFries. DeFries managed two of John's favorite acts: David Bowie and Iggy Pop. DeFries had formed the company in 1972 to manage Bowie and helped construct the Ziggy Stardust mystique. A crafty businessman, especially when it came to finances, DeFries built up Bowie's image by manipulating the press, making his protégé an exclusive and elusive subject by declaring him unavailable for interviews. He issued mountains of hype concerning Bowie's potential as the "ultimate star of the Seventies," not just some Rod Stewart rip-off. Industry insiders called DeFries, with his trendy clothes and permanently affixed cigar, "Tony Deep Freeze" because of his tendency to treat people like pawns in his ongoing, strategically executed promotional game.

John knew that Bowie had just ended his business relationship with DeFries (he fired him by telegram). John thought he would have a chance with the high-profile manager. He sent DeFries a copy of his demo and a photo of himself in a stiffly pressed suit that looked a size too big. He had perfectly parted, blow-dried hair and posed in a wingback chair in what looked like grandma's formal living room. Looking oddly out of place, George Green stood aloof in the background, wearing a black leather motorcycle jacket and a matching beret. Both held smoldering cigarettes.

John walked into MainMan's New York headquarters (they had offices in London and Tokyo, as well) wearing his more standard well-worn blue jeans and T-shirt. He felt more like himself than in the monkey suit he wore for his pictures but among the made-up, glammed-out David Bowie wannabes gathered in the lobby waiting for time with DeFries, John was the one that looked like a freak. Anticipating another rejection, he handed his tape to the receptionist, who happened to be from Indiana, and walked out...to an empty parking space. His car had been towed! That was the last straw. Beaten down, his perseverance stretched thin, he retrieved his car from the tow lot, packed his bags and drove back to Indiana. On the way back, he stopped at a small independent label in Louisville, Kentucky, his last ditch effort at a deal. Even these small-time players passed on John Mellencamp. His demo, they said quite simply, "sucks."

Maybe he should throw in the towel, he thought, and get some mindless factory or construction job. Maybe everyone else was right. The dejected, aspiring entertainer didn't realize, however, that the über-manager he had just tried to visit in New York heard something in John's rudimentary demo tape, an untapped talent that he could control, mold and manipulate into the next big star. He was a handsome bloke, a bit rough around the edges. A bad boy. The women would love that.

John stared at the newspaper, *almost* ready to look through the want ads when the phone rang. On the other end, he heard a man with a thick British accent—Tony DeFries—say that he actually listened to John's raw demo and thought they could do business together. Could he come out to New York to meet? By this time, John had had enough of Manhattan. Sure, he told DeFries, he'd like to meet but he couldn't afford the trip. DeFries promptly overnighted him a plane ticket and in short order, John found himself in DeFries' New York office for the second time. Once inside this zoo of an office—DeFries ring-leading a staff of ego-driven music business types, part-time actors and other colorful characters—John signed a five-year contract with MainMan without questioning its contents. He didn't consult with a lawyer and didn't understand, much less think to discuss, percentage points. He wanted a record deal so badly, he signed away his independence to a man who promised he would be a *big* star within a year. DeFries gave himself a nice pat on the back. He had just found himself another 24-year-old boy to mold; this one in the shape of an all-American rebel singing real rock 'n' roll.

The plan that MainMan developed to launch their new bad boy contained elements both logical and ludicrous. They sensibly decided to build John's fan base in and around Indiana first, then expand outward through the Midwest and ultimately the entire U.S. and beyond. Conversely, they produced one of the most overblown, borderline outrageous promotional campaigns to launch their new act. DeFries compared him to Dylan and early Elvis to the press and music business colleagues. While DeFries searched for a buyer for his "package," he gave John a monthly stipend so that he wouldn't have to crawl back to the phone company for income. DeFries then decided that John, Pricilla and Michelle must move—they deserved better than their tiny garage apartment. So he ensured that they move to a proper place, which happened to be former Governor Edgar Whitcomb's summer home. The citizens of Seymour must have raised their eyebrows as this "bad kid" moved into a stately abode. Even John himself started wondering if maybe he was a big deal.

But it was the visit from DeFries and the MainMan clan, who descended upon southern Indiana in a flurry of flash and cigar smoke, that generated the most gossip. DeFries' smooth-talking ways, stylish attire and endless cash flow marked him an obvious outsider in the tiny Seymour community, but he made the small town (and John's house) his home for a record nine weeks. The Mellencamp family didn't know what to make of the MainMan clan. Their blunt, East Coast attitude struck them as rude, and while DeFries convinced most that he was a serious mover-and-shaker, Pricilla Mellencamp sensed trouble.

DeFries did make good on his initial promise to find John a record deal. After knocking on nearly every record label door on the east and west coasts, he found a believer at MCA Records. One of the label's A&R execs, Bob Davis, took a liking to John and with his support, DeFries finagled a package deal for John and David Bowie guitarist Mick Ronson. Great! John got his wish and DeFries got label backing for two acts at once. John, although thrilled that he had come this close to his dream, worried. He had only written a handful of songs in his lifetime, and questionable ones at that. How the heck was he going to make a record? He had no band and only a couple of original songs. He had marginal skills as a lyricist, worse talents as a music composer, but a major record label expected an album. He called in for backup.

After high school graduation, friend and guitarist Larry Crane joined a country band based out of Columbia, Missouri. Obviously Trash was, well, trash, but Crane's urge to play and a feeling of wanderlust prompted him to put some more twang in his tone and hit the road for a bit. The group's meager earnings afforded them overnight stays in run-down motels, so the considerate Crane called his mom at least once a week to let her know that yes, he was alive, eating well and not getting into too much trouble. During one of their conversations, Mrs. Crane delivered the message, "That Mellencamp boy keeps calling here. He wants something."

"Mom didn't ever like John too much," Crane recalled. "So I told her I'd wait for 10 minutes; have John call me at the payphone. The phone rings, and it's John. He told me how he had a record deal. It sounded fairly goofy, but it was better than what I was doing."

With Crane back in the fold, John then recruited guitarist Dave Parman, who had played with John in a band called The Mason Brothers shortly after

Snakepit Banana Barn disbanded. He then brought in Wayne Hall to play sax and Tom "Bub"Wince to add some piano parts and dubbed the ensemble Tiger Force Band. John had the whole outfit together except for the drummer. The next step was to find a studio and figure out what the heck they were going to do once they got there.

Mike Wanchic grew up in Lexington, Kentucky in a home where traditional country music wafted through the house like the aroma of pecan pie. His mother worked as a program director for a Lexington radio station in the early '50s, and got Flatt and Scruggs their first radio show. He jokes that he cut his teeth on Flatt and Scruggs—literally! "They were so grateful, when I was born they bought me a teething cup that said, 'I cut my teeth on Flatt & Scruggs.'" He spent much of his childhood with his ear stuck to Nashville's legendary WLAC-AM, taking in the traditional country played on the Grand Ole Opry or the early soul music performed on Ernie's Record Mart. Later, he tuned in to The Beatles, the Rolling Stones and psychedelic rock on Louisville's high-powered radio station. About 130 miles away in Seymour, Indiana, a young John Mellencamp did the same thing.

After graduating from DePauw University in Greencastle, Indiana, in 1974, Wanchic—who played in such bands as the Wakefield Summit and Catch—decided to continue his music career as an audio engineer. In the 1970s, when only a scant few recording schools existed in the U.S., one learned the trade through apprenticing. This basically meant convincing a recording studio to let you sweep the floors for free. Then, if all went well, an engineer would mentor the apprentice, which *might* lead to a job as an assistant engineer and later, a promotion to chief engineer. Wanchic knocked on the door of Jack Gilfoy's Gilfoy Sound Studio in Bloomington, Indiana to get his start in the business. Gilfoy was the featured drummer for Henry Mancini and owned a small 16-track studio that catered mainly to classical and jazz musicians studying at Indiana University, Gilfoy's alma mater. Wanchic spent days apprenticing at Gilfoy's and nights gigging around town as a guitarist when John and his newly minted Tiger Force Band booked the studio on short notice in 1976. John walked into Gilfoy's with $7,000 fronted by DeFries to record an album's worth of material. They had zero time to rehearse—plus, with the exception of Crane, his motley crew didn't exactly know their craft. John had to take away the drummer's cymbals at one point, because he felt compelled to crash them on every beat. Despite their lack of proficiency, they forged ahead and with a small posse of friends cheering them on, recorded some of John's favorite cover songs. He hadn't written many originals yet, so the band deferred to bar band standards in order to give DeFries the album he wanted.

"When I first started making records," John told *Performing Songwriter*, "the idea of writing songs never really occurred to me, because I was in a bar band in Indiana and I was a singer. We did other people's material, so when I got a record deal, it was like, 'Oh, you have to write your own songs? I don't know how to do that.' Literally, the first song I wrote, which was probably 'Chestnut Street Incident,' ended up on my first record [Laughs]. All that early stuff was just Woody Guthrie and Bob Dylan. Everybody thought it was Springsteen, but it was really Guthrie and Dylan."

During their two weeks at Gilfoy's, the band laid down covers such as Roy Orbison's "Oh, Pretty Woman," "Do You Believe in Magic," "Jailhouse Rock," and "Hit the Road Jack." At night, Wanchic came in and replaced several of the guitar parts, unbeknownst to ol' Parman. John didn't want to hurt his feelings.

The collection was haphazardly assembled, not unusual for an artist with little direction but lots of ambition. DeFries wanted to release the material as-is, with the addition of the three original songs John had to his credit. He was mortified, but could he say no?

They recorded those originals at the Hit Factory in New York with DeFries making his debut as a record producer. "I know no one could have brought out what I heard in Johnny without losing the raw, vital energy inherent in the act—I had to do it," he brazenly told *Pittsburgh Phonograph Record*. Mick Ronson added some guitar parts and helped John remix some of the cover songs before DeFries released the whole lot as *Chestnut Street Incident*. This was John's first real record, and admittedly, it was terrible. They recorded on a shoestring budget with a sub-par band and the leader fumbled for direction in his career and his voice. Settled at home in Indiana, he worried that the public would think this was all he was capable of.

Back in New York, with their new artist out of their hair and his album at the pressing plant, DeFries and his team turned their attention to promotion, creating an image for their new "all-American M-A-L-E" and crafting overblown publicity stunts to get the boy mass attention.

At their insistence, John begrudgingly cut his thick brown hair and photographer Jamie Andrews guided him through a photo shoot for his first album cover. His new 'do made him appear more clean cut, but the black attire, turned-up collar and sullen expression hinted at the rebel inside. At MainMan headquarters, DeFries and staff agreed that "John Mellencamp" would have to go. John became Johnny (*a la* Johnny Angel), never mind that no one had ever called him that. They erased "Mellencamp" completely from his public identity in favor of the much hipper surname, Cougar. They changed John's name, changed his appearance and busied themselves planning his "World Debut." Meanwhile, John sat at home with his family, wondering when the money would start rolling in.

He flew to New York to see a mock-up of his first album cover, and that's when he saw it. In bold, two-tone type, his new name: *Johnny Cougar*.

What the hell?

The real John Mellencamp went into a near-rage at what had to be a horrible mistake. He was (and is) proud of his name; it's his heritage, and by God, if he was going to be known around the world, he wanted to be known by his real name! DeFries calmly told him that he would *not* sell records as John Mellencamp, the hayseed, but he *would* sell records as Johnny Cougar, the cool cat. "No fucking way," John retorted, to which, DeFries replied that either the record comes out by Johnny Cougar or the record doesn't come out at all. Humiliated, but backed into a corner that he didn't know how to get out of, he relented. He wanted his rock star status desperately, and couldn't imagine turning back now, back to a life stringing wire for the phone company, permanently stuck in Bloomington, frustrated and bitter because he threw away this one opportunity. So he sacrificed his dignity and let MainMan go on about their business of greasing the PR machine.

The company employed some of the same strategies used with David Bowie, such as purposely keeping Johnny Cougar from the press to create "mystique." "Oh, I'm sorry John isn't available for interviews right now," they'd tell the music journalists. They turned down all requests until Johnny Cougar's big coming out party, and remained elusive as to where and when that might happen. MCA Records' press release announcing the arrival of Johnny Cougar and his debut album played up the small town, all-American guy to a T. "In his search for happiness, Johnny was constantly being disappointed and that disappointment had left him with a tough exterior..."A lot of parents used to tell their kids not to hang out with me...that I was a bad kid. I wasn't bad, really. They just didn't understand." But on the rare occasions when Johnny Cougar spoke, whether on his own or through quotes fed to the press by MainMan, he came across as cocky rather than confident, small-minded rather than small town.

"Once you've had me, you know you've had the best," he bragged. "I can say I look real good 'cause every day of my life I've been told how good lookin' I am, how damn cute I am." His lyrics reflect this physical attention. In "American Dream," he writes, "I had a face so cute/made a young girl cry/And I could blow 'em away with just a wink of my eye."

DeFries unleashed Johnny Cougar by way of Seymour, Indiana, on the newly christened "Johnny Cougar Day," October 2, 1976. Then-mayor Donald H. Ernest declared the special holiday to honor John as a "member of the community with special and unique talents as an entertainer and performer," according to promotional material. Johnny Cougar Day celebrated the October 1 release of *Chestnut Street Incident* with a parade down Chestnut Street, Seymour's main drag from which the album takes its name, followed by a concert at Seymour's National Guard Armory. The festivities were held in conjunction with the city's annual Oktoberfest, one of the largest Oktoberfest festivals in the state, held the first weekend in October. Through the weekend, arts and crafts and food vendors line the streets of downtown Seymour, and myriad other events take place, including a flea market, a 5K run/walk, a hot air balloon race, a baking contest, a quilt show, carnival rides for the kids, a *Bier Garten* with nightly bluegrass and German music for the adults and the Seymour Oktoberfest Parade featuring an entourage of floats, school marching bands, antique cars, clowns and other participants. During its third year, 1976, the event also honored Johnny Cougar as the city's first bonafide rock star. John, wife Pricilla and Larry Crane sat perched in the requisite limousine flanked by a team of female "Cougarettes" who cheered in his honor as they slowly progressed down the city street. The locals didn't know what to make of the spectacle. They assumed that maybe this was just the way the music business does things. Some folded their arms and mumbled, "Why should I applaud that Mellencamp kid all of a sudden?" His former classmates heckled him, shouting, "Hey Mellencamp, you asshole!"

"The kid hadn't done anything," recalls friend Mark Ripley. "It's funny to see those things and compare them to where he ended up. Looking back on some of those things makes him wince!"

"I can remember me and Larry Crane getting in the limo for Johnny Cougar Day to drive through town and wave at these people," John told *Rolling Stone*. "Both of us went, 'Wait a minute,' then went behind a garage and threw up. I looked at him and thought, 'We're not gonna make it.' But we went out and did it."

The daytime drama concluded with a free concert at city hall with Cougar and band as featured entertainment, followed by their 9 P.M. Armory benefit concert. Huge searchlights beamed back and forth near the venue, which gradually filled with just about every Mellencamp in Indiana, followed by all of their friends, former classmates, DeFries and crew, MCA executives and writers and editors from *Rolling Stone, Creem, Village Voice*, the *Daily News*, the *Boston Globe* and *Penthouse*, not to mention the curious onlookers of Seymour. Before Johnny Cougar and Tiger Force went on stage, Larry Crane threw up again.

The lights dimmed at 9 P.M. and John bravely walked on stage alone with his acoustic guitar for an "unplugged" version of "Chestnut Street Incident." Following the introduction, John kicked off the full-tilt rock show with a "Hello. I'm Johnny Cougar, and this is Tiger Force!" They played their short set with unabashed energy, John staggering and jerking about, losing his shirt, and engaging the crowd in colorful between-song banter with liberal use of the F-word (his nervous habit coming out again). A sweating, panting "Cougar" lost himself in the performance, giving every ounce of energy and effort and pushing his band to their max. His encore that night was The

Rolling Stones' "Brown Sugar" which was received by the audience with screams and applause. Safely backstage, he collapsed, exhausted from working himself into a level of intensity he had never experienced before, but would many times more in the future.

The press attended an after-show party at Richard and Marilyn Mellencamp's house, spent the night in the Seymour Holiday Inn, then prepared themselves for an interview with the star of the Armory the next day. Most of the reporters had already judged him as having more swagger than substance, and considering he had a nasty habit of shooting his mouth off when thrust in socially uncomfortable situations, they also pegged him as hotheaded and rude. But a select few took time to look beyond the superficial words and discovered, as one reporter phrased it, a man "blessed/cursed with a vision that sees the utter bullshit in everything."

The grand Johnny Cougar Day, which cost DeFries a whopping $100,000, kicked off the first Johnny Cougar tour that hit five cities throughout Indiana and concluded with a show in Louisville, Kentucky. "We've started our campaign to break Johnny nationally in his home state," DeFries said in an interview with *Phonograph Record*. "We'll spread our efforts outward from here, throughout the Midwest, *then* beyond."

They hired Ted Mellencamp as roadie/tour manager and bussed in the Cougarettes and parents to most of the shows because the $5 tickets had sold so poorly. Nevertheless, the short junket proved a valuable learning experience for John and Tiger Force as it tightened up their live show and gave them a taste of life on the road, albeit on a small scale.

Put off by DeFries' aggressive marketing schemes, the press largely considered *Chestnut Street Incident* a joke. *Rolling Stone* claimed the album "full of ridiculous posturing," his Roy Orbison cover "nearly sacrilegious" and "Do You Believe in Magic" and "Twentieth Century Fox" "so unspeakably lame they defy belief." Ouch. Critic John Swenson went on to deem DeFries' "new scam" "just another ready-made pop throwaway."

Further complicating matters, MCA was reluctant to promote their new act. Even after label reps talked up his Armory performance to others within the company, they still didn't want to put forth much promotional muscle. John's inherent attitude problem didn't help matters. "I was a pretty snot-nosed kid back then," he later told *SPIN* magazine. "I mean, real arrogant— swaggering, loud-mouthed, beat-up-the-world type of guy. And I was under the illusion that record companies were kids. I went out to California for the very first time and I walk into the office and there's a bunch of old guys sitting there in suits. Flipped me out, man! 'Who are these guys?' 'These guys are going to be selling your records.'"

Well, at least MCA gave it a weak try. The album's title track received minimal airplay, and John's few promotional appearances were erratic at best. He landed a plum gig playing at the University of Toledo, but he bombed. His one nervous habit—abusing the F-word—kicked in full force during a live radio interview with WMMS. The program director did not welcome him back.

In total, *Chestnut Street Incident* sold approximately 12,000 units, mostly in Indiana, during its initial run. John received his first royalty check on December 16, 1977, for a whopping $27.59. Merry Christmas!

John wanted to put the *Chestnut Street Incident* behind him. He knew he could far exceed the content of his debut on his next release. He would record at New York's Hit Factory, he decided, and he would produce the record himself. He wrote 11 new songs and paid close attention to the arrangements, while the band put themselves through more rigorous rehearsals. With this album, to be called *The Kid Inside*, Crane noticed John's potential as a songwriter, although still in raw form. The lyrics, mainly focusing on the past two years of his life, contained lines about feeling wounded, rejected and out of control, and had the meter of a juvenile poem. However, he had improved in the past year. The music called forth Stones-inspired riffs, but a more polished sound void of memorable hooks. Still, the album did contain 11 original songs—more than three times the number on his debut!

As the delivery deadline approached for John's supposed sophomore release, signs of real trouble surfaced. His primary point of contention occurred during *The Kid Inside* photo shoot. The all-American rebel image wasn't working for DeFries, so MainMan decided to pretty up their rock 'n' roll experiment with heavy eye makeup, lip gloss and a pouty expression that made him look more like a lost little boy than a sex symbol. John naturally hated, resisted and protested the new look, but MainMan went ahead and used the new photos anyway.

Then, the day John delivered the album to MCA, the label went through a corporate housecleaning that led to the dismissal of nearly all of the staff that had any involvement with Johnny Cougar, including his few supporters. This wouldn't be the first time that corporate changeovers would damage his career, but the reality of big business hit him hard. A restructured MCA refused to release *The Kid Inside,* and really didn't want John on their roster anymore. DeFries knocked on a few doors on Johnny Cougar's behalf to try to find a new deal, but by this time he had made such a mockery of John's career, he got laughed out of most offices. With John's career a shambles, the two parted ways, leaving DeFries free to find another naive young act to mold, MCA holding a million dollar mess and a devastated, emerging rock star sulking at home in Indiana.

With the MCA and DeFries deals gone sour, John set his band free while he looked for a new manager and record deal. He moved his family from

Seymour to Bloomington, partly to escape the constant Johnny Cougar Day hauntings. He started working the phones again, and found that no matter which name he used, Cougar or Mellencamp, he got no response. He called up former MCA A&R man Bob Davis, one of his early supporters, and asked for his help in getting him a new record deal. He promised that if anything materialized, he would pay him.

Davis lived in L.A., and for six weeks, John did, too. Armed with cassette copies of *Chestnut Street Incident*, they knocked on more doors, both together and apart, but none opened. They had almost given up when Davis said he had one more person he could try—Billy Gaff, manager of Rod Stewart (who was at the height of his career at the time) and founder of a European independent label called Riva Records. Gaff might as well have lived on a different planet than John—their worlds were so different. "He was this jet-setting English guy—that, and the opulence that Gaff surrounded himself with was not real high up on the Bloomington agenda, lifestyle-wise," recalls guitarist and co-producer Mike Wanchic.

John agreed to visit Gaff, but this time, he would bring his acoustic guitar and play songs himself rather than play a recording that even he didn't like. They pulled into Gaff's Beverly Hills driveway, walked to the back of his house and found a tanned Gaff trimming hedges by the pool. He put down the shears and sat down for a long talk with Davis and John. John played an acoustic version of "Taxi Dancer." His audience of one loved it.

Go back home, he told a fidgety John, get your band together and write some new material. Call me in a few months. John followed his orders. He brought back Crane and, after putting the word out through a St. Louis music store, auditioned and hired drummer Tom Knowles and bassist Robert "Ferd" Frank. They all soon moved to Bloomington and the band, which John named Streetheart, rehearsed in a rented house in Elotsville.

With a new band in place, John needed some original songs to really impress Gaff. He looked outside of his own life for inspiration this time, and found it through an old friend who had fallen on hard times. "I need to find some chick I can be with who won't bug the shit out of me," the man confided. His words rolled around in John's head. He could relate to his friend's wishes, and jotted a few lines that didn't exactly rhyme but had a good meter: "I need a lover who won't drive me crazy/Some girl to thrill me and then go away..."

Crass, yes. Honest, that too. To compliment his primal, testosterone-fueled words, he heard brutal, pounding drums and a thick wall of guitars. If the song didn't stand out for its lyrics, it would make itself known through volume.

John and Streetheart played a one-song set at a talent night at a Chicago club called Beginnings. The band impressed Bob Davis and Mike Gil, who worked with Gaff, enough to report back their positive findings to their boss. In short order, Gaff set up a show for John in L.A. so that he could invite some of his music industry colleagues to hear him. Of course, he found an open slot at one of the hippest spots in the city.

British punk band The Jam booked their first U.S. performance in West Hollywood's famed Sunset Strip rock club Whisky-A-Go-Go. Johnny Cougar scored the opening act slot. The Jam emerged out of a movement that turned its nose up at the lavishes of fame, even though bands such as The Sex Pistols and The Clash eventually did become famous. Oddly, The Jam shared the bill with an artist who clamored for fame and had aligned with Gaff, who represented Rod Stewart, one of the most commercially successful artists of the era. Gaff invited PolyGram A&R rep Jerry Jaffe and producer Mike Chapman, among others, to the L.A. club and they all sought out a seat among the young, punk-rock audience.

John and Streetheart walked out to a barren stage, decorated only by a streetlamp that he had brought, which he would lean on from time to time for effect. "He ended up in his underwear at the show, but I don't remember how he made the transformation," recalls PR veteran Bob Merlis, who ironically became John's publicist years later. "He was posing, doing this kind of *Scorpio Rising* kind of thing. I went there to see The Jam, but John really won me over. "I Need a Lover" started to play in my head then, and it did not stop."

He, like a lot of others in the audience, realized that he was the real deal... even if he had no record deal. "I realized he was more of a rock 'n' roll throwback," says Merlis, "and you could see at the Whisky that his band was really important. He was the name, but there was a lot of interaction with the band members."

Chapman and Jaffe flipped over "I Need a Lover," and immediately wanted to talk business with Gaff. After some hushed conversations, Gaff told John and Streetheart to pack their bags. They were going to record an album—in England.

Gaff decided that since most of the U.S. record labels wouldn't come near Johnny Cougar, he would release his next album through Gaff's label, Riva Records, which had distribution in the U.K., Australia and a few other spots, but not the U.S. John signed another contract without really understanding the clauses, and Pricilla and Michelle Mellencamp got their affairs in order for a move to England. Pricilla enrolled Michelle in London's American School and set about taking care of the domestic duties for her family and the band: She cooked, kept the house that Gaff had rented for them and did the grocery shopping and other errands. There's an often-told tale from this time in John's life when during their first (and only) Thanksgiving outside of the U.S., Pricilla hit all the local markets in search of a turkey. She finally found one, a very expensive one, feathers still attached! Meanwhile, John and Streetheart caroused around London, presumably preparing for their upcoming recording sessions and playing an occasional nightclub—hicks from rural Indiana, proceed with caution. "I walked into a club with an acoustic guitar the night after The Sex Pistols played the same club," John recalled in a *SPIN* interview. "I could have been like, 'I'm not going to get over. They're going to kick my ass.' But I wasn't going to spike my hair up and put a safety pin through my nose just to fit in." The show didn't go so well, but he didn't get tossed out, either.

Gaff spared no expense on Riva Records' debut act. They recorded at Wessex Studios with John Punter, a producer best known for his work with Roxy Music. He got an earful from the young artist, and not just from singing. "I had a big chip on my shoulder during that album," John told author Martin Torgoff. "It was too soon after the MainMan thing, and I was still pissed off about it... My life in general was fucked up and so was my attitude."

Mr. I-hate-the-world and band laid down simplistic tracks, most of them a step up from John's previous two albums, but with only one real standout. "I Need a Lover," insidiously catchy and oddly structured, had very real potential. Crane experimented with guitar parts, working for hours on chord changes and layered tracks to build a fuller guitar sound. They miraculously discovered key changes, and once they started playing them, they couldn't stop—hence, the song's long instrumental intro. The band later moved to Basing Street Studios for overdubs, then mixed at George Martin's prestigious Air Studios. The album, titled *A Biography*, took a total of three months and nearly $50,000 to make. Gaff would spend nearly double that amount on promotion following its 1978 release. John bristled at the thought, memories of DeFries' overblown efforts fresh in his mind. "I've had this done before," he complained. True, but not by Gaff. "Gaff was instrumental because he had enough faith in John to bankroll him through the hard times, when most bands definitely would not have been able to survive," says Wanchic.

Like DeFries, Gaff revisited marketing strategies that had helped break his previous top-selling act. Unlike DeFries, he didn't manufacture quotes for John. He let John come up with curt winning lines all on his own. Gaff plastered London with posters of John wearing blue jeans and a sports coat, shirt collar rebelliously upturned, hair properly coifed. That same photograph ran in full-page magazine ads and accompanied "Hunk of the Month" features in teen magazines such as *My Guy* and *Pink*. His snarly, pretty boy image appealed to the teen female set, but didn't gel well with serious music fans or the press, both of whom had more interest in the punk and emerging post-punk trendsetters such as Human League, P.I.L., Joy Division and Talking Heads.

Nevertheless, the winds shifted ever so slightly and "I Need a Lover" hit Number 17 on the British singles charts, followed by a Number One slot in

Australia. When Gaff told him about his popularity in the Land Down Under, he had just finished nine months of touring with Nazareth and Blue Oyster Cult in Germany, France, Sweden and Belgium. He and Gaff argued continually over money, and John resisted Gaff's attempt at managing him. Things just weren't moving fast enough, John thought, and his frustration transmuted into a ferociously quick temper.

Australia offered some hope, and Gaff wasted no time in getting John and the band to the country for a series of promotional appearances. Fans gathered outside the hotel to greet him. He thought they were waiting for someone else! Gaff arranged a packed schedule of press interviews and radio and TV appearances, including a spot with well-known music journalist Molly Melbourne, who had given the artist several plugs since *A Biography*'s release. Unfortunately, word got out that John had called Melbourne's show "stupid," which resulted in a scathing Melbourne-penned article in a major Australian magazine. He apologized and the local celebrity forgave him, but the incident served as just one more blow to his shaky career.

Luckily, Jeff Franklin, founder of American Talent International Ltd.—which became one of the nation's foremost concert booking agencies—put together a record deal that would allow John to slither out of Australia to the U.S. of A. With that bit of news, he packed up his family, gave word to his band and returned home to sign a new deal (finally!) with Mercury-PolyGram. Ironically, Gaff had pitched "Johnny Cougar" to the label before shuttling him off to England, but they passed, partly due to personality conflicts with Gaff.

Once home, he received word that Phil Spector, creator of the legendary "Wall of Sound," wanted to produce a record for him. John flew to Los Angeles to meet with him, but got an uneasy feeling about Spector's unusual and controlling ways (he had become a recluse by the late '70s). John caught the next flight to Indianapolis before they even had a chance to grab dinner.

Although the Spector meeting went nowhere, John still had a commitment to deliver an album for PolyGram. He wanted to start off on the right foot with this company and promised himself he wouldn't repeat the mistakes he made with MCA. Before recording commenced, however, he wanted to add a second guitarist, then get the group rehearsed before the tape started rolling.

Mike Wanchic, the guitar player/engineer who had helped him out during the *Chestnut Street* sessions, appeared at the forefront of John's mind. At the time, Wanchic was a club fixture as the six-stringer for rock artist Randy Handley, Bloomington's hottest act next to a prog-rock band called Streamwinner. At the time, Dire Straits's stripped-down sound had started to win over U.S. and U.K. audiences, and John wanted to find someone who could replicate guitarist Mark Knopfler's classic style. Wanchic was one of the few guys in town that could. He signed on in 1978 and never left.

Wanchic's easygoing nature lent balance to John's high-strung, Type-A, hotheaded ways. "John was very volatile in those days," Wanchic said to author Martin Torgoff. "A lot of people couldn't work with him—you had to be very level-headed. He was hard to please, kind of like General Patton. If he didn't say anything, you knew you were doing okay." The people that stuck with John for the long haul also had to have a strong sense of self-worth and a skin thick enough to ignore a string of thoughtless insults and swear words. Wanchic had both, as well as the courage to stand by the frontman and support his vision no matter what got thrown their way.

PolyGram sent John and band to Criteria Studios in Miami to work with producers Ron and Howard Albert, the masterminds behind the country-tinged rock of the Allman Brothers, Stephen Stills, Byrds alum Roger McGuinn, Clark and Hillman and Firefall, among others. Legendary engineer/producer Tom Dowd—who had recorded everyone from Ray Charles to Aretha Franklin to Cream—oversaw the design and construction of Criteria, and had recorded a slew of albums there, including several for Rod Stewart. Hence, the Gaff connection. Gaff had approached Dowd about producing a Johnny Cougar record, but Dowd already had an overflowing plate of acts waiting to work with him, and wasn't completely moved by John's music anyway, so he passed the project on to the Albert brothers. Don Gehman, a staff engineer at the time, was their regular engineer. Gehman arrived at Criteria by way of Caribou Ranch in the Rocky Mountains near Nederland, Colorado, where he worked on Stephen Stills' *Illegal Stills* album. As a studio engineer, Gehman honed his craft with help from some of the best in the business—including Dowd, Phil Ramone and Bill Sczymczyk. When a young Johnny Cougar walked in the door, Gehman had seven years as a live sound engineer to his credit, and a few more as a studio engineer. He was still learning, but no newbie, by any means.

Much like Dowd, the Alberts didn't "get" John or his music. "They were nice guys, but they didn't really have a handle on who we were," Larry Crane recalled to Torgoff. "They were in a real Miami kind of cool groove, kind of behind the times." Wanchic added that they brought in a Dire Straits album to give the Albert brothers an idea of the sound they wanted, and they just turned up their noses. "It was volatile," says Gehman, "a situation where the Albert brothers were accustomed to cranking out records a certain way, and John was in the mood to explore. He was looking for who he was, and he didn't really know how to make records yet. The Alberts didn't have a lot of patience for that, so they put a lot of it on me. 'Don, if he wants to try something go ahead. When you're done, we'll come in and tell you whether we like it or not.' A lot of the record was made that way, where I took care of John and made him feel like he was getting a chance to make the record he wanted to make."

The majority of the album featured new songs such as "Miami," "Foxy" and "Small Paradise," among others, most of them focusing on lust in various settings and circumstances. They resurrected "Taxi Dancer" and "I Need a Lover" from *A Biography*, and promptly gave them a serious polish. In the process, the Alberts produced most of the life out of "I Need a Lover." John didn't like the new version, and after repeated listenings, neither did Gaff. He battled brutally with the producers over the song, and ultimately won out. The original version is what appears on record.

Wanchic agrees with Gehman that yes, John and Co. didn't really know what they were doing yet. They knew what they liked, but hadn't quite figured out how to turn that into their own sound. Because John was so green, the record label had an easier time extorting influence over his music. Ultimately, the record label and producer's vision overshadowed the artist's on John's PolyGram debut. Because he had such a hard time communicating what he wanted, others involved steamrolled over his ideas for raw, rock 'n' roll. This frustrated him, and, as we've learned, he didn't deal with frustration well. Rumors flew around the studio about that John Cougar...a *little bastard*. The name stuck.

The album hit the streets in the summer of 1979, a close-up of John looking less of a pretty boy now with a few days of stubble, a cigarette in his mouth and a head of dark hair that didn't look like it had lost a war with a blow-dryer. He's scowling now, has the expression of a man who's got a few scars, and he does. This Johnny crap, he decided, had to go; thus, PolyGram titled the album, simply, *John Cougar*.

Mike Chapman, who had first heard "I Need a Lover" at John's show at The Whisky, was producing an album for Pat Benetar. He never could get that darn chorus out of his head, and ultimately requested the song for his artist.

Her version, released on her *In the Heat of the Night* album, got heavy airplay—one of the most-played album cuts on FM radio—broke her career and gave the songwriter a chance at legitimate success. His version reached a respectable Number 28 on *Billboard*'s Hot 100 chart. Combined with the publicity from the Benetar cover, he had a reasonably successful album under his belt. He and his band, now called The Zone soon ventured out for a series of live dates. He expanded the lineup with Eric "Doc" Rosser, a pianist from Indiana University.

They played any club that would let them in and opened for just about any band they could—Ian Hunter, Kiss, Rainbow, Judas Priest, R.E.O. Speedwagon, you name it. No matter how cool the band, John found someone to butt heads with. Once, on a tour with Head East, he wanted to beat the lead singer with a club, but ended up pounding his dressing room door instead.

When they weren't warming up another band's audience, John and The

Zone played clubs and dives across the U.S. Sometimes they played to only the bartenders, who glared through the whole set hoping they would stop so they could go home. "We basically hit every dump in the world," says Wanchic. "I remember going to a restaurant/club one time in Albany. The marquee said, 'whale of a fish fry!' in big letters, and then underneath it said, in very small letters, John Cougar. The friggin' fish fry got top billing!"

But no matter where or to how many, John and his troops put on a frenetic performance. Their intense energy, combined with a heavy dose of humor, made them a formidable warm-up act. They combined John's originals with a set of covers that included everything from The Stones' "Honky Tonk Woman" to Iggy Pop's "Search and Destroy." While the band played with as much enthusiasm and precision as they could muster, their lead singer leapt onto speakers, onto Wanchic's shoulders or sometimes accidentally colliding right into his guitar, as in the case of a show at the Bottom Line in New York City. When the band opened for Kiss, he had a great time sprinting down a long runway specifically designated for the headliner. The tour manager told him not to, so that's exactly what he did!

In 1979, John made his first of what would be many *American Bandstand* appearances. He essentially tore himself down during his debut by telling host Dick Clark that he and his band were "just a bunch of hillbillies who don't know how to act." They certainly proved that point on national TV. He redeemed himself, monetarily at least, when he received his first significant royalty check—far more than that measly $27.59 statement awarded in 1977—for Benetar's version of "I Need a Lover." The check gave him enough money to buy a spacious redwood house not far from Lake Monroe. His father advised it, saying John had better invest that money because someday, all of this celebrity business would fade and he'd need a place to live. The frivolous stuff could come later.

John finally seemed to have his career headed in a credible direction when a vinyl single called "U.S. Male," released by a tiny Bloomington label called Gulcher Records appeared in 1978. Local resident Bob Richert pressed and released 2,000 copies of the single, which featured John's demo version of "Kicks" that he recorded while label-hunting in New York City. "I met Bob Richert years ago while he was working for a paper factory in Indiana," John said in a 1979 interview with *Blitz* magazine. "I was interested in buying a couple of reams of paper from him, but the price was a lot more than I could afford at the time. He knew that I was a musician and asked me if I had any demo tapes. I did—the four songs that were released on the EP. He said he'd give me the reams of paper if I'd turn the demo tapes and release the rights for them over to him, which I did. I never even knew that record was out until I saw it in a store a couple of months ago."

The press had a hard time saying goodbye to Johnny Cougar. Instead of recognizing his progress as an artist, they considered his small-town image and simple-life lyrics a pale comparison to Jersey boy Bruce Springsteen, and would continue to link the two artists for years to come. John bristled whenever he heard The Boss' name. "To be honest, I think the so-called 'street-wise' image built up around Bruce Springsteen is a scam," he told one reporter. He would go on to admit that he knew his music wasn't completely original, that he tried to emulate artists such as Donovan, Mitch Ryder, Eric Burdon and The Animals—artists whose music creates a "feeling of complete musical fulfillment." He wanted his music to elicit the same response, especially the songs on his next album, which he thought would have an "acoustic flavor" but with all the energy and intensity of classic rock 'n' roll. Now that more people were starting to take notice, he *really* had something to prove.

CHAPTER THREE

I NEED A DRUMMER WHO WON'T DRIVE ME CRAZY

I n 1976, some friends from drummer Kenny Aronoff's Indiana University days lured him back to Bloomington from his native Stockbridge, Massachusetts. He had returned to the East Coast after earning his Bachelor's of Music Performance degree at IU, where he was awarded the prestigious Performer's Certificate. Around this time, he started taking drum *set* lessons. Since he was old enough to drive, Aronoff had focused his studies on classical percussion and tympani, learning his craft with the Boston Symphony Orchestra and at the University of Massachusetts, before completing his degree at IU. In his heart of hearts, he knew he had more passion for rock 'n' roll than he did for tympani, so he gave 110 percent to the craft.

For months before his friends called him back to Bloomington, Aronoff practiced eight hours a day and played in a fusion rock band at night. Upon returning to the Midwest in the summer of 1977, he formed Streamwinner, a jazz fusion group that featured David Grissom on guitar. With Streamwinner on its feet and circulating the local club circuit, he resumed the ritual he had established back East: practice his ass off during the day; play with the band at night.

While Aronoff developed his reputation around town as a powerhouse drummer, Johnny Cougar inhabited the same area in a different orbit. "He was this guy that's famous!" recalls Aronoff. "He was going on tours, but it was all just beginning, so you just heard about it. This guy, Johnny Cougar, he's going on tour with Kiss, and he's got a record deal…but I wasn't even trying to be part of that." Aronoff, who had grown accustomed to jazz and fusion's complex time signatures and rhythmic structure, essentially turned away from Johnny

Cougar's commercial rock.

As much as he enjoyed playing in Streamwinner, in early 1980, a 27-year-old Aronoff decided that he would have to make a significant move—either to L.A. or New York—to take his career to the next level. He chose New York, where he had friends and contacts and could live near his family. Two weeks before his second departure from Bloomington, he auditioned for a job playing with Lou Rawls. On his way to the Indianapolis airport, he stopped in vegetarian Tao Restaurant in Bloomington to relax and grab a bite. There, he bumped into local singer-songwriter Ruthie Allen, who said, "Johnny Cougar fired his drummer last night. Do you know him?" Drummer Tom Knowles had found out that John issued guitarist Larry Crane a cash bonus for his work on "I Need a Lover." When Knowles demanded the same, he got his walking papers.

Aronoff paid his tab, calmly walked to a nearby phone booth and called up Mike Wanchic, whom he knew from his tenure with Randy Handley, Streamwinner's rival in the club scene. Wanchic confirmed that, yes, Cougar was auditioning drummers, but John was moving into a new house and was in a bit of a transition. Call back in a couple of weeks.

"In Kenny's tradition, he was aggressive," Wanchic recalled. "He said, 'Let me audition! Let me audition!' Kenny and I both came from a somewhat more sophisticated musical background, initially. John had a raw, intuitive nature about him: James Dean with a bigger edge."

Aronoff didn't get the Lou Rawls gig, but he wasn't disappointed. He had already decided that he wanted the job with John Cougar, bad. "I started thinking about John and I went, 'Wow. Radio, touring and records,'" Aronoff said. "When I was a kid, I wanted to be in The Beatles—I saw *Hard Day's Night*, and the next week I started a band. It suddenly hit me…My God, this is why I had Streamwinner: I wanted to be in a rock 'n' roll band, but I was picking music that wasn't going to get played on the radio. I thought, 'Wow, I could be in The Beatles, basically.' Suddenly, winning this audition meant everything to me."

Aronoff called back as instructed, and got the audition. To prepare, Wanchic told Aronoff to "be familiar" with the *John Cougar* album. "Be familiar…you could take that as listen to it in your car," says Aronoff. But he didn't. "I literally wrote out every note, practiced every song on the album six to eight hours a day for two weeks," he said. "When it came time to audition, I was definitely familiar with the material." That was an understatement.

Aronoff—driven, determined, but appearing as cool as could be—carried an enormous drum kit into Cougar's basement. His kit included nine toms, at least as many cymbals and two bass drums—the assemblage would have made Rush drummer Neil Peart proud. But John came from the Charlie Watts school: two tom-toms, a bass drum and a snare. That's it. He shot Aronoff a disgusted look as he carried in the second bass drum. Aronoff pretended not to notice and finished setting up his kit.

The band casually asked the eager drummer, who now took up most of the room, "Well, do you know anything off the record?" "Yeah, I think I do," he replied, not letting on to his nearly 80 hours of practice. He backed Wanchic, Crane and John for a run-through of "I Need a Lover," and ripped through the song with such force, his new home virtually rattled off its foundation. "It was the loudest thing I had ever heard in my life," Wanchic stated. "He split two cymbals in one song."

He broke some sticks, too. "I'm a very hard hitter, and back then I thought I should be *louder* than what I'm used to. I think John may have seen my intensity, which is really a big part of my playing. I don't even take credit for it—that's just the way I'm made. I'm hot, I'm intense." He's Italian. And he's a rock 'n' roll drummer.

When they finished the song, John looked startled, a rare expression for the fearless performer. They went into "Living in Miami," and again, Aronoff virtually rattled the walls.

After the audition, John charged upstairs without saying a word. A few minutes later, the band hears him scream, "Mike, come up here!" Wanchic looked at Aronoff with a grin, as if to say, 'This happens all the time.'

He disappeared upstairs to converse with his bandleader. When he came back to the rehearsal room, Wanchic walked over to their new drummer, stuck out his hand and said, "Congratulations. Welcome to hell."

About two weeks after Aronoff entered The Zone, the band received a visit from guitar legend Steve Cropper, who was tapped to produce John's next record. Cropper's exceedingly long track record starts in Memphis as a founding member of Booker T. and the MG's, songwriting partner of Otis Redding and guitarist, producer and/or songwriter for just about every Stax Records project from 1961 to 1970. He wrote or co-wrote some of soul's biggest hits, including "Sittin' By the Dock of the Bay," Eddie Floyd's "Knock On Wood" and Wilson Pickett's "In the Midnight Hour," to name a few. As a producer, his credits include albums for American songwriting great John Prine, Poco, Tower of Power and Jeff Beck, among others.

When Cropper flew from Los Angeles to Bloomington to meet with John and the band, he had just wrapped up two albums with Levon Helm's RCO All-Stars band; re-established his own solo career with the first of two MCA albums, *Playing' My Thang*; and had landed a gig with the Blues Brothers Band. Helm's manager introduced Cropper to talent agent Jeff Franklin, who then put Cropper and John together to discuss his second album for PolyGram. John had initially wanted Don Gehman, his patient engineer on the *John Cougar* album, to produce; but, alas, Barbra Streisand had booked him for her landmark

Guilty album—produced, co-written by Barry Gibb and recorded at the Gibb brothers' Middle Ear studio, where Gehman worked at the time. The album went on to sell more than 20 million units. No doubt he made the right choice.

John then deferred to Cropper, who seemed like a logical fit considering John's longtime love of early soul music, and his desire to bring more of an R&B feel to his music. Besides, Cropper had more experience and skill than John and his bandmates combined.

Cropper spent two weeks in Bloomington observing the rehearsal sessions, which usually ran from 1 P.M. to 5 P.M., then resumed after a dinner break at 7 P.M. One day, Aronoff and Cropper missed the 7 P.M. call time. They had gone out for drinks instead. "I knew Kenny had decided to suck up to Cropper," John said in an interview with *Billboard*. "So I tore Kenny a new asshole."

Aside from the local watering holes, Cropper spent his minimal time off cruising around the southern Indiana countryside, hanging out along Lake Monroe, frequenting the local meat and three diners or milling around antique stores. "That's when I got the education of the Little 500," says Cropper of Indiana University's popular cycling race. "I had never really been in that area, and John and the guys were the greatest hosts. We had a good time for a couple of weeks, then after I got back home we set up a time for them to come to the studio to record."

John and Larry Crane had four albums worth of studio experience, Wanchic and Aronoff had years of live experience, but all were still relatively green in terms of recording on a professional level. But John's manager, Billy Gaff, had high expectations for this album, to be titled *Nothin' Matters and What If It Did*, and so did John. He had achieved some notoriety with "I Need a Lover." The goal now was to exceed that by delivering an album with at least a couple of solid hits.

But even as he prepared for his trip to L.A., thoughts of ditching the music business altogether crept into his mind. He still carried a chip on his shoulder from the MainMan nightmare, and his personal life was a mess. His relationship with Pricilla had become strained to the point where she moved out of their home and into an apartment across town with their daughter, Michelle. As they grew apart, John had assumed a long-distance relationship with Vicky Granucci, a pretty blonde that he met in Los Angeles. When Pricilla moved out, he asked Vicky to come and live with him in Indiana. She said yes, but the transition wreaked havoc on John's anxiety level. The fact that some of his friends called her the "blonde home-wrecker from Los Angeles," behind her back didn't help. But John worried most about Michelle's well-being. "Michelle would come over and I'd have to leave and hang out at the mall," Granucci told author Martin Torgoff. "I'd feel terrible: She'd come over and eat this meal that this witch—the other woman—had prepared for her, and then leave. John was trying to protect everybody else's feelings, and it wasn't working; he was tearing himself apart."

Granucci took matters into her own hands by visiting Pricila at the property management office where she worked. The home-wrecker and the estranged wife had a heart-to-heart, shared their feelings about the situation and resolved to make it work for Michelle's sake. Over time, they even became friends.

John had to put all of this personal business aside for about four weeks in 1980 when Cropper booked time at Cherokee Studios, a premier L.A. recording facility that boasted such clients as Steely Dan, ELO, Aerosmith and Al Green, to record *Nothin' Matters and What If It Did*. On the docket were 10 of John's originals, including feisty tunes such as "Wild Angel," "Make Me Feel," "Cry Baby" and "This Time," as well as his version of "Hot Night in a Cold Town," a song also recorded by Steppenwolf and Uriah Heep. Studio owners Bruce and Dee Robb, friends of Cropper's, engineered the sessions with most of The Zone in place. First-call session musicians such as pedal steel player Jeff "Skunk" Baxter, pianist John Jarvis and sax man David Woodford enhanced the core lineup.

Cropper recalls that John had very strong ideas and entertained very few others from outsiders. Even Cropper, with his decades of experience, squeezed in only a few. "The bass line and the intro of 'Ain't Even Done With the Night' are taken from a song I had with the Mar-Keys called 'Philly Dog,'" he says. He did teach John and the band invaluable lessons in studio etiquette. "I thought John was a very strong entertainer, but at the time I was producing him I'd never seen him entertain," he continues. "I didn't really know quite what to expect until we got him on the microphone. I think we taught him a lot. He picked things up very quickly—how to stand, where to stand, how to treat a microphone and all that. He wasn't brand new at it, but I think by coming out to California and working with some pros, he got a pretty good education on how to make records."

Wanchic learned how to emphasize his unique strengths as a guitarist by playing what felt right to him, rather than copy an Eddie Van Halen lick. Crane refined his sense of tempo and rhythm. But Cropper's pal Aronoff probably learned the hardest lesson from the *Nothin' Matters* sessions. At Cropper's request, John fired Aronoff from the project within an hour of recording. "I felt that we needed some real heavy experience studio-wise on the record," says Cropper. "So I elected not to use Kenny, which was a tough decision to make."

Drum tracks serve as the foundation for an entire record, so naturally Cropper wanted a drummer with a proven track record in the studio. They had only a small window of time to record drums, and Aronoff, the newbie in the band, didn't make the cut. He didn't have the two-play tom heads that had become fashionable in L.A., and he didn't have tenure with the band. "I wasn't coming from the school of The Rolling Stones," Aronoff adds. "My heart wasn't there yet. But that's where John's heart was, and he was looking for that kind of drummer." Plus, he felt anxious in this new environment. "John gave me a chance to come in there and do it," he says. "But there was a lot of tension between me and John, and Cropper could see that." He could hear it, too. "If you feel tense, you sound tense. If you feel uptight you will sound uptight. We started, and the sounds weren't right, so they made the executive decision to bring in the session guys."

Cropper called in L.A. heavyweights Rich Schlosser and Ed Greene to play drums on the album. While they busied themselves getting new drum sounds, the band took the rest of the day off. John called Aronoff into his hotel room. "He basically said, 'I'll pay you for the rest of the week, you know, and so you go home and practice, and we're going to make this record, and maybe we'll go on tour later...' After he finished saying everything, I just said, 'No.' And I'm thinking to myself, 'I can't believe I just said that! I'm telling the boss no!'" John looked shocked. Maybe not as shocked as the first time he heard Aronoff smash cymbals, but his new drummer's moxie certainly took him by surprise. Aronoff wouldn't go down without a fight. He bluntly asked, "Am I still the drummer in your band?" John stared at him, perplexed. He said it again, a little louder: "Am I still the drummer in your band?"

"Well, yeah..."

"Fine, then I'm going to stay here. You don't have to pay me. I'll sleep on the floor, I don't care, but I'm going to watch these drummers play my parts. And I'm going to learn from them, and I'm going to benefit from that and because I'm the drummer in your band, you're going to benefit from me learning."

What could John say? He saw a fighter in his drummer. "This was the beginning of Kenny's aggressive stance. John admires that," recalls Wanchic, who saw the whole scene. "It had happened to me on the record before that. He took me into the parking lot and said, 'Mike, you're going home,' and I said, 'Fuck you.' If you want to stay in this band, that's the kind of attitude you've got to have, because the weak will fall. This is not a job for the mild-mannered."

Aronoff made it clear that he would play on the next record, period. The rest of the band—Crane, Wanchic, bassist Robert "Ferd" Frank, piano player Doc Rosser and their requisite sidemen—set about the somewhat laborious task of recording an album. The sessions yielded "This Time," John's first attempt at a commercial love song, influenced by his new love, Vicky. "The first time I heard it on the radio I almost puked," John said. "I decided never to try to write a formula song like that again." It made it up to Number 27 in 1980. Much to John's surprise, the second single, "Ain't Even Done With the Night," with its Stax sax solo, climbed to 17.

In the studio, Cropper didn't challenge John's strong opinions, though they did clash over some of the album's lyrics, with good reason. "Tonight" contains lines about the "son of a bitch" boss man and winners such as, 'Come here little boy/I'll put my pussy right on your face.'" "Cry Baby" offered equally enlightening lines:

> "My baby is a cry cry baby
> She sits on my lap and balls
> My baby is a top mechanic
> She works with my nuts until…"

PolyGram loved the album, in spite of the lead track, "Cheap Shot," which takes a stab at their very industry.

> "Well the PDs they won't play the record
> They're too worried about that book
> And the DJs they all hate the song
> But they're in love with the hook."

John did *not* love this album and made his feelings very clear. "I hated making that record…" he said in an interview with *Musician*. "It cost so much to make and it sounds horrible and I didn't care enough to do anything about it. That was the real problem. Everywhere I turned, people were ridiculing me, and I tried to say it didn't matter to cover my ass. But, of course, it did."

While the band plugged through John's material, Aronoff planted himself on the sofa in the Cherokee Studio One control room and watched Schlosser and Greene work. He took notes. He asked them questions during breaks. Upon studying their instruments, he changed his kit to include double-ply tom heads. When everyone else retreated to their hotel rooms, he crashed on the studio floor. It was a humiliating and humbling experience, but a turning point in Aronoff's career. Schlosser and Greene both gave him valuable advice about hitting with consistency and playing with flow. Ultimately, he did get an album credit…for playing vibes.

After a month of experiential learning, Aronoff flew back to Bloomington while the rest of the band stayed in town to shoot music videos for "This Time" and "Ain't Even Done With the Night," with Bruce and Dee Robb mixing the album. As producer, Cropper had to miss the mix sessions due to previously booked shows with Dan Ackroyd and John Belushi's Blues Brothers Band, but John offered up plenty of opinion in his absence. Meanwhile, Aronoff hunkered down in Indiana and transmuted his frustration into relentless determination. "Eight hours a day, seven days a week, I practiced, all based on what I'd learned in L.A.," he says. "I changed my whole style of playing."

The album title—*Nothin' Matters and What If It Did*—came from John's friend Gary Boebinger, who tossed off the slogan one day when they were up to their usual no good. As John recalled to *Billboard*, "I said, 'Well I don't think the consequences would be catastrophic if we did this. But everybody we know will hate us if we do this.' [Gary] just looked at me and said, 'Nothing matters, and what if it did?' I don't remember exactly what it was we were contemplating...but we were very cavalier young men at the time, so I assume it was something we weren't supposed to be doing."

Video producer Simon Fields and director Bruce Gowers guided the videos for "Ain't Even Done With the Night" and "This Time," the later of which co-starred Edith Massey, best known for her role as Edie The Egg Lady in John Waters' *Pink Flamingos*. She's also the buxom blonde that graces the cover of the album. In "This Time," John serenades voluptuous Edie, who flips off her ostrich feather boa and hangs on John's every word. The Zone, decked out in white tuxedoes, mimicked the background music.

The band also dressed handsomely for "Ain't Even Done With the Night," in which they sashayed through synchronized dance moves *a la* The Temptations while John lip-synched to the camera. The video's freeze-frames and white background display a modest attempt to point to John's '60s soul influences.

As much as he hated it, John hammed it up quite well for the camera. His successful 1980 appearance on *American Bandstand* marked the beginning of a long, fruitful relationship with the program, although a botched performance on that year's AMA Awards showed that he still had a bit of media training ahead of him. A quick glance at the formally dressed crowd at the Shrine Auditorium in Pasadena, California led to a heightened case of anxiety; next thing you know, his feet slid clumsily around the slick stage floor, the mic fell out of his hand, and his throat choked up so that he could barely breathe, which certainly didn't help his singing voice. Safely offstage, he experienced a full-on panic attack that was so intense, he checked himself into Cedars-Sinai Medical Center in Los Angeles.

When the band returned to Bloomington, there was no grand reunion with their dejected drummer, Kenny Aronoff. John seemed ambivalent about giving him a permanent place in the group. John's initial response: "Let's start rehearsing and see if it works out." It did. His reaction: "We're going on tour with The Kinks, why don't you go on tour with us and see how it goes." It went. Even after a long tour, Aronoff still didn't know if he was in or out, as though he still had to prove himself. He, and others within John's inner circle, would share these feelings for most of their career. John may have wanted them to feel ill at ease. The tension created a livewire type energy in the studio, and seemed to keep everyone on their toes. Aronoff held on to his confidence after

The Kinks tour and focused his energy on playing even better.

John and The Zone toured with The Kinks for 1,000 dates at $500 each, playing to crowds all over the U.S. They helped fill the Midwest venues, which was one of The Kinks' weaker markets, while audiences in other parts of the U.S. got one of their first tastes of John Cougar's boundless energy. John's onstage presence mimicked the bravado in his song material. He usually introduced himself with a series of acrobatics, then darted across the stage with fists pumping, then found himself mid-set rolling around on the floor and carrying on like a hyperactive kid at recess. He even went so far as to wrestle women on stage, encouraging the bravest (or stupidest) ones to climb up on stage for a match that they would never win. "She'll go down!" he'd yell. The set also included X-rated versions of "Louie, Louie" and "Hang On Sloopy." The whole 45-minute he-man display may have gone over well with some of the southern Indiana boys, but others left the venue scratching their heads. "His onstage persona, as seen at the Bottom Line last week, is cut from the same cloth as Mitch Ryder, Eric Burdon and other macho twits," wrote *Village Voice* critic Ed Naha, who went on to call John Cougar a "sexist nerd" and to suggest readers check their IQs at the door before catching his show. Naha later admits, however, that he performed "with such wide-eyed glee that very few people in the audience took offense. Well, at least no one threw anything at him..."

Not all reviews were that bad, and with the minor success of *Nothin' Matters'* two singles, radio programmers, label execs and concert promoters started paying attention to this Indiana brat. They doubted he had another album in him, but they would keep their eye on him all the same.

John lost more than $200,000 during those eight months on the road as the opening band for an act that didn't like him one bit. "We used to laugh at Ray and Dave [Davies] because they always used to fight and spit on each other," John told *Billboard*. "And they hated me, but I did two tours with them; I had to—it was either open for them or for Uriah Heep! [Laughs]" Sadly, most of John's tourmates didn't like him. He recalls these first few years on the road as a comedy of errors, from tin can-sounding venues, to destructive outbursts. The pretty girls made those eight months bearable though.

With the tour under wraps, John came home to Indiana to an equally chaotic life, reuniting with his girlfriend, his estranged wife and his daughter. On the brink of his thirtieth birthday, John again contemplated leaving the record business. (He would grapple with this issue after almost every album and tour.) The anxiety he felt from performing every night, traveling from city to city and dealing with myriad uncooperative people and business issues was almost unbearable. He had some money saved—a couple of cars, motorcycles and a nice house. Why not just quit while he was ahead?

While he struggled to figure out his next career move, he also had to sort out his personal life. Girlfriend Vicky Granucci, now in her early twenties, was pregnant. He wanted to do the right thing and marry her, but he had to divorce his wife first! He and Pricilla Mellencamp filed the proper papers and amicably reached an agreement. Their marriage had officially ended, but they vowed to maintain a friendly relationship for their daughter's sake.

On May 23, 1981, John Mellencamp married a six-months pregnant Granucci during a ceremony held at his parents' house in Seymour, Indiana. Not only did his former wife, Pricilla Esterline, attend the wedding, she helped Granucci pick out her dress! With the vows made and the rings exchanged, John kissed his new bride, accepted congratulatory words from friends and family, then promptly dragged his friends and bandmates into the backyard for a game of flag football, one of his favorite activities. They played with a vengeance.

With fatherhood only months away, John considered his future and his responsibilities to his new wife and child. He realized that aside from possibly manual labor, he had no real marketable skills outside of playing music. More importantly, he understood at a very deep level that he didn't want to do anything *but* make music. He knew now that quitting was not an option. But to make it work, he had to do things differently. He couldn't continue making the overly polished fare that other people wanted him to make and look his new child in the eye. It had to be his way or no way, which turned out to be the only way for him.

CHAPTER FOUR

NOTHIN' MATTERS TO AN AMERICAN FOOL

As much as John learned from Steve Cropper, *Nothin' Matters and What If It Did* only hinted at what John and his band could do. John wanted to make an even better next album, even though he didn't have a vision for it yet. Well, actually, he had to step up, as he had fulfilled his initial agreement with PolyGram and they informed him that if he didn't start taking his career more seriously, they would drop him, no questions asked. They had also had enough of his mouth, so he had better show them a smidge of respect and stop telling them "No," and "fuck you." John thought this over. He was serious about his music, but he was also seriously living the cavalier, rock 'n' roll lifestyle. He didn't want to get dropped now—he was just getting started! A new game plan slowly came into focus.

In order to deliver an album strong enough to please PolyGram and himself, John wanted to work alone, with no outside A&R men or record producers telling him what to do. But PolyGram didn't take to that request, and suggested several outside producers to John. He turned them all down while plotting a workaround with Mike Wanchic. "We thought, 'What about the engineer we worked with on the *John Cougar* record?' says Wanchic.

John called Don Gehman, hoping he wouldn't turn him down again. "Come on man! Let's go make a record together," he asked. Gehman hesitated at first, but ultimately agreed. "I realized it was an opportunity I had to take," he says.

Though he received a production credit on Stephen Stills' *Illegal Stills* album, Gehman worked mainly as an engineer at this time, albeit a very good one, which is exactly what John wanted. To appease the label, John declared Gehman co-producer, although John fully intended to produce the record himself with no outside influences. "With Gehman, we would have an engineer, *and* we could make our own record," says Wanchic. Reluctantly, PolyGram agreed that they could work with Gehman, although they didn't know about the workaround.

John stripped the band down to its core: Larry Crane on rhythm guitar, Wanchic on lead, Kenny Aronoff on drums and "Ferd" on bass. They rehearsed the songs John had written—about 30 of them, written in a flurry—for eight to 12 hours a day at The Bunker, the name given to the tiny space underneath John's carport. His dogs slept there. When he felt the band had learned the songs well enough, they made the pilgrimage to Miami to join Gehman at Criteria Studios. John hobbled in on crutches, having crashed his motorcycle one night after rehearsal. He wasn't wearing a helmet, but the lucky bastard limped away with nothing more than a big hole in his knee.

"Whatever you've heard before, I want it different and I want it better," John said, a career-long credo that began with this record, later titled *American Fool*. He wanted the songs to leap out of people's car speakers. He wanted pounding drums. He wanted it to sound "like the Pittsburgh Steelers on a power sweep, like 50,000 stomping fans in the bleachers, like the assembly line of a mill, like a fucking war; like every rock song I'd ever heard or dreamed about in my life," he told author Martin Torgoff. He wanted stripped down rock 'n' roll on steroids. Now they just had to figure out how to do that.

But before they even had a chance to get drum sounds, John's new bride went into labor—a month and a half early. John rushed back to Indiana, but the baby didn't wait. On July 1, 1981, Vicky Mellencamp gave birth to Teddi Jo Mellencamp, with John still in transit. He returned to Miami a week later to commence recording.

Most of the 30 songs they had on the docket were merely mediocre, a byproduct of John's underdeveloped songwriting skills. He had great melodic and lyrical ideas, but had a lot to learn about logically arranging them into a song. Arrangements often happened by quorum, with John always having the final word. Intimidating as it was, John encouraged everyone's input, even if he shot it right down. "Being totally candid is the most important thing about making records with John," Mike Wanchic explains. "Any stimuli that comes in could take you somewhere. We've operated like that from *American Fool* forward. For every 10 bad ideas, there might be one brilliant one."

It took endless trial and error to get the song and the sound right. The studio's acoustics added to the messiness of the project. They wanted a "live" drum sound, which meant that when Aronoff pummeled his kit, the sound would reverberate off the walls, giving it a full sound with a lot of echo. But the room they worked in was "as dead as it comes," which made the drums sound flat—the opposite of what they wanted. Gehman tried to liven it up by using various electronic echo boxes, but still had a hard time getting the desired sound. In addition, Gehman hadn't worked on anything like this before. The Bee Gees, whom he had worked with prior to *American Fool*, had a highly produced, layered, pristine sound, and his first production, with Stephen Stills, came from a quiet, acoustic school. "All of the hard rock records that John was trying to chase as far as attitude, I had no idea how they were made," he says. "So it was a mess, but it's always a mess with John. He's always trying to push things further than anyone else has, that's his thing: go further and compete on a higher level; do better...push, push, push."

Mick Ronson, a blast from the sorted DeFries past, came in for one day to record guitar parts. While he was there, he showed Gehman a gated echo trick for the snare drum that virtually solved their drum sound problem. The focus stayed on Aronoff, who had to come up with a drum solo for "Jack and Diane" on the spot. John wanted a break similar to Phil Collins' "In the Air Tonight," which was hot on pop radio at the time. "It was a lot of pressure and a lot of work to come up with a solo that people would remember forever," Aronoff recalls.

They spent five hours getting drum sounds for that one song alone, with Gehman moving around mics to find the appropriate "sweet spot" in the room. It was up to Aronoff to come up with a memorable drum fill.

"It didn't just roll off my tongue," he says. "I was trying one thing at a time, up the toms, down the toms, with eight people looking at me, everybody making suggestions, trying to put their two cents in. Then I just melded my fusion jazz background, and ideas from the [LinnDrum] machine part I programmed the night before, into what the song was."

Coincidentally, the Bee Gees were recording next door, and their engineer/producer for those sessions, Alby Galuten, lent them the LinnDrum. They made the handclaps on "Jack and Diane" with that machine too, though they never intended to keep them. "The real drums don't come in until halfway into the song," John told *Billboard*, "and we were a bar band that never noticed if our songs sped up or slowed down, and once we put the drum machine's handclaps on the track, you couldn't budge off of it. When we later took the handclaps out, we said, "Man, this song sucks now. [Laughs] Put the handclaps back in!"

The idea for the bridge, which is actually the closest thing to a chorus the song has, came from the same fella who sang the low harmonies on that part— platinum-haired Ronson, who not only saved the day, but also livened things up when the endless sessions became a drudge. "He was the consummate English guitar player," says Wanchic. "He said, 'You got to make it interesting, you got to put, like, baby rattles and stuff on it.' We looked at him like, what planet is he on? But his point was taken—come up with unusual sounds."

Another one of the song's defining elements is the little two-note staccato di-dit guitar part right before each verse. "When I came up with that," John told *Billboard*, "I remember telling [guitarist] Larry [Crane] to do it, and he said, "Fuck you, I'm not playing that. It's just one stupid note." I said, "Yeah, but it's the rhythm of it that's cool!" He wouldn't play it—I had to."

With John at the helm and Gehman as the voice of reason, the band pieced together the rest of the song over many, many tracks to become the tribute we know now as John's homage to lost youth. The story of "two American kids growing up in the heartland," spending afternoons "sucking on chili dogs outside the Tastee Freez" could have been about any teenage couple in any small town in America. But like most of the songs on *American Fool*, he said later that the song was just a "stream of consciousness thing," that he really didn't have anyone in particular in mind when he wrote it. But it speaks to so many.

John and band spent nine weeks and about $150,000 in Miami, but ended up with only three usable songs—partly because they didn't know how to arrange songs, partly because they spent a lot of time dicking around. John had no idea how much money he spent; whenever he ran out of whatever money the label fronted him, he'd turn to his manager, Billy Gaff, who presumably pulled from the Rod Stewart fund (also one of his clients). At one point, he and Wanchic got sick of staying in the rented band house, so they moved to Burt Reynolds' three-bedroom bachelor's lair. With so many buxom bombshells walking around, they could have easily forgotten all about Criteria, and darn near did. Gaff sent down their old A&R friend Bob Davis to give them the "put out or get out" speech, but he got too drunk to deliver.

John wanted to scrap "Jack and Diane," but the band and his wife convinced him otherwise. He also kept "Hand to Hold Onto," "Thundering Hearts" and seven more tunes for a 10-song composite to submit to PolyGram. "Well, there goes our Neil Diamond," remarked one A&R exec, who expected a smooth, MOR album. They wanted the Bee Gees; instead, they got something closer to Mitch Ryder. The drums were noisy, they complained, and the whole thing sounded like it was recorded in a garage. Exactly! That was the sound John was going for, but the label didn't get it. Shocked and unimpressed, PolyGram shelved the album. Gaff, for all of his shortcomings, stood by John and convinced PolyGram to let John record more material, provided he buckle down, which was what he was supposed to do in the first place.

John and band left Miami minus one bass player and keyboard player. After a huge blowout, John fired keyboardist Doc Rosser and "Ferd," who smashed his bass to bits on Criteria's floor and then disappeared from the building.

With the enormous debt to PolyGram hanging over his head, John stewed in Indiana to write more songs. Periodically, John called up Gehman to play him what he had written, some of it with lyricist friend George Green. It wasn't until December 1981 that John called him with a plan. He had a few songs that would fit the album, one of which he thought was a hit, and was ready to go back into the studio. But this time, he wanted to go to Cherokee Studios in L.A. and use the same room and the same assistant engineer from *Nothin' Matters and What If It Did*—sans Cropper and the Robb brothers.

Bruce Robb's wife and Cherokee studio manager, Susan Robb, booked the time. Almost immediately Steve Cropper got a call from Bruce Robb, saying, "Get this! I thought you might want to know that John Cougar's people just called..." But Cropper didn't take it personally. He was in the middle of several other projects, Blues Brothers included, but he did find the situation a bit amusing. "Obviously he realized the value of having been in that studio and the sound it created," he says.

The core group—John, Larry Crane, Kenny Aronoff, Mike Wanchic and Don Gehman—holed up in Cherokee's main studio for one intense week of recording, followed by two weeks of mixing. The band came up with straight-up three-chord rock for "Hurts So Good" pretty easily, although it would take them at least 55 takes before they got a "keeper." Thankfully, the remaining songs didn't require quite so many tries. In place of Ferd, Gehman brought in George "Chocolate" Perry on bass, who seemed to gel well with Aronoff, who started playing some songs left-handed; on "Hurts So Good," he could keep the cymbals going while doing tom fills with his right hand. Overall, the band had discovered feel as they continued to work on song structure. Some songs had mistakes, but if it felt good, they kept them in.

About midway through all of their hard work, PolyGram sent over one of their A&R reps to see how the album was progressing. After listening to the rough mixes, the poor paper pusher, who had visions of more vanilla "Ain't Even Done With the Night," suggested that John add horns to a few songs. They threw him out of the building—literally—and onto the sidewalk. "It was almost *Spinal Tap*-ish," recalls Wanchic. Neither he, nor anyone else from the record label, was allowed back.

"I want it different and I want it better," was the motto, and this time, that also meant big, raw and loud. Real loud. They even blew out the control room speakers because the record was so loud, much to the chagrin of the Robb brothers. "Hey, you can't do that!" they yelled when they realized how loud they were listening. The five-foot-seven firecracker tackled one of them, shouting, "Oh yes I can! I paid for this studio and I can do whatever the fuck I want!" They added speaker repair expenses to PolyGram's studio bill.

A total of eight months, more than $250,000 and mountains of tape later, John had a revised finished master of *American Fool*, named after a song that didn't make the cut, and a fitting testament to the comedy of errors that comprised the recordings and really, his whole life up to this point. He brought a cassette of the final mixes to PolyGram's New York office for another listening session, expecting them to like it every bit as much as he did. Finally, he had recorded an album that sounded just the way he wanted it to, and he felt confident about the results. The label *still* hated it—they didn't want authentic and different. They wanted a safe repeat of *Nothin' Matters*, which by this time had eked out 500,000 in sales. The new songs were too rough, too ragged and radio wasn't playing music like this. They didn't want to release it.

"This is the biggest mistake you're ever going to make," the label told a dispirited John Cougar. "This record sounds like The Clash." Wanchic recalls that John then told the label, "Tell you what. Give it back to me then. You don't like it? I'll take it somewhere else." Manager Billy Gaff challenged them, too. "Put the record out or let me out of the contract," he told them. He argued that John had a better idea of what the kids wanted, and reminded them that their job was not to like the album, but to sell it. Reluctantly, they released the record on April Fool's Day, 1982, with "Hurts So Good" as its first single. Bill Cataldo, who worked in PolyGram's promotions department, believed in the song, took it under his wing and started working the record on radio with no support from his employer. Initially, PolyGram planned to bury the album after "Hurts So Good" ran its course, hoping no one would notice how bad it sounded. The fans, however, told them otherwise.

America fell for this down-to-earth American Fool. They slowly got to know him as he bumbled around in his 20s, trying to find himself and his sound and showing off in any number of embarrassing ways to get their attention. Now 30, John was sick of banging his head against the wall trying to prove himself. He said he didn't care if anyone else liked it—although deep down he desperately wanted people to like and understand him. Apparently his determination to hold on to his vision paid off. "Hurts So Good" became his first U.S. Top 10.

As with many good ideas, the crux of "Hurts So Good" materialized in that steamy wellspring called the shower. Childhood friend/lyricist George Green came to visit John during his break between the Miami and L.A. sessions. Green relaxed while he waited for John to get cleaned up. He emerged with a towel and the words, "sometimes love don't feel like it should, you make it hurt so good." "I sang it into a tape machine, with my own handclaps, and the band had to figure out what the chords would be," he told *Billboard*. They assembled the rest of the words, the result of which combined the primal instincts of John's earlier writing ("sink your teeth into my bones") with a yearning for his "young boy days" that had crept into his consciousness. "The whole song deals with the breakdown of illusions when it says, 'maybe we can walk around all day long'," John told Bloomington's *Herald Times*. "I'm 30 years old and that's what I do for a good time. Of all the things being a successful artist means, most of it ain't no fun. What's fun is going down to Kirkwood and looking at the girls and shit like that. That's what I consider fun."

Obviously, his plan for creating rock 'n' roll with Pittsburgh Steelers power worked, as the album ended up the biggest seller of 1982. "It just goes to show that when you're really true to what you really want to do, you have a much better chance of having something work out," says Wanchic. "We're rough hewn. We're from the streets and this music reflected that. We weren't trying to pull wool over anybody's eyes—it's just two guitars, bass, drums. That we understood, and that's what we did. Finally, we could go out and deliver exactly who we are."

On April 10, 1982, John and band made their debut appearance on *Saturday Night Live*. The date would also mark the debut of their new bass player, Toby Myers, who had joined the group only a month before. Myers had become something of a local luminary around Bloomington. In 1972, he joined a cover band called Pure Funk, a slick combo that became quite the popular outfit around the Indiana University campus. When the group inked a three-album record deal with Mercury Records, they changed their name to Roadmaster and started playing original songs. They released their first album, *Sweet Music*, in 1978, then hit the road with such bands as Rush, ZZ Top, Peter Frampton and Cheap Trick. "I played bigger shows with Roadmaster than I ever played with John," says Myers. We were doing these huge summer festivals with ZZ Top, The Cars, Eddy Money...we did that for two summers and toured pretty much nonstop." In 1980, Mercury dropped the band. Their talented lead singer, Steve McNally, quit and Roadmaster the band resigned itself to being barmasters.

Myers was "hating life" when Larry Crane and Mike Wanchic came by a Roadmaster show at the Bloomington club Oscars in late 1981. "There was one bass player in Indiana that I knew," recalls Wanchic, "and he was this guy...he kind of looked like a rock star, carried himself like a rock star...he was much more rock star than we were." Not long after, Myers got a call from Wanchic: "You wanna play with us?" Gee, let me think about that...stay with a bar band, or play with a major-label recording artist with a hit single? He signed on in March 1982.

With Myers in the new-guy hot seat, the band (not John) rehearsed "Hurts So Good" and "Ain't Even Done With the Night" for three solid weeks, working from 11 A.M. to 5 P.M. at Kenny Aronoff's house. They usually took a dinner break from 5 P.M. to 7 P.M. and then met John at The Bunker, the practice space at his house, for the "nighttime torture sessions," as Myers calls them.

Myers and John "connected" after landing at LaGuardia Airport in New York en route to *SNL*. "We were in one car by ourselves, and I barely knew

John," says Myers. "We were driving into Manhattan, and I was just so excited I put John in a headlock! I think that was a good thing, because from then on, he and I had a real kind of physical relationship. I couldn't take a punch from him because I knew he'd knock me out, but I would challenge him: I'd say, 'I will run you a 100-yard dash and beat your ass!' He was always into that shit because he knew he was faster than me, but it never came to pass."

John was more anxious than excited about the *Saturday Night Live* gig. A great performance on this high-profile show could mean major radio adds for his first single, but a bad performance would kill it before the closing credits. Plus, they had a brand new bass player, albeit a good one, who had never played on national television before. Adding to the pressure, as the name suggests, the show was truly *live*. "We were all scared shitless," says Wanchic. The tension escalated during soundcheck, but when John stepped onstage in his black leather pants, he appeared calm, collected and confident delivering his new material, and the band nailed their two songs: "Hurts So Good" and "Ain't Even Done With the Night." Myers says that he was so excited to be there, he "smiled like an absolute goofball idiot through both songs."

Almost immediately after the *SNL* gig, the band made two more highly rated appearances: on *American Bandstand* and *SCTV*. With the exception of Myers, the band knew the *American Bandstand* routine. They entered unfamiliar territory, however, with the comedy show *SCTV*. "It was the coolest thing in the world!" recalls Myers. "It was hysterical! For 'Hand to Hold On To,' John Candy had all these stripper chicks in his apartment. He had a stereo that was so great that all he had to do was push a button and real people came out of the speakers. We came out of the speakers and played that song. In the second skit, Martin Short drinks a potion and turns into John! We did 'Jack and Diane'."

Relaxing in her tiny Manhattan apartment, vocalist Pat Peterson caught John's *Saturday Night Live* performance. She had just wrapped up a two-year stint singing backup with Ray Charles, preceded by a tour with Pink Floyd. But her work had slowed somewhat in 1982, and she considered returning to her hometown of Smithville, Texas (the small town now known as the setting for the film *Hope Floats*). She enjoyed singing, and didn't mind touring, but wanted a career with more stability than what the music business had offered her so far. She considered joining the Army, like her sister. As she plotted her future course, she received a call from friend P.P. Arnold, another well-known backup singer whom she had met in Los Angeles. "Pat. What are you *doing*?" she asked. She said she might join the Army, because, you know, time was moving on and she needed some stability. Arnold replied, "Well, before you go, give this guy John Cougar a call. I met him at Criteria Studios, and he's got this hit out. He's looking for backup singers, so you might want to check it out."

She had the number jotted down when she tuned into NBC. "He was dancing around, and I had the biggest laugh!" Peterson recalls, laughing now. She has a large, joy-filled laugh of a woman with unwavering faith and optimism. "I thought, if he's got the nerve to dance around like that and show his self, that's pretty cool. I was a dancer when I was younger, and I understood that emotion when he moved. It was an awkward way, but it was cool."

Within two weeks, she found herself at the Indianapolis airport, where Mike Wanchic and Toby Myers waited at the gate to take her straight to Kenny Aronoff's house to rehearse for their upcoming tour with Heart. In that cramped space, Peterson met fellow backup singer, Lisa Mordente, Larry Crane and Aronoff. They worked up a 45-minute set culled from *American Fool* and some of John's earlier singles. "After several days of getting acquainted with material and learning parts, John drove up on his motorcycle," recalls Peterson. "He comes tearing in, and he says, 'Let me hear something.' So we picked some nice harmonies that he had wanted, and the harmonies he had on his record. It was fantastic. [Lisa] had a wonderful voice; she and I sang well together. He didn't say anything, just listened. Finally he went, 'Mmmm Hmmm.' And that was it!"

For a while, that's about all John said to Peterson. This was apparently part of the initiation process, as he didn't talk to Myers either during the entire four months of rehearsals. If Myers made a mistake, he'd turn to Larry Crane and say, "Tell Myers not to fucking do that," even though the lanky bassist stood a few feet away. He hadn't completely warmed up to Aronoff either, as he still wasn't sure if he was a permanent member of the band. Peterson, a warm, jubilant person, found John's standoffish behavior troubling. She likes to joke around, and she loves to laugh, both a byproduct of loving life. This irritated John. He spent most his life surrounded by grouches. He didn't know how to deal with someone so happy. "Why's she smiling?" he'd mumble. Even worse, his daughter Michelle would ask the same thing! She, too, had inherited some of the infamous "bad Mellencamp attitude." Peterson didn't let this get to her, though, and to this day, those negative moments roll off her.

The rehearsal schedule for the Heart tour mimicked the *SNL* rigors: days at Aronoff's; nights at The Bunker. John put a tambourine in the middle of the room, and if anyone made a mistake they had to toss a quarter in the middle of it. "We were so cheap that after the first week, the tambourine really had no money in it," recalls Myers. "We got tight really quickly."

Their set list included "Hurts So Good," "Jack and Diane," "Thundering Hearts," "Hand to Hold Onto," "I Need a Lover" and "30 Days in the Hole," a Humble Pie cover. July 15, 1982 arrived soon enough, and everyone prepared for the first of 110 dates with Ann and Nancy Wilson's hard rock band. After getting kicked off of tours with Kiss, The Kinks and REO Speedwagon, Heart was a dream of a group to work with. They were the nicest group they had worked with to date—or rather, they argued with John the least. Not that there weren't issues to deal with. "Part of my deal with Heart was that I wanted my name on the marquee," John told *Billboard*. "With The Kinks, we played a few arenas, but generally it was clubs and theaters. I remember being in Baton Rouge, and I looked up and it said, APPEARING TONIGHT: HEART. We were, like, 50 shows into it, and I thought, "Hey, look! John Mellencamp's not playing tonight. Let's pack up and get out of here." I got in the car and went back to the airport to the single-engine plane I rented. But the road manager came out, gave me some extra dough and said my name was back on the marquee. I went and did the show, which started 20 minutes late, and made my point."

John, The Zone, brother/road manager Ted Mellencamp and assistant manager Russel Shaw from manager Billy Gaff's office hit three to four cities a week on that rented Beech King Air six-seater. Their guarantee had risen to $17,000 a night, the highest paid opening act at that time.

Even though most of his sets were only five songs long, John kept some of the acrobatics of his earlier live performances, but refined the routine so that it became less football tackle, more high-energy live show. He danced and prowled the stage like a pro this time, his jumps well timed, his remarks, less crass but still blunt. He and Peterson worked out a trick they called "the flip." "I'd jump up on him, fall down into some sort of fit on the floor, and then flip over," she explains. "It was real dangerous." But they made it work with very few mishaps. He usually concluded his set with "Hurts So Good," at which time he'd dive into the crowd and bring a bunch of teenage girls up on stage to sing and dance with him.

The band played loud, raw and uninhibited—their talent not overshadowed by a few off notes. "His show was hardly the last word in slick showmanship," wrote Mark Rowland in a review for *Musician*, "yet Cougar remains such an ingratiating presence that all the raw edges worked in his favor."

As they traversed the U.S., John had to tape the name of each town on his guitar case to remember where he was. "Hurts So Good" continued its climb up the charts, hitting Number Two in August 1982 and sitting there for a nice four weeks. The song dominated radio and MTV, and as a result, hordes of female fans wanted to be all over John!

The attention worked fine on stage, but now, hordes of fans approached him at restaurants, in the airport, heck, even in the drugstore. The attention made him feel uncomfortable, and he wondered how so many people knew what he looked like. Well, aside from having his scowling face on the album cover, a new cable network, MTV, started broadcasting music videos 24 hours a day in 1981 and they had "Hurts So Good" in high rotation. Annoyed and intrigued at the same time, he called up the company headquarters. "I don't know who the Hell you are or who owns you, but because of you I can't get through the airport anymore without people bothering me," he announced. He didn't like the results in his personal life, but assumed it must be good for his career. He kept an eye on the fledgling network, particularly co-founder John Sykes, who then oversaw music, talent and promotion.

By summer's last breath, "Jack and Diane" had entered AOR and pop radio, on its way to becoming the largest added record in PolyGram history at that time. By September, it had moved into the Top 10 with "Hurts So Good," which would hold the top spot on the "Mainstream Rock" charts for 12 weeks. The album subsequently reached Number One, making John the first male artist to have two Top 10 singles and a Number One album simultaneously. The album held the top spot for nine weeks—through their entire Heart tour—and would go on to sell three million copies. Take that, PolyGram, for wanting to shove the album under the rug.

As fame surrounded John, he dismissed his songwriting as silly, meaningless stuff. Sure, he assembled simple words, but by writing about his immediate world, he found for the first time that he could touch a wide audience. "It's a celebration of immaturity," says publicist Bob Merlis of "Jack and Diane." "It speaks to people: You don't know how great it is to be a kid until you're not a kid anymore. These are the greatest years of your life whether you know it or not."

"When I was a kid, I couldn't wait to get away from home," John told the *Herald Times*. "I said, 'When I get to be a certain age I'm gettin' out of here.' But once you get out...you encounter things that you never thought would be the way they really are. Just like when you're a kid you say, 'I can't wait until I turn 21 so I can go into the bars.' But once I turned 21, I didn't want to go into the bars anymore. It's like, God, what do I want to go in there for? A lot of things in life are never what you expect them to be, even on the smaller levels."

As the tour moved forward, so did *American Fool's* success. The public loved the record, but the lofty music critics couldn't let go of the Bruce Springsteen and Bob Seger comparisons, and had not accepted John as a legitimate talent. Infamous rock critics such as Dave Marsh and Robert Christgau called John's smoke-stained voice and Heartland rock "phony," "overfamiliar" and "trite," and considered his popularity merely a result of good timing. Others fixated on his surly attitude, which showed itself on tour, in print, even on national TV. The most notable example occured during an episode of *Nightwatch*, where he got defensive with host Felicia Jeter when she challenges his beliefs and parenting skills, and criticizes the whips and chains in his "Hurts So Good" video. He stiffened, shifted uncomfortably in his seat and ultimately took off his mic and walked off the set. The media loves to blow these sorts of outbursts out of proportion, and they had a field day with John in the early '80s. A few journalists however, including Chris Connelly and Andrew Slater from *Rolling Stone*, bravely took the time to get to know the man behind the music, and aimed to bring forth the honest, hardworking side of John in more flattering prose.

On the road, which is where he remained for the rest of 1982, John didn't pay too much attention to the PR machine, though bad reviews did trouble him. Instead, he focused his energy and emotion on the stage, putting on knockout after knockout show for the people that scraped up $10 or more to hear him play. He knew that a lot of his fans probably had to work overtime a few nights in order to pay for a night out with their wife and/or girlfriend and he made darn sure they walked away happy, or at least entertained. "Onstage, the newness, the freshness, the rawness, the fun of it—it was really exciting," says backup singer Pat Peterson. "No matter what we had to go through to get to the gig, or what circumstances weren't seen on stage, onstage with John...there's an energy there that I cannot explain. It moves, it has its highs and lows and...I'm addicted to it!"

The fans brought the energy level up higher. Not long after the album went Platinum, they played a show in Indianapolis at Market Square Arena for 18,500 fans, all of whom went "nuts before we even hit the stage," Mike Wanchic recalled to author Martin Torgoff. "You couldn't even hear the P.A., it was so loud!" John's childhood friend Tim Elsner sat in the audience that night. "It was one of the only shows I've ever walked in to where everybody was in their seat when the opening act started, the crowd went crazy and then after John played, a lot of them got up and left!"

Toward the end of the year, John and band received a plum opportunity to open for The Who. "The first show we did was in Boulder, Colorado, at the football stadium: 50,000 people. They did *not* want to see us," bass player Toby Myers told Indianapolis alt-weekly *NUVO*. "They were throwing shit like crazy. Mike [Wanchic] and the guys who'd toured England extensively were used to this. They'd been spit on; this was nothing new. But I couldn't believe it. The next one was the Jack Murphy Stadium in San Diego and it rocked like a motherfucker that night. Third night was sold out, a full moon on Halloween, 55,000 people in Sun Devil Stadium in Tempe, Arizona. It was rockin' and I was diggin' it. I turned and looked and in the middle of the stage, John was flat out, lying there unconscious. Some dude in the crowd had thrown a whiskey bottle and knocked him out. We were four songs into our five-song set, almost done. When John came to, we got in a huddle and he said, 'Let's get the fuck off this stage.' John got his head sutured up and found a hard hat. We came back on the stage and played "Hurt So Good," but before we did, John invited the guy who threw the bottle to come up to the stage to meet us. I don't think it would have been a very pleasant meeting."

Thankfully, they didn't have to dodge many liquor bottles off stage. If they weren't stuffed in a plane or a car jetting from city to city, the band whiled away hours in a hotel room or backstage, counting down until soundcheck, then maybe seeking out some food afterward. Before each show, the band gathered in a dressing room and rehearsed the entire set, top to bottom, and *then* walked onstage for the real thing. In whatever free time they had, the band might rally for a game of flag football now and then, but overall their whirlwind schedule—often five shows a week—left them with little energy to carouse. On their days off, John usually had hours of interviews with the press scheduled. Wanchic often had to take care of random tasks that John didn't have time for, and Myers, Crane, Peterson and Mordente were left to fend for themselves, which often meant sleeping late and room service…and, well, maybe a little bit of carousing. Their antics were mild, however, compared to the typical rock band of the '80s. John hadn't drank or done drugs since college, and the rest of the band just worked too damn hard to consider flying high. Wanchic, for one, has never walked onstage with alcohol or drugs in his system. "Our stage was so aggressive, you couldn't really be high," he told *NUVO*. "You had to watch yourself, you could get hurt up there. I knocked John unconscious once onstage, whirling around with my guitar, knocking him in the head."

Sometimes they worked through their days off, such as the case with the infamous nightmare show in London, Ontario. Del Shannon and the Beach Boys had an outdoor concert booked the day after one of John's shows in Toronto. In an effort to boost sales for the slow-selling Beach Boys show—2,000 of a 10,000-seat soccer stadium sold—promoter Don Jones asked John Cougar to join the bill. All of the band's equipment was packed up with Heart's, but the promoter assured that they would provide everything. The show nearly sold out with John's name added, and man, did that audience get their money's worth! The band got no soundcheck before the show, a sign of trouble to come. Then the set got shortened from 55 to 35 minutes because of delays, which *really* ticked John off, because he didn't want to let down his fans. (He later promised to return to London on his own dime to make it up to them.) Things went from bad to worse when the provided equipment broke down piece by miserable piece.

"We get there and it's the most imitation gear you've ever seen in your life; like gear you would buy for your kids," says bassist Toby Myers. "The amplifiers were tiny, the drum set was pretend and the mic stands were just pretend. I think we made it through four songs before stuff blew up." Kenny Aronoff busted the snare and a cymbal during the first song. Mike Wanchic's amp blew on the next one, followed by Myers' bass amp. "For those of you who came to see me, we're not able to do our show tonight because this gear ain't worth a shit, and if it was up to me I'd give you your money back," John told the crowd. "Instead, here, you can have this shit gear."

"John was so mad," recalls Myers. "Kenny was playing and John started taking the drum kit apart and handing it to people in the front rows! I saw a guy walking out with a bass drum over his head. It was hysterical." After he passed out the drums, mics and amplifiers, John found out that the Beach Boys were supposed to use the equipment for their upcoming performance. The promoters were none too pleased.

The band got a break from the road around Christmastime when the marathon Heart tour concluded. John was exhausted, but pleased with his career's upward turn. But just as he was feeling good, the ghost of Tony DeFries came back to haunt him when MainMan seeped out *The Kid Inside* to the U.S. market, obviously aiming to cash in on his ex-clients' newfound success. He had legal rights to do this, but he went way out of bounds morally. John didn't want to see or hear the record again, a bitter memory of his 23-year-old self in smeared eyeliner. Luckily, the public didn't seem to pay much attention to the release; it sold only a handful of units and received minimal publicity, save for the unknowing record reviewer who assumed the album was a new release and promptly trashed it.

Rather than let DeFries get the better of him, he let the album fall quickly off people's radars and focused his attention on work as a producer. With the phenomenal success of *American Fool*, he had achieved one of his initial goals: to have enough money to sit around, watch TV and drink as much Big Red as he wanted to. Only problem was, he didn't want to loaf anymore (though a can of Big Red was still okay). This restless soul needed to continually challenge himself. At present, he also needed a project to work on while he sorted out some financial issues with manager Billy Gaff and Riva Records, the imprint to which he was still signed. He had always wanted to produce, and now that he had the opportunity, he came up with a short wish list of artists, all hugely influential in his own music: Donovan, Terry Reid and Mitch Ryder. He flipped the proverbial coin and chose Ryder.

"The relationship was fortuitous for two reasons," says Ryder. "It allowed me the opportunity to have a huge star help me try to re-enter the marketplace, and it allowed him to go into the studio and work while his other matters were legally frozen."

Ryder had only met John once before. In 1979, John opened for Ryder in Canton, Michigan. As he watched him perform, Ryder knew he would become a star, even though he had no real hits at the time. Only three years later, John would produce Ryder's first U.S. release in many years and help him get it released through Riva Records.

If Mellencamp's music blasted louder than anything else on early '80s FM radio, Ryder did the same with his Detroit Wheels band on '60s AM. Ryder's Motown-informed rock 'n' roll made a huge impact on John as a young boy glued to the radio in Seymour, Indiana. Years later, the two realized they had much in common. After cracking the Top 10 in 1967 with "Sock It to Me Baby!" Ryder got tangled up with a producer/label owner named Bob Crewe who made a mockery of his solo career by enforcing such unpleasant tactics as adding saccharine-sweet string sections to his recordings. Just as John took some bad advice from DeFries, Ryder listened to Crewe, who turned him into a manufactured, unnatural star and Ryder fought like hell to become his own person again. Ironically, Ryder even recorded an album with producer Steve Cropper, (*The Detroit-Memphis Experiment*) with Booker T. and the MG's and the Memphis Horns, on which he clawed his way out of a superficial music machine.

Aside from their career commonalities, they both hailed from the Midwest and operated from the philosophy that when someone pushes you, you push back, no matter how "important" they are. This won them both more enemies than friends in a business that's more about fake smiles than directness, and served as the root for conflicts between them in the studio.

John did not want to record Ryder's album in L.A. The glitzy city offered too many distractions from his work. He stayed up too late; the women were too pretty. He wanted to write and record at home. He felt more grounded there with his friends and family around him, and there was less activity to distract him from work. His sister Laura Gill and her then-boyfriend had just bought a run-down farmhouse halfway between Brownstown and Seymour. They planned to fix up the place and move in after they got married, but had run out of money before they finished the job. They approached John for a loan, and he agreed, with one catch. He would give them the money to finish the house, on the condition that he could use it as a recording studio first. Hence, the Gill family now has a soundproof kitchen.

With the help of Criteria Recording's chief engineer Ross Alexander and staff engineer Greg Edward, producer Don Gehman gutted the Miami studio's mobile unit and moved its equipment—an MCI console, 16-track tape machine and a few other items—into the kitchen of Gill's home, which became the control room. They blew a hole in the wall so that they could see into the living room, now the live room, put up a little bit of drywall to create a drum room and isolation booth, and *viola!*: a raw recording environment, if there ever was one.

They dubbed the Gill house "The Shack," because it really wasn't much more than that. John used Ryder's sessions as a test run for The Shack, to work out some of the kinks before he made a record of his own there. John brought in Kenny Aronoff, Mike Wanchic, Larry Crane and Pat Peterson to play on the sessions, and Ryder brought in his bass player, Mark Gougeon, and a few other Detroit characters.

As expected, the road between Motor City and Dudleytown, Indiana, had some bumps and potholes. John took his producer role a bit too seriously for Ryder, who didn't like to be told what to do any more than John did. "Cougar had to forget that he was a singer," Ryder later told the *Detroit Free Press*. "In the beginning, he was listening to every note I was singing. I felt a bit smothered. He wanted me to sing what his perception of Mitch Ryder was. He had to get in tune with my perspective." When he backed off a little, Ryder gave some of his best performances in years. "There was a mutual respect, but I wasn't about to get pushed around by some young upstart, and he wasn't about to be told what to do by somebody he thought he was resurrecting," says Ryder. "Even though my time as a big star had passed, I still had my pride that I had to hold on to. Being both Midwesterners helped because we knew exactly what we meant when we told each other to go fuck yourself!"

At one point, the tension got so thick, someone from Ryder's camp came into the studio and shot a gun toward the control room. He wasn't joking. They had similar experiences during their time off when they visited nearby dive bars for lack of anything else to do. One night, Ryder's gang almost got shot by a group of Indiana hoodlums. Turns out the Seymour boys were armed and likely drunk, but Ryder and gang skated out of the bar before anyone's hands got near a trigger. "We were stuck down there for months with nothing to do but go to these crazy bars if we wanted to have any social life at all," he recalls.

In the more isolated environment of The Shack, John had Ryder and band record a few songs from Ryder's previous albums, as well as some Mellencamp originals and random covers, including "B.I.G.T.I.M.E.," written and recorded by Keith Sykes, Prince's "When You Were Mine" and "A Thrill's a Thrill," a duet with Marianne Faithful.

Midway through recording, the entourage migrated to the Deep South— Miami—to work at Criteria Recording. There, Ryder met and saved the life of singer Marianne Faithful, who sang the B. Amesbury cover with him. Had he not prevented her from falling off of her fifteenth-story balcony, another standout song wouldn't have happened and the life of a remarkable performer would have been cut short.

"We were sitting on the balcony, and she got up to get a whiff of the mighty Atlantic air and she started to fall, over the side," says Ryder, in charge of babysitting the still-addicted vocalist. "I was able to stop her fall but in order to do that, I had to push her back toward the building. She hit the building and fell down. I was crazy with fear. I pulled her up and said, 'Are you okay?' She railed back and said, 'Don't you ever touch me again.' And slapped me. That's the thanks I got for saving her life. So I said to John, 'I can't babysit her anymore, you've got to get somebody else.'"

Shortly after wrapping up the album, the 1983 Grammy Awards took place and the Academy nominated Cougar for "Male Rock Artist of the Year" and the coveted "Album of the Year." He won "Best Rock Vocal Performance—Male" for "Hurts So Good," his only Grammy win to date. Toto got the Album award.

Riva Records released *Never Kick a Sleeping Dog* later that year, and Ryder watched "When You Were Mine" climb into the Top 50 on *Billboard*'s rock singles charts. The positive reviews in the *New York Times* and other high-profile publications gave him a positive charge; he saw it as confirmation of his credibility and longevity as an artist, brought to their attention by John's fame.

Also in 1983, Dick Clark Productions invited John to perform on the American Music Awards. He had a nomination for "Favorite Pop Male," and they expected him to sing "Jack and Diane." Instead, he insisted on showcasing his "new" act, Mitch Ryder. "He basically told Clark, 'If I'm going to be on the show, then you've got to allow me to promote this artist,'" says Ryder. "So he was my advocate all along. There was no question about that."

The two Midwest rockers ran through "B.I.G.T.I.M.E." with John sporting a three-month old beard, and Ryder so full of nervous energy that he teetered perilously to one side. The AMAs awarded John the "Favorite Pop Male" trophy, and when he returned to the stage to claim his statue, he thanked the audience, called himself an idiot and walked away. He had sold mountains of albums and played to thousands of screaming, fans, but he sloughed off his success, as if he still thought of himself as the n'er-do-well installing phone lines in Seymour.

CHAPTER FIVE

FIRST IMPRESSION SESSIONS

American Fool fought the good fight even a year after its release. But a few singles down the line, PolyGram execs began prodding Cougar, "How do you plan to top *American Fool*?"

"I'm going to do a polka record," he joked in an interview with Bloomington's *Herald Times*. Not exactly the response they wanted, but by this point, they knew to expect the unexpected. His philosophy held true. "Doing something different makes you credible," he continued. "It also means taking a risk."

Cougar had no qualms about taking risks. With his "do it different, and do it better" credo firmly in mind, Cougar started thinking about his next album, and how he could one-up songs like "Hurts So Good."

Early one summer morning, John drove himself home to Bloomington from the Indianapolis airport. Cruising along an overpass, still high off of his AMA and Grammy wins, he looked down and saw a black man sitting with a cat in his arms on the front porch of his weathered, pink shotgun shack. The Interstate ran within feet of the man's front yard, but the man didn't seem disturbed by the commotion around him. "He waved, and I waved back," he told *Rolling Stone*. That's how ['Pink Houses'] started."

John, still learning the craft of songwriting and arranging, sat down with a tape machine and described the black man, and didn't stop reporting until he had "Pink Houses" fully written. He knew there was something special about this song, because he felt a personal attachment to it. From this point on, with only a few exceptions, he would write without a collaborator.

Men, women and families lived in pink houses (figuratively speaking) all over the U.S., especially in those nondescript small towns where wide-open spaces interact with strip malls. What John touched on with "Jack and Diane" tumbled more freely now, and rather than censor himself or over-analyze his writing, he let it flow through him, uncensored, and onto tape or paper. He knew exactly how to top *American Fool*, and it wasn't going to be with some remake of "Hurts So Good."

Propelled by his creative surge, he called up Don Gehman. It was time to record that next album. Could he get himself back out to Indiana? Gehman signed on as co-producer/engineer, the same arrangement as with *American Fool*, and prepared himself for another stay in rural Indiana.

The Shack, even with Criteria's mobile equipment, still fell far from a professional studio, although recording in bedrooms, hallways and kitchens lent a certain rustic charm. "Since it was being taken apart after recording, there was no need to make it pretty, and it wasn't," recalls David Thoener, who engineered and mixed the album with Don Gehman. He was a 29-year-old New Yorker at the time, near the start of his career when he joined Gehman in Indiana. "The air conditioning ducts were hanging out of the ceilings, it was quite a sight. But it had an amazing sound."

"The control room was so small you literally couldn't turn around," adds Wanchic. "You had to just pick your spot and plant!" Between takes, the band hung out in the upstairs bedroom, converted to a makeshift lounge. "It was upstairs to hang; downstairs to work," says Wanchic.

Another downside: The house sat on a pig farm, so the smell was "pretty unbelievable." The back of the album has pictures of the band goofing off in the mud. The whole scene, from the muddy pigpens outside to the close quarters inside, lent itself well to John's vision for his *American Fool* follow-up.

"We decided to just go out there and make the rawest, most natural sounding, off-the-cuff, first-impression record that we could come up with, and we did it very spontaneously," says Wanchic. "First ideas were exploited heavily, and it was done with great vigor and aggression."

Admittedly, many of their ideas came from external sources. "The *Uh-Huh* record was heavily influenced by the Rolling Stones, very heavily," Wanchic said in an interview with *NUVO*. "We were feeling our oats as a young American rock band with a lot of success at that moment, we felt we could take the liberty; hell, we even thanked the Rolling Stones on the record."

As with the previous Cougar-Gehman collaborations, Gehman's presence was integral to the success of this off-kilter recording session. Aside from being an excellent engineer, he had a calming influence over the hotheaded, young artist. He wasn't intimidated by his client's demanding nature, and made for an honest sounding board for John's ideas, as well as one who could keep him from going too far over the edge. But John pushed him, and his band, by routinely taking them to unfamiliar, and unconventional, territory. For *Uh Huh*, John wanted to call forth not just an aggressive sound, but irritating and aggravating—the very opposite of the clean and more pleasant sound of his earlier records. Recording in a half-finished house with wires covering the floor and minimal equipment was one way to instill some of the tension that would lead to this raw, aggressive sound. "Because of my background in live sound, I was accustomed to moving equipment in and out, wiring things up and making them work," says Gehman, who got his start as a live sound engineer. "Getting used to what an environment does to you acoustically and making judgments [in that environment], I knew nothing about. I'm out in the boonies, with gear that I'd rented, in some acoustic space where I really couldn't hear anything, and then he wanted me to create something that I had never done before. Everybody was pushed to this place where they're teetering."

They recorded "Pink Houses" in about a day. As with many of John's songs, he had the lyrics down and the basic melodic idea, but had to communicate what he heard in his head to the band. Frustration came when they didn't get it right. Luckily, Crane and Wanchic had enough experience with John to come close most times. Crane usually fiddled around until he got the basic rhythm. Once he got a good groove going, the rest of the band would come in behind him, adding parts little by little until they had the structure of the song formed.

"Pink Houses" especially "captured the ambience of the acoustics," recalls Thoener. "There is no reverb on the drums; that sound is only the living room. Even John's tracking vocal was recorded in the same room. We used gobos with a Plexiglas window, put John in a corner of the room and made a triangle. He stood there looking at Kenny and the entire band. Everyone was in the same room. We put a guitar amp in one bathroom, the bass in another small room and the other guitar [amp] in another separate room off the living room. The backing vocals were an overdub but recorded in the same room so the ambience on the backing vocals is the living room also."

John and the band recorded together, their instruments bleeding into one another, which only added to the album's raw, natural sound. They kept most of John's original vocal takes, a rarity in recording, with John going back to maybe fix a line or two. "He is meticulous, but you can't deny a great performance," says Thoener. "If you're lucky to get it on the live take, you'd be a fool to not recognize it and keep it. He's always after his best performance, and not one for punching in syllables."

Much like Aronoff's *Nothin' Matters* experience, John kept bassist Toby Myers off the record, even though he had written all of the bass parts and later taught them to studio musicians Willie Weeks and Brother Louis Johnson. "He didn't know what I would be like when the red light turned on, he didn't know how I'd respond, but I wasn't scared," says Myers. Both Weeks and Johnson would tell Myers, "Man, I don't know why we're here, because you're totally capable of doing this." Toward the end of the tracking sessions, the great day came when neither Weeks nor Johnson could make it, and Myers had his golden opportunity. The band was going to cut "Authority Song" that day. "I went in and just kicked it out of the park," recalls Myers. John wouldn't bring in another bass player until 1994.

John and band worked at The Shack from 10 A.M. to midnight for 16 days and recorded 15 songs, some of them written at 2 A.M., and recorded the next morning. The schedule didn't allow for many "happy hours," but Thoener fondly recalls breaking for dinner at the local meat-and-threes for three bucks. "Coming from New York, that was something, and really good!" He had never visited a meat-and-three diner before, nor had he been in such close proximity to a family of pigs.

All said and done, John's spontaneous, homespun recording cost him a third of *American Fool* and a fraction of the time. Remember: Think fast. Make mistakes. Move on. "Don't let me go back and touch any of these songs, even if I want to," John would often say to Gehman.

Before taking the finished product to PolyGram, John listened to the masters again, then decided that the record needed one more "hit." He called up his ever-reliable pal George Green for assistance. Green had a few lines jotted down for a song about crumbling walls. With that foundation, John and Green traded off line by line—attempting to outdo each other each time—to create "Crumblin' Down," which became the album's lead track and the additional hit he wanted.

They structured the song with a traditional verse-chorus foundation, but lyrically, John crammed a lot of words into each line to deliver a fierce statement of his rock star status, the unsavory characters he'd encountered and the fear of falling out of favor. He also communicated that he knew darn well how people felt about him, good or bad, and really didn't give a damn.

> *Some people say I'm obnoxious and lazy*
> *That I'm uneducated and my opinion means nothin'*
> *But I know I'm a real good dancer,*
> *Don't need to look over my shoulder to see what I'm after*

"People thought John was expressing that it wasn't such a big deal to be a rock star..." Green told author Martin Torgoff. "The feeling we worked with is, 'What are you going to do when it's over, when the big-time deal falls through? I'll be here, how 'bout you?'"

Though the song alluded to John's own celebrity, the frustration conveyed in the verses came from watching his older cousin struggle after losing his electrical engineering job. "This guy's spirit is being broken by America, and that's crazy, because he loves his country and he works so hard," John told *New York Daily News*. "I've been lucky. I know that. But there are a lot of people, people close to me, who haven't been so lucky, and I'd rather write about them than me...It's a very frightening thing when you realize the industrial revolution is over and there's no place to go."

The album title, *Uh-Huh*, made reference to those same unsavory characters who made John their "whipping boy" years ago, and to his younger self who naively listened to them. The album also marked the introduction of his real name—Mellencamp—to his professional identity, showing that he really was coming into his own as an artist and entitled to getting what he wanted. Case in point: The *Uh-Huh* listening sessions with PolyGram went far better the *American Fool* meeting. They had doubts about "Pink Houses," but when John's East Coast contemporary, Bruce Springsteen, released *Born in the U.S.A.* in June 1983—four months before *Uh-Huh*—they figured they better catch this wave of patriotic rock. Maybe they were right.

Uh-Huh shipped Gold and was certified Platinum five weeks after its release. "Crumblin' Down" kicked off a string of singles from the album; the song eventually climbed to Number Nine on the Pop Singles Chart. "At that time, we matched out radio nicely," says Wanchic. He thinks it over for a minute, then clarifies, "Actually, we made radio match to us. Making records is a trying proposition. You bleed yourself dry, you make yourself vulnerable and if that's the case, you might as well shoot straight. If you're going to fail, you might as well fail doing what you want to do."

The video for "Crumblin' Down," with John chain-smoking, dancing, lip synching, kicking over chairs and nervously twitching a penny-loafer-and-white-socks clad foot, almost immediately went into high rotation on MTV. Denim with purposely ripped knees became the hot fashion trend, and he and Michael Jackson initiated a boom in loafer sales.

"*Uh-Huh* was Mellencamp's revenge on elitism," wrote Jon Pareles for the *New York Times*, who cites John as the "voice of the underdog." "Song after song put down authority, pomposity and hip insincerity." But the album also contains an American anthem, he continues, "Pink Houses," about "making do with disillusionment."

"Pink Houses" the follow-up single, made it to Number Eight, enjoying equally frequent play on MTV. Produced by Simon Fields, the "Pink Houses" video featured a quintessential pink house that John spotted in Austin, Texas. Joe Todd, an 83-year-old man living in a nursing home in Madison, Texas, sat on the porch and Austin Mayor Harvey Gooden made a cameo dressed in hillbilly garb. Fields, John and crew traveled between Austin, Little York, Seymour and other rural communities to shoot the varying landscapes featured in the video.

During MTV's early years, only a handful of acts spent this sort of time and money to create artistic three-minute video clips. "John realized that you could use the visuals to enhance and really help define the song even further," says John Sykes. "His videos were fun to program, and the audience loved them; as a result [of MTV] he found himself a lot more fans. He understood the delivery medium that had just emerged and embraced it."

In early 1984, MTV had a reputation for devising outlandish contests and promotions, and Sykes came up with the mother of them all for "Pink Houses." In a contest called "Paint the Mother Pink," one lucky winner would receive a pink house in Monroe County, Indiana. To sweeten the pot, the grand prize winner would receive round-trip airfare to Bloomington for 20 people, where John and band would host a barbecue and party at the house, followed by an informal concert in the living room for the winner's house party. Hotel accommodations, a pink Jeep CJ7, a Pioneer stereo system, a wide-screen TV and 500 cases of Hawaiian Punch soft drink rounded out the prize purse.

John taped the promo spots just outside of Bloomington in front of the house to be given away. Unfortunately, the house that MTV purchased sat next to Neal's Landfill, which in 1981 was identified by the Environmental Protection Agency as one of the 114 most hazardous waste sites in the United States due to PCB contamination. When John found out, he refused to let them give it away. "We had to basically push that house aside and buy another one," says Sykes, who was involved in finding and purchasing both toxic and non-toxic homes. "The good news was, houses like that in Bloomington weren't that expensive! It turned out to be one of the biggest promotions we did. It was a great day, the winner [Susan Miles] came in from Bellevue, Washington, John played and she sold the house the next day.

Although "Pink Houses" shows that the American Dream "isn't always what it's cracked up to be," its amber waves of grain caught the eyes and ears of then-President Ronald Reagan's camp, who asked John if they could use it for his 1984 re-election campaign. He refused. He was flattered that the President liked his music, but no way did he want the song used for political purposes, especially by a leader he didn't support. "What Reagan wants to do has nothing to do with [Bruce Springsteen's] 'Born in the U.S.A.,' 'Pink Houses' or working-class people," John said in a 1986 interview with *Creem* magazine. "But Reagan doesn't appeal to logic. He appeals to the emotional. Let's not forget the guy was an actor, and he's not stupid...Yeah, it's kind of scary, but there's also the type of patriotism that says maybe we can change things and make them better. That's my type." This wouldn't be the first time he would choose values over publicity or sponsorship dollars, although his anti-corporate sponsorship stance would soften some years later.

In March 1984, John and The Zone embarked on the Uh-Huh Tour, a relatively short jaunt that targeted mid-size halls and theaters (of about 7,000 seats or so), and lasted only about six weeks. The days of the fish fry getting top billing had long passed. Now, he could easily pull off his own tour, but since it was his first real headlining outing, he proceeded with caution and gave himself an opportunity to play in smaller cities to smaller crowds, in turn giving fans a more intimate experience.

He called up his old friend Tim Elsner to help organize the tour. "It was sort of the 'get your feet wet tour'," says Elsner, who had worked for John in 1978 during a brief jaunt in England. "He called me up and said, 'Hey, things are going good, I'm ready for you to come back to work for me.' And I said, 'Doing what?' And he said, 'Well, you can be like an accountant business manager kind of guy for me.' I wasn't really an accountant, and he said, 'Oh, that doesn't matter. You can keep a checkbook, right? Well, it's just like keeping a big checkbook.' So I came back to work for him and we figured it out."

He also brought back brother Ted to manage the tour, and together they plotted their course. Over 40 shows, they played to a total of 350,000 fans, hitting clubs and old theaters in larger cities, but also Florence, Alabama; Danville, Illinois; Davenport, Iowa; and a few places chosen at random by John. When his finger hit the map, it was up to Ted Mellencamp to find the venue, up to Elsner to negotiate the guarantee and up to John and his band to give the people a hellacious performance.

For all 40 gigs, John, Kenny Aronoff, Mike Wanchic, Larry Crane and Toby Myers stepped out in tuxedos, white shirts, string ties and white socks, with backup singers Carol Sue Hill and Pat Peterson in complementary attire. John's trademark acrobatics remained—he and Peterson still did "The Flip," but the man fighting for attention had evolved into a more confident frontman. He started the show by doing the splits in a move that called to mind the "Crumblin' Down" video, then he and band launched into a 30-minute medley of oldies, including "Heartbreak Hotel," The Animals' "Please Don't Let Me Be Misunderstood" and "Pretty Ballerina," among others. "As the headliner, we had a lot more room on stage, and whatever John decided to do, we could do," says Myers. "We played some great songs, we looked great and that record went bezerk!" John didn't curse as much, nor did he deviate into some cocky diatribe. He thanked the crowd and he played a 20-minute encore. When he had to drudge up the past and play "I Need a Lover," the "new" John held the mic out to the front few rows and let the fans sing the words.

Those fans went wild in middle-American towns, large and small, but the real test would come in New York on April 10, 1984, the date he would appear at the venerable Radio City Music Hall. The New York market, aka Springsteen country, had been slow to warm to John and he didn't know how they would respond. Adding to the pressure, many of the music critics that had rejected him early on, plus numerous other music business folks, would have some of the house's best seats. If there was one show that desperately needed to be flawless, this was the one.

Backstage, just minutes before they were to step on to Radio City Music Hall's historic stage, the band watched James Brown's famous T.A.M.I. concert from 1964, where he preceded the Rolling Stones. Really primed and ready now, they turned off the VCR, walked downstairs and on stage to deliver one of their best performances *ever*. Aronoff lost 16 sticks.

Critics that had stood back with their arms crossed since Johnny Cougar debuted, now admitted the singer had some talent and a long career ahead of him. John finally accepted this, too. When *American Fool* became the biggest-selling album of 1982, he realized that a whole lot of people wanted to hear his music, and they related to his simple, direct lyrics. When he began working on *Uh-Huh*, he toed the line between mindlessness ("Play Guitar" for example), and consciousness, exploring issues that he felt strongly about. He knew he had the ears of a few million people, but he was still figuring out what he wanted to say to them. He had mostly knocked the chip off his shoulder, his erratic hot-headedness had evolved into more of a stern attitude and an absolute demand for respect. He saw that he could be the ambassador for the everyman, fighting for the underdog and shedding light on America's dysfunction. As the Uh-Huh Tour came to a close, John "sharpened the saw" for his next step forward.

Back at home after the tour, John and the band had some time apart, which freed him to take on a smattering of side projects, including developing a film with James McMurtry, putting music to Barbra Streisand's words for "You're a Step in the Right Direction" from her 1984 release *Emotion* and producing the song "Colored Lights," for The Blasters.

He also had plans to build his own recording studio—a professionally built facility, not the wires and drywall of The Shack—so that he could have his business operations and creative workspace all near his home. He also knew how hard it was for regional acts to record a major-label-quality album on a tight budget, so he decided to open his doors to outside clients from time to time.

He already had a clear idea of what he wanted in a studio, but his band didn't know that. One weekend, he took them on a road trip to Nashville, presumably to check out studios as research for his forthcoming facility. "That's what we were supposed to think it was about," says Toby Myers, "but I think John wanted to rally us all together to get us ready for the next step. This was somewhat out of character for John, and out of character for all of us to hang out for two days. But we drove to Nashville, and we looked at studios, ate ribs, went to clubs and heard blues, and then when we came home, John bought this place in Brown County that I still live 15 minutes from."

The Blasters sessions had brought John and Don Gehman to Rumbo Recorders, a three-room studio in Canoga Park, California, designed and built by Daryl Dragon, aka the "Captain" of Captain and Tenille. They worked in Studio B, which Dragon patterned after Caribou Ranch in Colorado. Interestingly, Gehman and Rumbo staff engineer Greg Edward worked at both Caribou Ranch and Criteria Studios, and would later helm The Blasters sessions. With the final track mixed, Alvin and band walked away with a killer track written and produced by John for their *Hard Line* album, and John saw a perfect model for his own studio.

John wanted a control room that felt the same, looked the same, had the same design, woodwork, equipment and feel as Rumbo's Studio B. "Basically when you sit at Belmont Mall, in the control room, if you put drapes over the glass and change the color of the interior cloth, you wouldn't know where you were," says Ross Hogarth, Edward's assistant at the time who helped build the studio. All the way down to the woodworking on the equipment racks, it is identical to Rumbo."

John found a house down a side road off of State Road 46, in a remote area called Belmont, about 15 miles from Lake Monroe. In terms of modern conveniences, the town doesn't offer much more than a combination gas station and truck stop, but its history as a creative community dates back to the early 1900s. Prior to the construction of the Central Illinois Railroad, the wooded area was virtually inaccessible, with many residents spending their entire lives there without even straying to nearby Nashville, Indiana. But that all changed with the railroad, and as people came and went between Bloomington and Nashville, a few paused to marvel at the evergreen trees and other foliage that make up Belmont's lush landscape. The environment, which some believe to have a creative, psychic pull, attracted Wisconsin artist Adolph Shulz, followed closely by impressionist painter T.C. Steele, who arrived with his wife Selma and purchased 211 acres. They built a home there that they named the "House of the Singing Winds." Others, including woodblock artist Gus Baumann, illustrator Will Vawter, photographer Frank Hohenberger and cartoonist Kin Hubbard, established the first major summer art colony in the Midwest. Steele was also a member of the Hoosier Group, a collective of regional impressionist painters. Through the next several decades, artists visited for the plein air painting, and a variety of craftsmen, from pottery makers to weavers to woodworkers, settled among the hills and valleys of Belmont, believing, as Selma Steele once said, that the area would "command of us our best and finest spirit."

Years later, an instinctually driven musician established his own creative colony in Belmont, seven miles from his two-story home, down a long, windy driveway hidden from view by the woods. The house, bought for $20,000, contained his recording studio, as well as offices for business manager Tim Elsner, his father Richard Mellencamp and the rest of the small clan that kept the John's artistic enterprises running. He named the site Belmont Mall, sort of as a joke. There's nothing even remotely close to a mall in Belmont, only a few dusty old stores many miles down the road.

Greg Edward, a highly respected though erratic engineer, knew Rumbo's Studio B right down to the wire. Under Gehman's supervision, he managed the design and construction of the studio. Hogarth, Edward's assistant, flew out to Indiana to help build the studio, which often meant taking on tough tasks both indoors and out in the middle of Indiana's harsh winter. With assigned "grunt work" complete, he often had to fly back to L.A. to work on a recording session at Rumbo. "Greg was my boss at the time," says Hogarth. "He was this absolutely driven, incredibly genius engineer, but pissed people off right and left wherever he went." In 1983, his passion for recording drove him to make Belmont Mall a state-of-the-art facility, while the level-headed Gehman made sure his obsessive nature didn't spin out of control.

Belmont Mall's 550-square-foot control room housed a Trident 80C console and Studer 24-track tape machine, identical to Rumbo's. It connected to a spacious studio designed to accommodate John's style of recording, with everyone playing together in the same room so that their sound and infectious energy reverberated against the nonparallel walls and high ceilings and onto the 2-inch analog tape. The peripheral areas felt like a family's country home, with plush, comfortable furniture and views of the tall trees. The Gold and Platinum albums and photos of James Dean gave guests a clue who's the head of the household.

With all troughs filled, nails hammered, equipment installed and wired and hardwood floors thoroughly polished, John called a meeting with his band at the new studio. He had more than 30 songs written by now, and the time had come to discuss what to do with them. "He calls up and says, 'Well, we're meeting for the first time at Belmont. I've got a song that we're going to arrange tonight,'" says Toby Myers. "It was springtime, there were beautiful skylights on the ceiling, so it was bright as could be. We started working on 'Scarecrow,' and within 45 minutes we had it. It rocked like a monster! He was so happy from that, and we were too! We were expecting one of those marathon, like seven until three in the morning deals, but 45 minutes later he goes, 'Well, we're done.' and we all thought, 'Man, this place is going to be gooooood.'"

Even better, the band just had to drive a few miles back to their respective homes after a day's work; no sterile hotel rooms and long distance calls to the family were necessary. "We were on the road from 1978 to 1986, pretty much around the clock," says Wanchic. "We were either making a record or touring 200 dates a year. Everybody's family life was paying the price. It was time to bring it back home."

But John didn't like to stay home for long periods of time. He was restless. He continually raises the bar to success higher each year, and therefore, each day he has to take at least some step toward his goals. Thankfully, he didn't get as anxious as he used to about going into the studio. He didn't feel like he was about to pass out anymore. Walking into his own place, he felt more confident than ever about himself and his songs. His latest batch of material reflected a heightened sense of awareness of his immediate world, although his rebellious side—evidenced by the tattoos on his arms, his three Harley Davidson motorcycles, his Corvette and his Chevrolet '56 Bel-Air—hadn't gone away.

Instead of scribbling words down as soon as they popped into his brain, John put some thought into his lyrics this time. He had never used a typewriter before, but now he wrote down lyrics and then pecked them out on the typewriter his wife bought him. He studied them and rewrote and retyped them if he needed to. With a pregnant Vicki nearby to help keep him organized, an almost four-year old Teddi Jo, German shepherd Griff running around to keep him entertained and 14-year-old daughter Michelle and friends such as Mark Ripley visiting often, John's home and family life—and the struggles of his friends and families' lives—easily worked their way in to his music. In the '70s, he had attended the Vietnam moratoriums in Washington, D.C.; he remembered those times, but never wrote about them because he worried that people would consider it pretentious. But now, he had the maturity and life experience to write about such things. "When I think of the '60s songs that I liked, they were never politically or socially oriented," he told *Rolling Stone*. "For a long time I thought, as far as my career goes, it would have been ridiculous for me to make a record and talk about anything other than 'Hurts So Good.' People just didn't see me that way. I didn't think anybody would take it seriously."

But now, the time was right for him to take a stand, and he did so without preaching or becoming overtly political. "Rain on the Scarecrow," co-written with George Green would become the album's lead track, makes it immediately clear that he was no American Fool. The grim lyrics pointed to the deterioration of the independent, American farmer through a man who lost his family farm to foreclosure and was now reduced to "400 dusty acres."

Son I'm just sorry they're just memories for you now

"My younger sister [Laura] married into a big farming family in Dudleytown," he told *Rolling Stone*. "Let's take Mark, her husband. He works

18 hours a day. Last year, he mathematically figured out how much money he made. His wage was $1.15 an hour. And he's got hundreds of hogs. Here's a 28-year-old kid who has a very heavy debt hanging over his head. I know he's scared to death of that. He doesn't sleep at night worrying about it." This is part of the reason John lent them a hand prior to recording *Uh-Huh*. He also watched some of his childhood friends struggle as they tried to make their own family farms work, sometimes to no avail, and knew about the tough times his great grandfather endured as a farmer and why his succeeding family members committed themselves to other vocations.

When I was five I walked the fence, while Grandpa held my hand

George Green co-wrote "Rain on the Scarecrow" with John after months of hearing about the farm problem on TV while sitting at John's kitchen table, smoking cigarettes and drinking tea. The "97 crosses" reference came straight from the news. Whenever a farm foreclosure took place, a cross was planted in the local courthouse yard.

In "Minutes to Memories," another Green co-write, John reports back the words of a retired steelworker who gave up on the American Dream long ago.

Life sweeps away the dreams that we have planned

Through the eyes of this 77-year-old man, we come to know the values and beliefs of the songwriter himself. An underlying theme of hope, an inner voice that says, 'don't give up,' runs through the song and would reappear in much of John's material:

You are young and you are the future
So suck it up and tough it out and be the best you can

We also learn that he values his friends and family above all:

My family and friends are the best things I've known
Through the eye of the needle I'll carry them home

And he's stubborn:

I do things my way and I pay a high price

Throughout the album, John tells the stories of the helpless and hopeless, the brokenhearted and disillusioned and those starving in our supposed land of opportunity. He protests corporate America's high-dollar endorsements and sponsorships and the mega-chains that drive the mom and pops out of business. "Stand for Something" tells us—with humor—to stand up for your own truth, whatever that truth may be. He kept the lyrics intentionally vague—he never says what we should stand for—so that listeners could apply it to their own lives. Believe in something, or you'll believe anything!

John's grandmother Laura Mellencamp sings on the aptly titled "Grandma's Theme," a 55-second prelude to "Small Town." On the prelude she sang "The Baggage Coach," her childhood favorite about a man riding a train with his child. When asked where the baby's mother is, the passengers discover she's in the baggage coach—in a coffin. She often sang this song to John and his cousins when they were babies, and thus the song has remained a cherished memory in the family. Terrified at the thought of singing in the studio, Laura Mellencamp nonetheless delivered the song wonderfully with her naturally thick accent, the mics placed far away from her to give the track its scratchy old 45 sound.

Written in the tradition of Woody Guthrie, "Small Town" sets its simple intention clearly: this is why I like living in a small town. In an in-depth feature for SPIN magazine, Bob Guccione, Jr. pointed out that even though he was living in a small town, John, having achieved such phenomenal success, knew that he is no longer one of them. But he still knew how to write about his surroundings just as they are; no hidden meanings, no plays on words. "He doesn't wear small towns the way Springsteen wears the boardwalk or Lou Reed wears leather." When he sang, "My job is so small town, provides little opportunity," he was certainly not referring to his own career, but could easily had been referring to that job he left at the telephone company, or one of the jobs held by his friend Mark Ripley or the guy who lives quietly down the road working at a nearby factory to support his family.

"Lonely Ol' Night" is named for some lines from Larry McMurtry's book Hud, and the Paul Newman movie based on it. John saw the film for the first time in 1963, and Newman's classic bad seed character and his strained relationship with his father left a deep impression on the young man. "I watched that movie a thousand times during that time in my life," he said. As an adult he identified less with Hud, but got many song ideas from the film and its classic lines.

Songs such as "R.O.C.K. in the USA" add levity to this otherwise weighty album, and imply that John still has a bit of that freewheeling, cavalier spirit left in him. That's also the reason he didn't want it on the record. It was too poppy, he thought, too formula, and it didn't match the rest of the album. He was right, but nevertheless, the single shot up to Number Two, stayed there for three weeks and was soon certified Gold. Slam dunk.

On *Scarecrow*, John replaces a lot of the rock 'n' roll shrieking of his previous two albums with a mix of lower register singing and hushed tones, allowing the pleasing melodies to roll easily along, guided by acoustic instruments and a rock-oriented beat.

The album weaves classic rock, folk and even reggae together into one simmering musical stew, evoking images of dusty, deserted farmland in the summertime and late-night back porch jams. To prepare, he had his band learn hundreds of old '60s songs, including everything from Lou Christie, the Four Seasons and the Beach Boys to Music Machine. They learned the songs note-by-note so that their essence might seep into John's songs. As a result, The Troggs' "Wild Thing" and Neil Diamond's "Cherry Cherry" rear their heads on "R.O.C.K. in the USA," while a guitar solo on "Face the Nation" takes its influence from an Animals organ solo.

"If you listen to the lead Larry plays on 'Face The Nation,' he never would have played that [otherwise] 'cause he didn't really know who the Animals were," John said in an interview with *Creem*. "He's young, and he grew up on Grand Funk Railroad. You hear it, and it's like, 'where did that come from?' It had to be from hearing those old records."

By the time the band walked into Belmont Mall to record *Scarecrow*, they had these songs imprinted deeply in their minds. With the evening sky peeking through the skylights, John played "Rain on the Scarecrow" once on acoustic guitar, and as Myers indicated earlier, the band worked up their respective parts in the control room within 20 minutes. After that, they walked into the studio and nailed the song on the first take. They went home knowing that something special was starting to happen, but they had also worked together for so long, they knew they could have many more first-take moments. "There was a ton of spontaneity, but it was backed up by endless rehearsals," says Mike Wanchic. "You get to know the songs so well, you feel like you've lived them."

Ross Hogarth, who returned to Indiana to assist engineer Greg Edward and co-producer Don Gehman, watched as the band spontaneously composed songs in the control room. "Kenny [Aronoff] would create a beat by using his leg as a snare, tapping his foot for the kick drum and using his chest and knee for toms," he says. "Toby had the acoustic bass, Mike would have the acoustic guitar and they would figure out the parts, go out into the room and cut it in one take—*boom!* Those guys made records in takes! Every song had its own life and if it didn't come in a couple of takes, it was revisited in a different way. But that band was a one-, two- or three-take band. Part of it came from John wanting that, but the other part was the band delivering it."

John expected his band to deliver a spot-on performance once they stepped into the studio, but at the same time, he gave them the freedom to experiment and offer up ideas. In fact, he expected it. "Your job was not just to be prepared and play your instrument," Aronoff told *NUVO*. "You had to constantly come up with ideas for everybody else's inspiration. It's as though we were each mini producers and arrangers. To work for John Mellencamp, if you couldn't relate to his drive, you'd quit."

Larry Crane changed his guitar sound for the album. "I went from Gibson guitars to playing a Fender Telecaster, started listening to all the guys who played rhythm guitar on Telecasters—Willy Nile, Keith Richards—and figured out what they were doing," he told *NUVO*. "It changed our core guitar sound. In recording, John always had a good idea of how he wanted the arrangements to go. It was my job to interpret that into musical terms. He'd say, "I want it to feel like that," then I'd go through this brain process and say, "Take the guitar and do this, the drums will do this here," and it would make that sound that he was hearing."

On *Scarecrow*, the band explored and expanded their creative abilities, discovering talents they didn't know they had. "John gave us the latitude to try anything," recalls bassist Toby Myers. But I must say, the band was very well rehearsed and we were expected to cut really quickly. We would cut a song a day; after dinner we would at least have a rough mix and then we'd talk about what was going to happen the next day. If it was a hard song, we'd spend no more than two days, but there were songs that took at least four days."

John's albums build on one another, each one taking him notches higher in quality, and step by step closer to his authentic creative potential. *Nothin' Matters and What If It Did* hinted at the more stripped down rock sound he wanted, but slick production and horn sections clouded that message. *American Fool* hit the mark in achieving his vision of raw rock 'n' roll, although the songwriting reflected a man after catchy rhymes and commercial hits. His songwriting became more honest, the music even more raw on *Uh-Huh*. But with *Scarecrow*, he would give his songwriting a higher purpose and transform the raw, electric energy of his past albums into organic, acoustic power. That sound—Americana before the public knew it as such—held its own amongst the upbeat synthesizer-driven music played by pretty boys and girls such as Duran Duran, Culture Club and Madonna.

"I'm real proud of these songs because I think they give a good indication of where I've come to," Mellencamp confirmed to the *Herald Times* in Bloomington. "As crazy as it sounds, after all I've been through, I feel that I'm just beginning to hit my stride as a songwriter and singer. The way I feel now is that I'm not the kid I used to be anymore; and what happens is when you grow up you take more responsibility. That's what I've done on this album."

"*Scarecrow* was the first record of the rest of our lives where we really found what we're looking for," says guitarist Mike Wanchic. John dedicated the album to his grandfather, Harry "Speck" Mellencamp, who fought a hard battle with lung cancer through most of the album's gestation. He put his fists down on Christmas night, 1985, but didn't bow down easily. Hell, a couple of years before he passed, he beat up a man at his son Joe's Rok-Sey Roller Rink. Speck endured rounds of intense chemotherapy treatments the year he passed away, yet still had enough energy to flirt with his nurses. John went with him to the doctor's office, but he hated hospitals and vowed that when Speck's health deteriorated to the point where he had to go to one, he wouldn't go in. Speck understood; he and his grandfather said their real goodbye at the elder Mellencamp's house in Seymour, with the cornfields standing by across the street.

Speck had to stay in the hospital during his final days, and during this time, a priest came to visit. "Do you accept Christ as your Savior?" the priest asked. "Fuck no," replied Speck, his fierce pride still intact. He refused to admit his fear or give in to faith. As Christmas approached, most of the Mellencamp family gathered daily in Speck's room to spend as much time with him as they could, while they could. John never showed up, but on Christmas Day, he ignored his hatred of hospitals and walked into Speck's room with his acoustic guitar. He had a gift for his grandfather, his role model throughout his life. He pulled up a chair next to the bed, propped his guitar on one leg and softly sang "Silent Night." There wasn't a dry eye in the room, Laura Mellencamp recalled. Then he left. Speck's wife of 60 years believed it was the best gift of her husband's life. He died, as peacefully as someone as tough as him could, later that evening.

CHAPTER SIX

WOODEN CROSSES, LONELY NIGHTS

Mercury released *Scarecrow* in November 1985 to both critical acclaim and the long-awaited respect of John's peers. Along with Springsteen's *Born in the U.S.A.*, Madonna's *Like a Virgin* and Michael Jackson's *Thriller*, the album defined the musical landscape of the early- to mid-1980s. The album soared to Number Two on *Billboard*'s Album chart and its debut single, "Lonely Ol' Night," would inch all the way up to Number One on the Mainstream Rock chart, Number Six on the Hot 100. "Small Town" would climb to the same position the following month and reach Number Two on the Mainstream Rock chart. The album continued to deliver hits through 1986.

A couple of months before the album hit stores, John shot the video "Lonely Ol' Night" in and around Bloomington. George Green's wife starred as John's girlfriend. Prior to shooting, she had told him, "Listen, Mellencamp, you better not be putting a lot of real pretty girls in this video, because real pretty girls don't have lonely ol' nights!" "Fine," he said. "I'll put you in it." Mrs. Green's realistic beauty worked well for the video. She could turn some heads, but wouldn't feel or look out of place meandering through the carnival at a local state fair. The porch where John sat and played guitar and the old church from the "Rain on the Scarecrow" video weren't far away.

Everything clicked into place during the *Scarecrow* era, on many levels. John and Vicky enjoyed a solid relationship; sure, they still had their occasional tiffs and a blowout or two, but their loving bond won out over any argument. She took care of Teddi Jo and newborn Justice, born August 14, 1985, and kept their newly renovated home in order. She supported John, despite a demanding career that kept him away from home more often than not. When he was home, the pressure of the music business, combined with the high expectations he set for himself, caused his temper to flare at random. An innocent "What would you like for dinner, John?" might elicit a loud "Get off my case!" Vicky had the patience to deal with his antics, combined with the strength to stand up for herself when things got out of hand. John's ex-wife Pricilla Esterline lived at his old house near Lake Monroe with daughter Michelle, now a teenager with almost as much attitude as her father. She split her time between each parental household, though she probably saw more of her step-mom than her father.

John would soon have to leave his growing family to embark on his most ambitious tour to date. Thankfully, Vicky had the large Mellencamp clan for support. After Speck's death, Richard Mellencamp tried to repair his relationship with his sons, and the family grew stronger as a result. As John's career became more demanding, they took on various roles in his business affairs. Friend Tim Elsner continued to serve as John's business manager, Esterline worked as production coordinator, brother Ted Mellencamp stuck around to handle various road manager duties, cousin Tracy worked as a bodyguard for a while and Richard Mellencamp oversaw John's financial affairs. Through his career at Robbins Electric, he knew how to manage large amounts of money, and having him and the rest of his family involved meant he had a network of people he could trust and who would keep him grounded. "You need people around you that can sometimes say, 'John. Come on,'" says Elsner. "If your father can't tell you that, who can?"

Around the time that John emerged from Belmont Mall with *Scarecrow* in hand, American singing-songwriting great Willie Nelson got the idea to organize a benefit concert for American family farmers. He got inspiration from Bob Dylan, who wondered aloud between songs during the Live Aid concert in 1985 if maybe some of the money they raised could benefit local growers. Nelson, who grew up in the farming community of Abbott, Texas, responded to his suggestion; initially, he thought that one concert would be enough. More than 20 years later, they're still holding concerts to support this ongoing issue.

A perfect chain of coincidences brought Nelson and John, his first recruit for the benefit concert, together. Ironically, John had turned down the enormous Live Aid extravaganza. The concert follow-up to the über-all-star Band Aid collaboration single, "Do They Know It's Christmas," raised millions to relieve famine in Africa. The Live Aid concert, held July 13, 1985, was considered the biggest live rock event ever, spanning two continents and viewed by 1.5 billion people worldwide. The show raised many more millions.

Phil Collins, David Bowie, Sting, Santana, Neil Young and dozens of others performed at the event, but John stayed away. "I knew it was going to be on [inter]national TV, satellite linkup and it was all about that," he said in the book *Farm Aid: A Song for America*. "Being here in Indiana, I felt weird about it." He felt he could do more good if he focused his energy on local issues, and he got his opportunity when Nelson called. "Willie was out here playing golf," John recalled. "He was with some guys I knew here in town. He was talking about the [first] concert, and one of the guys was a good friend of mine. He said, 'John Mellencamp made a record called *Scarecrow*, and in it is exactly what you're talking about.' They played about nine holes, and Willie called me from the clubhouse, I think. He said, 'Do you want to do this?' We talked about farming and how I felt about it. I said I'd try to get some rock bands to come and play."

Nelson enlisted Neil Young in August 1985 while they worked together on the video for "Are There Any More Real Cowboys?" for Young's album, *Old Ways*. Young, who also performed at Live Aid, agreed with John and Willie that our country's farmers desperately needed help. They immediately started planning the concert.

"I talked about no corporate sponsorship," John recalled to *Rolling Stone*. "I talked about low ticket prices for the concert. I talked about not making this a concert for the rich. I said, up front, my education on this is limited. I'll help because I know a lot of people in rock bands. But I didn't want to get into a situation where people would be asking me about what happened to the money for Farm Aid. I told Willie, 'I don't want to know about this money. It's not why I'm doing it.'"

The first show, held September 22, 1985 in Champaign, Illinois, featured performances from the founding fathers, plus a mixed bag of guests that included Tom Petty and the Heartbreakers, Bob Dylan, the Beach Boys, Daryl Hall, Van Halen, Johnny Cash, X, John Fogerty and Lou Reed, among others. Billed like Live Aid as an "all star" concert, performers left their egos at the door, focusing more on the mission than publicity. "It was good having people like X and Lou [Reed]," John told *Creem*. "It changed the spirit of the thing, and there wasn't any of this 'Am I going to get a prime time spot? Who am I following?'—which wasn't why we were doing this. I really think there was such community there. It was, in many ways, what the '60s pretended to be for that one day."

Also in the mid-1980s, John became one of the most vocal opponents of the Parents Music Resource Center (PMRC), a committee formed in 1985 by a group of Washington wives, including then-Senator Al Gore's wife, Tipper. Their goal, they claimed was to "educate and inform" parents about purportedly sexually explicit, violent or drug/alcohol-endorsing lyrics and they even convinced record labels to mark albums with a "Parental Guidance: Explicit Lyrics" label. Many prominent recording artists publicly protested their efforts. Frank Zappa called the PMRC proposal an "ill conceived piece of nonsense," and even artists as "vanilla" as John Denver opposed the censorship. John also fell into this category. He demanded a contract from his record company declaring that his records 'wouldn't be rated, and compared the ratings system to McCarthy blacklisting. "It's a wolf in sheep's clothing," he said. "I don't really like 'Fuck Like a Beast,' but if you look forward and backwards, you can see what's coming. Before long, K-Mart'll say we got too many X and R records, and then you'll be lucky to get Olivia Newton-John because her clothes are too tight. We'll be lucky if we end up with the Archies."

While John fought against the PMRC and for the family farm, the rest of the band took the summer off, sort of. Larry Crane teamed with members of Tom Petty's Heartbreakers to record a few songs for Rosanne Cash's *Rhythm and Romance* album. Mike Wanchic caught up with some old friends in Greencastle to play a few club gigs with their Average House Band, played some vicious rounds of basketball and plucked around on various stringed instruments. Toby Myers chilled out and contemplated building a home recording studio, a project he would tackle after the Scarecrow Tour. Kenny Aronoff played drums on Stray Cat Brian Setzer's album and sat in with various jazz, fusion and rock bands. The exceedingly ambitious Aronoff also decided to learn country drumming that summer so that he could land more work as a session player in Nashville. To hone his skills, he got himself a gig at the Opry—not *the* Opry, but the Little Nashville Opry, and not *that* Nashville, but Nashville, Indiana. Big difference.

The Little Nashville Opry has a lot in common with nightclubs in Branson, Missouri—a tourist trap surrounded by campgrounds and antique malls that hosts a smattering of country music artists on select nights, and a house band playing Top 40 country and traditional tunes on the weekends and off nights. A pretty 20-something named Lisa Germano played fiddle in this house band and hated every minute of it. Ever since she was a little girl, she dreamed of having her music on the radio, though she hadn't performed much farther than her back yard. But she showed signs of prodigy, having written her first piece of music—a 15-minute opera—at age seven, and later studied the violin. The middle child of six, born to musician/teacher parents, she had given up the dream in her teens, become a high school cheerleader and famously got kicked off the squad for not smiling enough. A sensitive soul with a gentle spirit, Germano had more depth than pep. Over time, her confusion manifested as agoraphobia and depression, and she continued on through young adulthood a very isolated, lonely woman.

She worked her way out of the downward spiral through therapy and the violin and joined the Little Nashville Opry band as a way to pursue her lifelong goal as a performer, as well as reconnect with the world around her. When Kenny Aronoff showed up in the summer of 1985 to fulfill their need for a drummer, Germano's much-hated job became much more enjoyable. She gained a friend and soon, her life changed dramatically. "We had so much fun!" she recalls. "We had these little hidden jokes...when people that would come up and sing who were really bad, he'd use this gong and I would be the only one that knew that's what he was doing. We'd usually ride out [to the club] together, so we became very good friends."

After one summer with Little Nashville Opry, Aronoff left to rejoin John for the inaugural Farm Aid performance and other projects. A couple of months later, he gave Germano a call. "Hey, come by the studio on your way back from the Opry—John needs someone to put fiddle on a song," he told her. One subtle fiddle part may have seemed like no big deal to Aronoff, but it was a huge opportunity for Germano, who saw herself moving one step closer to her goal of performing on records, preferably ones that would get played on the radio.

Since Belmont Mall was right on her way home from the Little Nashville Opry, Germano didn't bother changing out of her requisite "Hee Haw" overalls. When she walked in, John gave Kenny a 'who the hell is this chick' look, but let her play the part just the same. She exceeded his expectations. She understood how to play what he heard in his head, which is what he needed: another mind reader. Bassist Toby Myers stared in a daze, she was so "drop-dead gorgeous." After that night, they knew they had their fiddle player. About a week later, John called and asked if she would join them on the Scarecrow Tour as a wardrobe person, but also play violin on that one song. As Germano recalls, "he had this idea of using me on his next record, and wanted another voice that could carry out what he wanted."

She accepted his offer, despite the fact that the idea of touring terrified her. She had just emerged from a completely isolated life; the idea of sharing a bus with a tightly knit group of men's men, including new addition John Cascella on accordion, plus two backup singers, Pat Peterson and another newcomer, multi-instrumentalist/vocalist Crystal Taliefero, to play for huge crowds and interact with dozens of strangers brought about a level of anxiety that required additional therapy.

Taliefero, however, practically grew up on stage. The Gary, Indiana, native started playing R&B songs in local clubs when she was 11 years old. John procured another prodigy when he recruited her into the group. A student of classical, opera and jazz, the young performer could sing, dance and play the sax, guitar, harmonica, percussion, bass and keyboards. She bonded quickly with Peterson, who could educate her to John's strict protocol.

"Crystal was right out of college when she joined," says Peterson. "I feel like I'm her big sister. We did some phenomenal backup work together. She was very athletic also, so she would flip, jump over John's head and dance. It was exciting because we challenged each other. This was her first real gig as an artist, and I was glad to be there at the beginning."

On the road, Germano found herself lonelier than ever. The men hadn't accepted her as part of the band, and the two other women—Peterson and Taliefero—usually palled around without her. They called this the "scare Lisa" tour behind her back, and whether consciously or not, maybe that was their intention. "It would be scary for any woman coming on the road with us," says Wanchic. "We weren't exactly *consummate* gentlemen at the time!"

All of the conflicts washed away on stage though, where, with her fiddle perched underneath her delicate chin, she wowed the crowds with her solo in the middle of "Small Town" and became a defining presence in the group. She didn't always enjoy being on the road and on several occasions, considered backing out. She would take John aside and say, "I don't know if I really want to do this!" "Hang in there, he assured her; I have ideas for you. I really want you to be on the next record. She focused on that light at the end of the tunnel, her goal of playing on records, though she wouldn't reach that light for many, many more months.

For his headlining performances, John and band played a two-and-a-half hour set...no gimmicks, a feat compared (again) to Bruce Springsteen for its marathon length. The tour would cover more than 100 U.S. and Canadian cities over six months, hitting some of the largest venues of his career to date. Overseas, they played 11 sold-out arena shows in Sydney, Australia alone.

To get revved up for these long, intense performances, John and the band worked up their aggression with a fierce game of three-on-three basketball. "We carried our own sports locker," Wanchic recalled to *NUVO*. "It had a full flag football rig, and we carried our own basketball goal. We'd get to the venue, have dinner, do a soundcheck and then play three-on-three basketball, shower and then go on. We'd try to get a full body sweat going before we went on." Wanchic always played on John's team, usually with another crewmember. Toby Myers, Kenny Aronoff and Larry Crane formed the other team. Ninety percent of the time, Wanchic says, John's team won. It was a good idea to let them win.

In the middle of his long set, John usually asked the audience to write their local congressmen to ask them to help the family farmer. The day after the show, he would run an ad in every local paper giving the senators' names and where to write to them. "I don't know if it's going to mean anything at all," he told the *Herald Times*. "I mean, some guy in a rock band isn't going to make a hell of a lot of difference with these guys." He underestimated his influence.

Numerous corporations approached John and new manager Tommy Mattola regarding sponsorships, but he turned them all down, still retaliating against "the Man." "I don't need to make money that way," he said. "I didn't write these songs or play these shows so they can offer me money in return for sticking their logo above my name. The beer ones get to me. I don't even drink! Cigarette ones gall me too, because I hate that I smoke." Even his parents tried to convince him to take the money. "Strike while the poker's hot," Richard Mellencamp would tell him. But like so many times before, he ignored their advice. Ex-manager Billy Gaff didn't understand his resistance to corporate dollars, either. Gaff wanted to license "Hurts So Good" to a ketchup company, and John loudly protested. No way would he let his song become synonymous with hot sauce. He didn't write the song with hot sauce in mind, and he didn't want it to be used for that purpose. The argument, compiled with many others, led to the dissolution of his relationship with Gaff.

Prior to the Scarecrow Tour, John assembled a new team of professionals— all leaders in their field—to keep his broadening career on track. He signed with Mottola, then head of Champion Entertainment Organization, for personal management. Elsner stayed on as a business manager in Indiana. Mottola also managed Hall and Oates and Carly Simon, among others. Mottola then approached Rob Light, Hall and Oates' booking agent at powerhouse Creative Artists Agency (CAA), to join John's team. Well aware of Mellencamp's talent, he agreed, but they had to convince John that this was a wise decision. Light recalls their initial meeting:

"Mottola introduced John to [colleague] Tom Ross and myself, and left," Light recalls. "John wouldn't even sit down, he sat on the arm of the couch. He looked at us and said, 'I'm not really sure why I'm here, because I think that agents are the lowest form of humanity on the music food chain.' And Tom, without missing a beat, said, 'John, we're not the lowest on the food chain. *You*, the artist, are the lowest rung. We're second!' And John laughed, he goes, 'Alright, I buy that.' And he sat down. He wants people around him who are strong. I've worked with him ever since, and we've been friends ever since."

To further prove their strength, Mottola once challenged John and the band's flag football team, dubbed the MFL, to a game against Champion. The two made a serious bet on the outcome. "Mottola showed up with a New York championship flag team, and these motherfuckers were brutal, all serious college players, semi-professional rugby players," Wanchic recalled to *NUVO*. "They annihilated us, beat us 70 to nothing, the worst ass-kicking I've ever had in my life. So, then the challenge was on."

The MFL played hard in between dates. Their season took place during the band's days off on the road. Wanchic, Toby Myers and John would team against anyone brave enough to play them. Crew members, PolyGram execs, even the Cincinnati firefighters all took their shot. Jam Productions, a tour promotion company based in Chicago, once assembled a team that included a starting quarterback for the Chicago Bears. As with basketball, John's team usually won, but during MFL season, they hired a referee.

No doubt CAA and Champion's presence ensured the Scarecrow tour's success, and created a stable foundation for John to build an even larger vision. The extra support on the business end also gave John a few spare minutes to relax, which helped tame a man known for savage outbursts. "It was pretty manic on the American Fool and Uh-Huh [tours], mainly because John's fame was coming so quickly and he had to do so much shit and it really wasn't organized that well yet," says Toby Myers. "By the time we got to *Scarecrow*, he had more people taking care of stuff and more time to be a human being. And once he got that time, he had more time to spend with us and more time to flesh out ideas."

As one would expect when an artist plays multiple large venues, not every show ran flawlessly. One of the band's highest profile dates—Madison Square Garden in New York City—came to a screeching halt, twice. Apparently a circuit breaker blew, causing the high-end loudspeaker system to cut out twice during his lengthy set. With as much calm as he could muster at the time, he informed his 20,000 fans, each of whom had paid $17.50 a ticket, that if they kept their stubs, they would get their money back. He only lost half of his shirt, as only about that much of the crowd took him up on the offer.

The Scarecrow Tour raged on until spring of 1986, when the band held their grand finale in Bloomington, Indiana's Memorial Stadium on April 27. The concert capped off that year's "World's Greatest College Weekend." With 43,000 tickets sold, and 12,000 more fans gathered in parking lots across the street, the show drew the largest crowd ever for the event. It would also serve as a sweet homecoming after a long and grueling tour. "I'm looking so forward to Saturday, you wouldn't believe it," bassist Toby Myers told the *Herald Times*. "If the weather's great, it's going to be the best gig of my life."

They took the stage at 7:35 P.M., playing in front of an enormous setup left over from the Farm Aid concert the year before. They kicked off the set with "Small Town," followed by other songs from the current album. Mid-set they played earlier hits such as "Ain't Even Done With the Night" and "I Need a Lover," then devoted most of the encore to The Drifters' "Under the Boardwalk" and a steaming medley that included the Holland/Dozier/Holland song, "Mickey's Monkey," Neil Diamond's "Turn on Your Love Light" and James Brown's "Cold Sweat."

MTV held another Indiana-centered promotion around the event, this one proving much less "toxic" than the "Pink Houses" debacle. Contest winner

Patricia Cross emceed the concert and took home one of John's Fender Telecaster guitars. MTV VJ J.J. Jackson attended the concert; this was his first visit to Bloomington. Like a lot of people, he knew nothing about the college weekend event until he saw the movie *Breaking Away* (the 1979 Academy Award-winning film shot in Bloomington that features the "Little 500" bicycle race—arguably the second biggest thing to happen in the city).

The happy occasion differed drastically from a sobering show John played right before coming home. In the spring of 1986, he detoured to Chillicothe, Missouri, to perform during a 145-day protest action at the USDA office held by the newly formed Missouri Rural Crisis Center (MRCC), a statewide organization comprised of farmers and rural families throughout the state. Farm Aid supported the organization early on by awarding them a $10,000 grant for emergency food distribution. Hundreds of farmers stood in line to get food in Chillicothe and surrounding areas, because they couldn't afford to buy it themselves. Farm Aid gave them hope.

The purpose of the rally was to oust the county supervisor who was foreclosing farms against the law. It also aimed to put pressure on policy makers to pass the 1987 Credit Act, which stated that the Farmer's Home Administration (FmHA) could not foreclose on any family farmer unless the FmHA made more money through foreclosure than they would by investing in making the farm profitable. The parking lot in front of the USDA office served as a hub for local farmers and community and civil rights organizations for that entire 145 days. When John showed up to play his songs on the back of a flatbed truck, 15,000 people listened. When he finished, he wrote a $15,000 check to the MRCC and never forgot the impact the rally had on the farming community.

When John came off of the Scarecrow Tour (and presumably back down to earth), he was exhausted—spent from the tour and tired of the music business again. But every time he walked by his indoor pool, down the hall, past the laundry room where he wrote some of the songs for *Scarecrow* and by his guitar, he couldn't keep himself from picking it up and writing more songs. In the past, he put off writing until the deadline of an album mounted. But now, he couldn't seem to turn off the flow of verses and choruses. The words that came forth from that unexplainable well were some of his most revealing yet, mostly about ordinary people with complex emotions. He had his own complicated emotions to sift through; some of them came out in these songs. He still grieved for his grandfather and recently his Uncle Joe, a brute of a guy strong enough "to lift a tree," died from cancer at age 57, the same disease that killed Speck not long before.

He found it easier, or more realistic anyway, to write about other people's life challenges than about *his* real life. His world had become too surreal, overblown. On the road, he found himself giving in to the temptation that always seemed to taunt him.

He had a wife, three kids, a large extended family and a tight band, but he has said he felt lonely and alone. He made selfish decisions and didn't want to be bothered with much of anything.

He wanted love / Without involvement

The band (they had dropped the name The Zone, thank goodness) had earned a reputation as a monster unit, just blazing hot, arguably on par with Bruce Springsteen's E Street Band. They deserved every word of praise after years of exhausting rehearsals, tours and an unwavering commitment to excel. "We had consciously in our minds the idea of being the best rock band in the world, whether or not we ever would be was open to question," Mike Wanchic said. "We went into rehearsal at a level that no one ever has. We rehearsed for six months before a major tour; it took forever. At one point we did a study of American music, and we spent three months learning 90 songs of other bands. We learned them not just listening to them, but we learned every single nuance of every single song, whether it was "ABC" by the Jackson Five or "White Room" by Cream, "Dancing Days" by Zeppelin, the Rascals catalog, a bunch of Motown. We made a thorough study of what we could bring back to the table. When you really analyze what makes Motown Motown, you understand the various components of what makes the music work."

The band propelled swiftly toward their goal of "world's best rock band," but their personal lives paid the price. Some of the guys, married for 10 years or more, were going through hard times with their wives. Some felt the heat (and guilt) of missing their children grow up; ultimately all suffered divorce. "I think we had a 100 percent attrition rate, actually," says Wanchic.

While the Scarecrow Tour wove its way around the globe, producer/engineer Don Gehman and engineer Ross Hogarth kept Belmont Mall warm with other projects, most notably R.E.M, who used the studio to record *Life's Rich Pageant*. When that album wrapped, Hogarth returned to Rumbo to work on albums for RATT, Dio, Motley Crüe and a slew of other then-popular hair metal bands, but would come back to Indiana a few years later. Greg Edward, however, was permanently dismissed from the Mellen-camp after the *Scarecrow* sessions.

Though haunted still by the ghosts of Speck and Uncle Joe, John didn't rest on his *Scarecrow* fortune long before rounding up the band to record another album. Having spent several months together on the road, John had time to talk about this next record with them before they started rehearsals in September 1986. They entertained the idea of a double album, but at least 10 of the songs John had written ultimately wouldn't fit as the album began to take shape. He originally titled it *Bobtown*, after the small Jackson County town where his grandparents once lived. As the album became more serious, he replaced that notion with *The Lonesome Jubilee*, a nod to his own lonesome state of mind, as well as to those all around him who had reached middle age and thought, "Is this it?"

His days of screwing around musically had dissipated with his last album, and when the band convened in Indiana to presumably top it, he followed a similar roadmap: He gave them the lyrics and the seeds of the song, and expected the band to help grow that into something better than he anticipated. And under no circumstances do you screw it up! This time, however, they had an idea of how John wanted the album to sound musically before they entered rehearsals; basically, *Scarecrow* times 10. "There was a natural progression from *Scarecrow*, which had certain thematic content, to the expanded instrumentation on *The Lonesome Jubilee*, which completed what we started with *Scarecrow*," Wanchic explains.

The rehearsal sessions came first, with John and the band working up the songs until they were suitable for a record. The actual album recording, when the songs evolved from raw demo recordings to fully flavored radio-ready gems, would occur shortly thereafter.

Don Gehman and engineer David Leonard, who had worked with Gehman on several projects through the '80s, came in for both the demo and master sessions. Though a few band members had only played with John on the road prior to *The Lonesome Jubilee*, Leonard was the only completely new variable in the equation. "It was exciting, and a little bit intimidating, because it was John's private studio," says Leonard. "So it was his studio, his mics, his people and I was the new guy. But it turned out to be probably the best record that we did together."

Leonard replaced the talented, fearless but "manic" Greg Edward, who helped build Belmont Mall and engineered *Scarecrow*. His strong personality clashed with the equally dynamic man-in-charge who fired him. But even though he wasn't around, his presence was felt within those four walls he helped build. The core lineup of John, Mike Wanchic, Toby Myers, Larry Crane and Kenny Aronoff was on hand from beginning to end, while keyboardist/accordionist John Cascella, fiddle player Lisa Germano and background vocalists/percussionists Pat Peterson and Crystal Taliefero—all newcomers to John's studio routine (save for a single part here and there)—would arrive slightly later in the process. All played pivotal roles.

Though John claims to have mellowed out by the ripe old age of 35, in the studio, he remained a live wire. John thrives under pressure. He *wants* to experience anxiety, and pushes his band to feel that too. Whereas most people tend to avoid tension, he creates it. Push, push, push, as Gehman related on *Uh-Huh*, he straddles the line between motivation and meltdown. On a typical day, John might walk into the studio with lyrics written and some basic melody ideas. He'd turn to his band and say, "Okay guys, this is the best song I ever wrote. Don't fuck it up." "It's his way of saying, 'This really means a lot to me guys.' I know that feeling now when I write," says Germano. "Every song you finish you think, 'This is the accumulation of everything I've learned my whole life.'"

Rehearsals usually began with John playing a song for the band on acoustic guitar. Mike Wanchic and Larry Crane would then fall in, followed by Kenny Aronoff on hand percussion. Much like the *Scarecrow* sessions, one member would come up with a few bars of a song, another might suggest a bridge. In the case of Germano and Cascella, casual playing around led to melody lines and an instrumental combination that defined the album.

"The minute I heard John Cascella and Lisa Germano playing together like RANNT! RANNT! in the rehearsals for "Paper in Fire," I knew that was a sound people hadn't heard before—or at least not with the kind of parts we had them playing," John told *Billboard*. "See, I was anti-guitar then and sick of guitar solos, and I asked them to play a hook line together that would provide the same melodic part on that record as a guitar sound." The song came together in just a few hours, a sign of magic in the making.

They aimed to record a song a day—some days the song formed in just a few hours, sometimes it took all day. Other days, seemingly nothing got accomplished, as the band would take a song in a different direction than what John had in mind. That's when he joked around that, indeed, they did fuck it up. Sometimes he got mad, kicked machines, walked out of the studio and went home. Then he would come back the next day with a fresh perspective, and possibly a new idea or another way to communicate what he wanted.

"The pressure was on even more, and the desire to experiment was even greater," says Toby Myers of *The Lonesome Jubilee*. We cut so many songs; I have a CD of songs that didn't make it that most artists would cut their left arm off to release."

The passing around of instruments continued with this album *a la* Sly and the Family Stone, complete with similar closeness and dysfunction. "You could get so mad, but you'd come back because it's your family and you love them. It had that kind of dysfunction," says Germano. They even wrote "We Are the People" with Sly and band in mind. Penny whistle, banjo, pedal steel, hammered dulcimer, mandolin and dobro, among other instruments, all found their way onto the record...a sign of their "that sounds good, let's try that" approach, as well as the frontman's reverence for his rural roots.

Toby Myers sang lead on one track, a new thing for him, and got to play a little funk bass on "Rooty Toot Toot." "I used to say really off the wall shit just to get John agitated—not to make him mad, but just get him going a little bit," recalls Myers. "John hated 'Rooty,' but it was the first time that I was allowed to play a slappin' bass part. It was so fun for me to cut, and I thought the song grooved so friggin' hard. Toward the end of us cutting tracks I said, "John, that's the best friggin' song you ever wrote,' and he leaped across the room and put me in a headlock!"

The family feel was most apparent on "Cherry Bomb." Pat Peterson recalls that John gave everyone a particular role to play, whether it was a vocal line or a solo. On the vocals, first Peterson would sing a line, then Taliefero, then maybe Mike Wanchic. Peterson's memorable addition came toward the end of the song, when she follows John's "and if we've done any wrong" with a soulful "I hope that we're forgiven." "It had this 'we're all in this together,' kind of sound," recalls Germano of the vocal trade-offs. The line that Pat sang, for example, sounded like she wrote it, to have that real *band* feeling." When she and John discussed how she would sing the part, she mentioned that those words were very humbling, very honest. "Oh, I didn't mean that," he said gruffly. "I just write songs, you know." Uh-huh.

"Check It Out," a nod to the poets "screamin' out their words," hoping that "future generations" have a better understanding of living and happiness than we do, had the most memorable fiddle/accordion hook on the album, not to mention the hardest to sing two words—"Future generations." It tumbles out of John's mouth, a mountain of verbiage in a short span of time. But when the accordion and fiddle play in unison, the phrasing and combination of instruments sounds perfectly natural. Germano says that the demo version is even nicer than the album cut. "The version they ended up using is more rock and pop, so I understand why they used it. They wanted it played on the radio. The demo version is gorgeous and beautiful...more magical. But those songs don't get played on the radio."

With the tour ordeal and some studio time behind her, Germano had gotten comfortable enough to contribute ideas, and she often got so excited about the album-making process (her dream, remember), she found it hard to stop! "John allowed everyone to speak their minds but there was a definite point...it's a political thing, you've got to be careful not to speak your mind when too many other things are going on."

During the recording of the album, Belmont Mall was about as crowded as a shopping mall during Christmas rush. Musicians gathered in the studio, the hallways, iso booths, all at the same time to create John's signature organic sound. Even if they weren't needed on a song, they stayed close by. "Nobody was hanging out in the lounge," says Leonard. "If we were working, everybody's working."

Basic tracks—drums, bass, guitar—came first, with other instruments and

John's vocals added later. When John's wasn't singing, he chain-smoked and directed the band.

In addition to delivering powerhouse vocals, Taliefero played multiple instruments, including percussion and saxophone. Cascella played sax too, which meant the two of them could join together and form a mini-James Brown horn section, which they did. "It was a creative, exciting time," says Peterson, who cites *The Lonesome Jubilee* as her most meaningful recording experience. "The feelings, as this music was being laid down...you could feel the openings. Even the toil over it, and the listening at the end of the day, it was creativity at its best."

They had the album almost finished when John decided to record one more song: Woody Guthrie's "Do Re Mi." He wanted it as a B-side for one of his next singles, as well as a the forthcoming Guthrie benefit album *A Vision Shared: A Tribute to Woody Guthrie & Leadbelly.*

The band, along with Tim Elsner and John's assistant/runner/friend Rick Fettig gathered around the coffee table in the control room, fiddling with their instruments before the tape machine turned on. As *SPIN*'s Bob Guccione, Jr. recalled, "John sits on the edge of the couch, a cigarette in his right hand, his left arm hanging over the top of his acoustic guitar, keeping it on his knee. Dave Leonard, his engineer, and Don Gehman, his co-producer, sit to his right; opposite them is Mike Wanchic, who has a steel guitar on his knees, and smiles and laughs easily. Larry Crane sits next to him, holding his guitar in his lap like a deputy riding shotgun. Lisa Germano sits on a tall stool between Larry and the couch, leaning slightly off of it into the circle. She has large curious eyes and round cheeks, and the movements and feel of a small bird. When she sits up to play, tucking the violin under her left cheek, she has a delicate curve to her back. She plays intensely and exquisitely, and her body moves with the sound as her foot taps gently on the run of the stool. John Cascella sits on the edge of the recording console, one foot on the ground, opening and closing the accordion."

They hadn't rehearsed "Do Re Mi" before this day, but John played the band the melody and they picked it up easily. Like many of John's own songs, they created the arrangement on the spot, with John leaning over to read the lyrics as he sings them. They record the song much the same way, reconfiguring their positions out in the studio, with Cascella moving into the reception area, Wanchic putting his amp in the office/lounge to isolate its sound. Toby Myers is out sick that day, so Cascella plays his part on a sampler, which must have looked like a foreign object next to all of the acoustic instruments.

After Leonard and Gehman finished mixing the album, and Stephen Marcussen gave it the final in mastering at Precision Lacquer in Hollywood, John faced the unpleasant ritual of playing his latest work for the label. He suggested "Paper in Fire" as its first single. As with every other album, the label didn't feel confident about the song's potential as a single, or the album as a whole. They wanted something safer—more like *Scarecrow*. But there wasn't anything safe about *The Lonesome Jubilee*. There were no surefire "radio hits" *a la* "R.O.C.K. in the USA." The album held honest, experimental and pure songs. "Radio friendly" didn't come to mind.

With *The Lonesome Jubilee*, John wasn't trying to "hold on to 16" anymore. Instead, songs such as "Cherry Bomb" offered, "Seventeen has turned 35/I'm surprised that we're still living." *College Media Journal* voted him college act of the year in '85 and '86, even though most college-age kids couldn't necessarily relate to his new album's subject matter. The people that identified with him mostly had reached their mid-'30s, disillusioned with life, but trying to hang on, even though they were exhausted from years spent fighting to keep their place in life's rat race. At 21 or 25, you've got energy to burn, life is just beginning. But a decade later, many adults start getting that "stick a fork in me, I'm done" feeling. "Unless you know what it's like to spend your whole life or the majority of your young adulthood doing what you're *supposed* to do, then you can't relate to it," John said in an interview with *Creem*. "Because some of these young guys are thinking, 'Well, I'm doing what I *want* to do'—but that's not true. They're doing what they're supposed to do." John based "The Real Life's" Jackson Jackson character on his Uncle Jay, who got married at 17 to a wife he didn't love, then worked at the same job pouring concrete so that he could support her and his children. In his 40s, he found himself divorced, having spent nearly 30 years doing what he was *supposed* to. He wanted to do something for himself now, but he just didn't know what. Seventeen turned 35.

In the midst of the middle-aged crisis, he characteristically offers some hope. Be grateful for what you have, and know that whatever disappointments come your way, things will get better. "Without hope, without love, you've got nothing but pain/just makes a man not give a damn," he sings in "Empty Hands" in the spirit of Guthrie himself.

His family values come forth in "Rooty Toot Toot," a nursery rhyme written for his daughter Teddi Jo. When he first played it for Larry Crane, it didn't have any music, just the rhymes. John and band then worked it into a song—the song that Myers jokingly told John was the best he'd ever written.

But no matter how starkly honest the stories, and despite the virtuous Ecclesiastes quote printed inside the album sleeve, John admits that these songs didn't completely reflect the *real* John Mellencamp, but merely the ideal of the man he would have liked to have been. "At the time, I was going right down the shitter, and for a time I was kinda proud of it. That's the truth," he told *Billboard*. "I thought, personally, because of my age or the success of my records or a combination of all of it, that you really could not talk to me on a personal level. I didn't want to know about anything. Every decision I made was totally selfish, very clichéd."

In one act of selflessness, he donated his efforts to rock producer Jimmy Iovine (soon to be founder of Interscope Records) and wife Vicky's benefit CD for Special Olympics, *A Very Special Christmas*, released in mid-October 1987 on A&M. John had always wanted to sing Jimmy Boyd's 1952 holiday classic "I Saw Mommy Kissing Santa Claus," and now he had his chance. Still heard in shopping malls everywhere, the song joins other holiday tunes sung by Madonna, Bruce Springsteen, U2, Sting and Whitney Houston, among others, on an album with the most massive rock lineup since *We Are the World*.

Though his personal life was starting to crumble, his professional life had peaked to heady heights. Critics hailed his latest album as one of the finest of the decade, and even more importantly, he was proud of it too. Mercury released *The Lonesome Jubilee* on August 24, 1987, and watched it climb to Number Six on *Billboard*'s album chart. Not too bad compared to *American Fool*'s Number One and *Scarecrow*'s Top Three. "Paper in Fire" and "Cherry Bomb" inched their way to Top 10, and "Check It Out" reached a respectable Number 14 in April 1988. The videos that accompanied them would now get played on MTV, as well as its sister station, VH-1, the network that catered to the disenchanted middle-age adults that John now sang about.

John shot videos for "Paper in Fire," "Cherry Bomb," "Rooty Toot Toot," Check It Out" and "Hard Times for an Honest Man" in some of the poorest parts of South Carolina and Savannah, Georgia, the later of which he chose for "Paper in Fire." For these scenes, he wanted to show a dream that *really* burnt up. He and the video crew passed by plantations, ramshackle mobile homes and churches until they found the oldest street in the city, a desolate dirt road that runs through downtown. Roll camera. For "Hard Times for an Honest Man," he shot video footage on the stone steps of a building where slaves were displayed and auctioned off as they came off the boats from Africa. "It was gruesome. Scary and gruesome," John says of the building's history. He chose these locations and characters to point out the equally "scary and gruesome" fact that racism was still alive in America, and that a large number of people living in our country are still very, very poor, and they're still scraping to make ends meet, no matter how much Reagan and the government ignored them. A lot of people missed that message in John's video, assuming it was just another rural location for John to shoot videos. They didn't understand the meaning behind having "all those blacks running around." He intended to use the videos as a platform, but a lot of people, whether consciously or unconsciously, looked the other way.

No sooner had *The Lonesome Jubilee* hit record stores around the world than John and band said goodbye to their pastoral Indiana surroundings for one arduous but exciting nine-month, 10-country, 130-city tour. The Lonesome Jubilee Tour reached large venues worldwide, selling out in record time in nearly every city they played. Crowds of more than 20,000 to 30,000 people packed hockey rinks in Canada, arenas in the U.S. and other venues worldwide. The tour earned rave reviews nearly everywhere it went, with the band earning as much praise as Mr. Lonesome himself. Considered one of the greatest, if not *the* greatest, ensemble in rock, each member made a deep impression on John's fans. Kenny Aronoff's passionate, muscular drumming, combined with Crane and Wanchic's twang-fueled rock riffs; Myers' solid grooves; and Germano, Cascella and Taliefero's enhancements, got audiences on their feet, while John's energetic stage presence kept them there. After their Madison Square Garden show in November 1987, *New York Times* music critic Jon Pareles writes: "He treated Madison Square Garden like a club with a giant stage, one that gave him room to dance, to clown with band members and backup singers, even to do a James Brown-style split in the middle of 'Lonely Ol' Night.'" "Even songs with a conscience," he writes, "can pack a rock 'n' roll wallop."

The band played two one-and-a-half hour sets with a short intermission in between. John didn't believe in encores, and at the time, he didn't believe in an opening (aka warm-up) act. They were determined to do it on their own. "The stage was gigantic, it went completely across the arena floor, and we were jumping off risers, sliding all over the place, a seriously athletic endeavor," Wanchic told *NUVO* of their live set-up during The Lonesome Jubilee Tour. "We resisted having an opening act until well into the '90s. We didn't want any other focus whatsoever, so that the audience could focus on nothing but us. The whole concept was to bring the eye and the ear of the listener dead center stage, no gimmicks, nothing like that." And they were still committed to being the absolute best band, period. "We were driven to not be denied; we'd been denied for so many years in the early days, jeered at, laughed at and made fun of, that our first taste of success sparked a defiant enthusiasm that has driven us until, pretty much last night," Wanchic continued. "Above the door of the studio and above the door of the rehearsal room there's a sign that says, "'You think you're good when you walk in this room, you'll be great when you walk out.'" It's an attitude."

For some fans, The Lonesome Jubilee Tour not only ended up on their personal "best concerts" list, but inspired them to take up an instrument themselves.

In his native Australia, a young Keith Urban caught one of John's 1987 concerts and it defined his path as an artist. "If there's a vision I've always had for my music, it's a rock band with organic instruments," Urban told *Entertainment Weekly*. He bounced between rock and country until he heard

John and band play songs from *Scarecrow* and *The Lonesome Jubilee*. Then his musical direction fell into place. "Oh, right: straight-up rock band, but there's accordion, fiddle and acoustic guitars. Okay!" In the mid-'90s, Urban fell in love with the banjo—"not in a country sense [but] more as a rock instrument. I like it when it's [used] in a stomp situation, as opposed to a bluegrassy thing." As one of country music's hottest celebrities, Urban continues to marry traditional country and rock, and acoustic and electric instruments, into his chart-topping hits.

Toby Myers experienced his own life-altering experiences, many with an effect on his social life. "Sean Penn and Madonna had just started dating, and they were so famous, they were hanging out with John in his dressing room [at The Forum in Los Angeles], and when it came time for him to play, all they could do was just stand back there and listen to us, but not really stick their faces out," says Myers. "The same night, Barbra Streisand was so close to the stage I could see her—she read a book the entire night we played. It was the best!" She must have remembered John from their 1984 songwriting partnership for "You're a Step in the Right Direction."

Myers also recalls spotting Phil Collins with his kids watching from a specially built riser, and then bumping into comedian Sam Kinneson after the show. "I went up to the Forum club after we finished playing to look for a buddy of mine, and I saw Kinneson at the bar. I said, 'Dude, I saw you on *Letterman* a few nights ago, you were the best!' He says 'I'll be doing the late show at the Comedy Store, I'll leave your name at the door.' So I went, I met Pauley Shore, who was probably 12 at the time, and Sam Kinneson and I hung out for two days straight. It nearly killed me!"

While the rest of the band was having their own fun and games, calling home periodically in between, John was in many ways living his own private hell. He knew he wasn't like his audience in terms of lifestyle and income tax bracket, but night after night, he sang about issues that were supposed to stir their emotions. Night after night for nearly a year, he entertained more than 20,000 people and he took this job seriously, but one man can only give so much. He's said in the past he felt like a jukebox up there, the dancer/singer for money and at times, he just wanted a break. As a performer, every show has to be the best, because that's what those thousands of ticket-holders expected. But he would find himself slacking off in some "off" city. Dubuque, Iowa maybe. Other times, he'd be in a dead sleep, only to be rousted up for a headlining show some 20 minutes later. Other times, he would walk off stage and vomit because of the pressure of performing onstage was so great, and because he was dead tired and sick of the road.

Throughout the tour, possibly to keep himself grounded, he maintained contact with his close friends in Indiana. Childhood buddy Mark Ripley would get calls from John from time to time, and invitations to join him on the road. These small gestures meant the world to Ripley. "My wife and I had gotten divorced, and he knew I was having a really hard time with it," he says. "He'd be backstage, and it might be a half hour before he walked on stage, but he would just call to see how I was doing. He'd make jokes: 'Have you killed her yet?' The thing I thought that was nice was that even in the midst of going on stage, he would think, 'I'll call Ripley and see how he's doing.' He'd let me blow off some steam, make fun of me and just make things more tolerable. That's the kind of guy he is—he'd just call to let you know he's thinking about you, or he'd say, 'Why don't you come out on tour with us for a few days? Then I'll fly you home.' We had a great time."

Ripley, Tim Elsner and others close to John agree that he's the friend in their circle that remembers to keep in touch, which is a rare and valued trait, especially once people get married, have children and lead busy lives of their own. "You can almost count on if he's in a certain town and there are friends of his that live there, they'll be at the show and get to go back and see him," says Ripley. Aside from keeping the bond of friendship tight, staying in contact with old friends assures him that he's got people around he can trust. "He's put in a position where you've got a lot of people patting you on the back, shaking your hand and they really want to put their hand in your back pocket," says Ripley. "John grew up in a typical Midwest atmosphere where if a guy tells you something, you have no reason to doubt him. He's been around a lot of [fake] people. But for whatever reason, he trusts us."

After nearly a decade together (longer for Wanchic and Crane), John's band had put in enough tenure to earn his trust, even if they weren't personally close. To show his appreciation, he would occasionally surprise them by renting a boat on their day off to take everyone out on the lakes around Adirondack Park in upstate New York, if they happened to have a break there. The hotels got much nicer, and the restaurants got better. Life on the road became more comfortable, but no less exhausting. Physically and emotionally exhausted, John engulfed himself in the bubble that the tour and its entourage created, putting himself at the center. His skewed state of mind and selfish attitude led to an affair with another woman, despite his friends' warnings. He had turned into someone they didn't like so much, and John didn't much like himself, either. When the tour finally ended, he told his band to take time to explore individual projects, then did the same himself. He took his first real break from touring and recording, took up painting and promptly watched his personal life continue its descent down, down the shitter.

Chapter Seven

Who's Your Big Daddy Now

Fights with Vicky escalated through the end of The Lonesome Jubilee Tour. Throughout their marriage, they always had what they called their annual "blowouts," but after six years, Vicky had likely had enough of his mouth, his self-absorbed tendencies and his wandering eye. In 1988, Michelle was about to graduate high school, Teddi Jo was in primary school and Justice was three years old and growing like a weed, although their Dad wasn't around much to see all of this activity. He likely assumed his absentee trait from his father, who didn't see much of his sons' childhoods, either.

Shit hit the fan when Vicki found out about John's affair. Their strained relationship couldn't take any more damage, and the news likely did more than push Vicki over the edge; it gave her a legitimate reason to get out. In August 1988, she filed for divorce. The same month, Michelle gave birth to a baby girl, making John a grandfather at age 37. She got married the following year, a nervous bride following in the footsteps of her stepmom (pregnant with Teddi Jo when she married John) and Dad (a father before he became a husband...twice).

Now they all see through you / And you're sinking like a stone

Just the year before, John ruled the mountaintop in his business and personal life, but now, he found himself on his way back to ground level. Like the stock market, which can only sustain a boom for so long before it bursts, John's world crashed. He was tired of fighting with his estranged wife and sick of fighting with his label over money and creative control, a battle that had gone on for some time. Devastated, guilty and overall disgusted with himself, John fell into a depressive slump. It's a dark and lonely place, but he got some good songs out of it.

In the fall of 1988, engineer Ross Hogarth got a call from producer/engineer Don Gehman informing him that John wanted to record some more material soon, so be ready. He made note of the upcoming sessions and returned to the project at hand, knowing he might have to jet off to Indiana soon. Not long after, he had John's then-tour manager Harry Sandler on the line with an update. "We need you to leave tomorrow." So soon! Sandler assured him that, yes, he needed to catch a plane to Indianapolis the next day. He arrived at LAX, found his gate and glanced around the terminal hoping to see Gehman. He continued watching and waiting, but never saw his longtime studio comrade. He boarded the plane, assuming Gehman would catch a later flight.

John's assistant Rick Fettig picked up Hogarth at the airport. "Where's Don?" he asked. "He's not here," Fettig responded, and pulled the car onto the Interstate for one silent trip to Belmont Mall. No Gehman. How strange. Hogarth felt a little uneasy, but still assumed Gehman was just scheduled to arrive on a different date. Fettig took Hogarth to the studio so that he could drop off some random items for the next day's session before proceeding to The Pointe, a complex of condominiums in Bloomington where the out-of-towners usually stayed. The next morning, Hogarth returned to the studio to start setting up for John's session and noticed that no one was even mentioning Gehman. Then, he found out why: John fired him—his rock of an engineer for nearly a decade, his patient voice of reason.

Wanchic says that there was no huge fight, no bad blood. "We were ready to move on, simple as that." When John first brought Gehman into the fold as co-producer on *American Fool*, he hired him mainly for his excellent engineering skills, and as a way to appease the label by appearing to hire a producer when, in fact, John wanted to produce his records himself. But from *American Fool* forward, Gehman's career blossomed and he did, in fact, become a very successful producer. "Exactly what we didn't want," says Wanchic. "We loved him and his engineering, but all of a sudden he was bringing in outside engineers. He still had a calming influence around John, which was always one of his finest points. But we found ourselves with a producer again when we ultimately didn't want one."

On *Scarecrow* and *The Lonesome Jubilee*, Gehman did have some influence on the production, but for the most part, John and the band had their course clearly mapped. "We already know what parts to play, vocals to sing, what kind of vibe we're looking for and don't really need to be told by anybody. We had a definite sound in mind, although certainly Don was a big, big help on all of those records."

It was seemingly a mutual decision. Spending so much time away from home was hard on Gehman's family. Add that to the fact that he spent most of his time in Indiana working with a man who continually pushed his limits into the red for long periods of time. After five albums, that sort of intensity would wear anyone down.

Gehman's departure gave John's next album, to be called *Big Daddy*, a rocky start. "The beginning of *Big Daddy* was an interesting experience," recalls Hogarth. "John was going through his divorce and was in this absolutely raspy mood. When I get to the studio, he has this pile of songs about all this heavy stuff going on in his life, and at the same time, Larry Crane was doing another session, so he wasn't available right away." Not so coincidentally, Crane was playing on an album by John Eddie, *Cold Hard Truth*, engineered by designer of Belmont Mall/engineer of *Scarecrow* Greg Edward. "John was pissed at Larry for not being around, so they hired David Grissom to come in an play guitar on those [first] sessions. So for the initial tracks, we had no Gehman, no Larry Crane and just me in the control room. And it was the first time Grissom had played with John." John's sessions were usually tense, but this time, the tension was exceedingly thick.

Grissom may have walked into a very odd and uncomfortable situation, to say the least, but he had some old friends in the room with him. He and drummer Kenny Aronoff had known each other since the late '70s, when both attended Indiana University School of Music and played in the rock fusion band Streamwinner together. "Talk about a situation where I had to keep up," recalls Grissom to *Guitar Player*. "Kenny is one of those guys who plays with so much soul and feeling, yet you know he could handle anything thrown at him—a guy with chops, but who never lost sight of why he started playing." He also met Mike Wanchic, Larry Crane and John back in college when the guys would visit the record store where Grissom worked. Through the years, Grissom tried to catch their shows when he could, whether in Austin while working on a session, or at home in Bloomington. John often chided Wanchic and Crane by pointing to Grissom and saying, "There's your replacement, right there."

When he stepped in to play on the *Big Daddy* sessions, he was in the midst of a five-year touring stint with Austin rocker Joe Ely. His presence and firey playing brought an edge to these recordings enhanced by the razor-sharp feelings in the studio. "I was in town four days and we recorded four songs," Grissom told *Guitar Player*. "Everything I played was a first take, spur-of-the-moment. John's deal is, if you don't have it the first or second time, it's not gonna get any better. For the most part, that proved itself to be true."

When Crane finished his work with Eddie, he drove to Belmont Mall and joined Grissom and the rest of John's band for the remainder of the sessions, presumably not before getting ripped a new asshole by The Little Bastard.

John wrote dozens of songs for *Big Daddy*, but he didn't spend as much time crafting material as he did with his last two albums. Instead, he reverted back to his first-instinct approach, letting the words pour out of him as a sort of catharsis. Similarly, in the studio, he didn't labor over the music, but let it flow out of himself and his band in a tumble of acoustic beauty. "*Big Daddy* was certainly a melancholy record, and it came at a time in John's life when he was very reflective," Wanchic told *NUVO*. "It was a very spontaneous record, a record that we hadn't planned to make. I was in the middle of Lake Cumberland on a houseboat when John called me. We had no intention of making a record, but he had some inspiration for a few weeks and he wrote the whole record. We just got together and put it down."

As with many of his albums, John aimed to record a song a day; this time, he wanted a rough mix finished before they went home. More pressure. He sang in hushed tones while the band played as proficiently as always, choosing mainly acoustic arrangements. The very first line of the opening track, "Big Daddy of Them All," states, "You used to raise your voice so that it could be heard." He's clearly out of tune, but he won't sing it again. "We said, 'John we've got to redo that vocal,'" recalls Hogarth. "But it was a first take tracking vocal with a first take track on a song that was the most painful thing for him to sing, so there was no way he was going to sing it again. He said what he had to say, whether other people appreciated it or not."

Beginning with this track, John wrote not about the John Mellencamp he aspired to be, as he did for *The Lonesome Jubilee*, but about the man he had become. That person disgusted him. "To me, at 37 years old, I'm finding that I should have been kinder to a lot of people," he said in an interview with *Musician*. "I should have given more to my kids...I've Sammy Davised out. I did it my way. Big deal. They don't give me no medals at the end of the day. That's truth. That's the reality...I should have been more awake. I should have heard things that my wife was saying to me, but I wrote 'em off because I was in the middle of a recording session. 'Baby I'm out there making these records and playing every night, and you got a brand-new car and the kids'll go to college!' But you get right down to it, and it don't mean shit if you don't know how to act. I don't know how to act."

> You're sad and disgusted, Is what you've grown up to be
> Bet you had no idea what your dream would turn out to be
> But when you live for yourself
> Hell, it's hard on everyone

The hopelessness that he expressed on *The Lonesome Jubilee* as an observer had him in a headlock now. He learned the hard way that his actions and words really do affect the people around him. But at the same time he believes that when it's all said and done, nothing he says or does really matters. The man who abided so fiercely to his strong ideals wonders if they really got him anywhere. In the end, he decides idealism is for kids, and he's not a kid anymore. As an adult, he just wants to live above board. Up to this point, John operated as a "do as I say, not as I do" kind of guy. He carries boundless wisdom, but he doesn't apply it to his own life. In this case, he knows good and well that infidelity will ruin a family, but he does it anyway. It's as if he's ridden his motorcycle without a helmet his whole life, and he finally took a spill nasty enough to prompt him to follow the rules of the road.

A number of characters make up the songs on *Big Daddy*. John modeled Martha in "Martha Say" partially after his estranged wife, Vicky.

> *Martha say she don't need no stinking man making no decisions for her*
> *She don't need his money, she don't need him between the sheets*

Vicky was 19 when she met then-25-year-old John, but now she's 30. Eleven years of living with John and his celebrity can take a toll on even a strong woman such as Vicky. John admits he contributed to the shield of armor that's around her heart now, the same armor Martha wears. "It's like, 'If you wanna hang around here baby, you gotta be tough,'" John said of himself to *Musician*. "That's something I always preach to everyone around me. 'This ain't no fucking picnic. I ain't here to have a good time. We're here to learn something, and to push each other till we blow up! If you ain't gonna do that, we're not playin' 'cause with me it's all or nothing.' Young girls like that, you know? Older women don't. And I can't blame 'em, 'cause I don't like that anymore."

But rather than write specifically about someone so close to his heart, he backs up a step and allows Martha to speak for the independent women who defied traditional female roles, and consequently leave traditional men's men like John confused.

"Jackie Brown," on the other hand, represents, "every fucking guy in the streets of Savannah."

> *Is this your home, Jackie Brown?*
> *This three-room shack*
> *With no running water*
> *And the bathroom out back*
> *Is this your grave, Jackie Brown?*
> *This little piece of limestone that says another desperate man took himself out*
> *Is this your dream, Jackie Brown?*

The song goes on to point out that much of America doesn't really give a damn about Jackie Brown; in the Reagan era, people turned their backs on poverty.

"Jackie Brown" made a strong statement, but the sardonic "Pop Singer" got the most rouse out of people for its stab at the music business and at his own career. For the last decade, those two words pushed his buttons, because he personally took the title as an insult. "Any time anybody would want to diminish what I might have accomplished, they would refer to me as a pop singer," he said to *Billboard*. "In reality, my songs were rock-folk songs that were on pop radio, which was a bigger accomplishment than if I had rerecorded 'Hurts So Good' again and again. It really pissed me off."

At the same time, he retaliates against the empty life of the "pop singer," aka the song and dance man that he had to become to keep his job. He may have poured out his soul onto his most artful record to date, with some of his finest songwriting, but the record label cares less about his art and more about how much money they can make from it. There's a definite disconnect between making music that matters and "How many singles are on the record?" These are the issues he rebukes on "Pop Singer." "I committed public suicide with that song," he said in an interview with *Entertainment Weekly*. "It pissed everybody off, and was probably intended to piss people off. We had just played like 160 shows, and it just made me literally sick to walk into an arena. At that point, I figured anything was better than that."

As Hogarth mentioned, John only wanted to sing these songs through once, maybe twice, because they came from such a personal place. He demanded the same of his band for different reasons. The band that *Rolling Stone* had named "The best band in the U.S. today" could certainly handle recording everything on the first or second take. He wanted to keep them on their toes, and continually challenge them with new recording ideas. But now, most of the band members had side and solo projects to juggle, and they were well aware of John's penchant for tension. They had all ascended to a level of musicianship and confidence where scare tactics didn't work anymore. The atmosphere was more relaxed, partly because everyone's constant fears of getting fired had lessened. Sometimes, the scene became too relaxed. Toby Myers noticed that the phone rang "off the hook" with production coordinators and other music bizzers wanting to book or otherwise occupy the attention of the various band members. When John wanted to record a song, it often took longer to locate and assemble the entire gang. It got to the point where John would have to yell from the control room, "Get off the fucking phone and come in here and fucking record!" He had his tension back!

While the band felt less pressured, their engineer felt more pressure than ever before. Without patient, rational Gehman around to offer his technical talents and ego-soothing skills, Hogarth was left solely responsible for the technical duties, with assistant Rick Fettig on hand to handle basic tasks. Hogarth took orders from John directly now, and without Gehman as a "buffer," that direction could sound pretty harsh. The pressure to capture these tracks on the first or second take was intense, and there was no guidance or support from anyone else. "We recorded on one 24-track analog tape machine," Hogarth recalls. "John would come in each day and say, 'I don't like that part, erase that and that off, but right after that note I want you to come out of Record.' He arranged his songs on tape. We used one piece of 24-track tape, and when that tape was full you had to either erase something or move something to have more space."

As with previous albums, they recorded twice the amount of songs needed for an album, with many good ones cast aside because they didn't fit the focus of *Big Daddy*. The band played beautifully, their uplifting melodies balancing John's weighty words. The same cast that played on *The Lonesome Jubilee* returned for this album, with the addition of Grissom on acoustic and electric guitar and Willie Weeks on bass for "Martha Say." John added that track late in the game, after the rest of the album was finished. When he told the band, "We're done!" Myers took it to heart and left for a month-long trip to Thailand. Not long into his vacation, he called John to check in: "'Myers! What are you fucking doing! We're cutting a song today!'" "'Oh Jesus, no,'" he thought. "I'm on the other side of the world!" There was nothing he could do. John called in Weeks for the last-minute session and Myers continued his session of R&R.

Mercury released *Big Daddy* in May 1989, with "Pop Singer" as its debut single. Despite naysayers who believed he had cut his own throat with such a rant, the single reached Number Two on the Mainstream Rock chart, Number 15 on the Pop Singles chart and the album made it up to a respectable Number Seven on the *Billboard* 200. *Big Daddy* sold a million copies in its first year, reaching a total of two million overall—no small potatoes, but nowhere near the phenomenal multi-Platinum success of his previous two albums. For an Americana-rooted rock artist, *Big Daddy* was an art record: a somber, intimate collection of songs born out of personal pain. Some of his longtime fans didn't understand the album and wondered if its acoustic folk leanings meant that John had grown too serious to rock. Hardly, but he had to make this album in order to have the energy to R.O.C.K. again. He made a glitzy video for "Pop Singer" in Hollywood, and let it serve as the final encore in a trilogy of albums that served as the pinnacle of his career. He gave the band another extended vacation from him, and he retreated to his Indiana home. He had built an extension onto his house for a studio, but instead of recording equipment and guitars, he stocked it with canvases, an easel, oil paints and a blade. With a steady supply of cigarettes and a morning cup of coffee to keep him company, he stayed there until 1992. He felt content (or as content as a restless soul can feel) for the first time in years.

John didn't take *Big Daddy* on tour. He wanted a break from the music business; hell, maybe he would leave it altogether this time. In reality, his break from the music business translated to a shift toward other projects. He had written a screenplay back in 1985 called *Ridin' the Cage*, which remained "under discussion" for many years. The screenplay starred a character called "Dud," (a reference to *Hud*) which would be played by John. Dud and his friends felt trapped by their small-town environment and their desire to escape led to much drama. When Warner Bros. received a copy of the script, they agreed with John that the story needed work, and the film company asked John to find someone to re-write it. He sent a copy to his idol, novelist/screenwriter Larry McMurtry, who rewrote the story while keeping some of the characters' identities intact.

Returning the favor, in a sense, Larry McMurtry later passed his son James' demo tape to John when the two were working together on the filming of *Ridin' the Cage*, later named *Falling from Grace*. James had won the New Folk songwriting award at the Kerrville Folk Festival in 1987 and was gaining serious attention as a lyricist and guitar player. He hoped John Mellencamp would record one of his songs.

John did him one step better. Instead of covering one of his songs, he let James McMurtry sing it himself. His stark storytelling set to music would work best told by McMurtry's rich Texas drawl. John helped him land a record deal with Columbia and produced his well-received debut, *Too Long the Wasteland*, in 1989. Later, McMurtry was asked to play alongside Mellencamp, John Prine, Dwight Yoakam and Joe Ely in a one-off band called The Buzzin' Cousins for the film soundtrack. They recorded McMurtry's debut at Belmont Mall, with Mike Wanchic adding his wise guitar licks, dobro and co-production skills, and the entire "Mellencamp family band" adding backup. David Pomeroy on upright bass and powerhouse vocalist/songwriter Ashley Cleveland provided stellar support. Ross Hogarth stuck around to engineer this one, with assistance from Rick Fettig. While Belmont Mall served as John's personal studio first and foremost, he had no problem loaning it to outside clients. Wanchic brought in more acts of his own to produce, including performing songwriter Sue Medley and Hearts and Minds, a group formed by roots-rock artist/songwriter Bruce Henderson in 1983. Hearts and Minds featured red-hot guitar player Andy York, fresh off a stint with Nashville rock band Jason and The Scorchers. They traveled to Indiana to record their self-titled A&M debut, with Wanchic at the helm, Kenny Aronoff lending a couple hands on drums and Toby Myers on bass. The album didn't make much of an impact when it came out in 1989, but York made an impression on John and his team. Hogarth then produced, engineered and mixed Kevin Welch's Reprise debut, recording a portion of the songs with some of Nashville's top session players at Belmont Mall. John may have taken a sabbatical, but his studio hummed with activity.

Secluded in his spacious estate, John isolated himself as much as possible to work on a new art form—painting. An obsessive man by nature, he had no problem spending 14 hours a day in his small studio surrounded by oil paints and cigarette butts. In short order, the new extension to his house filled with canvases—one stacked in front of another on the floor along each wall. An old white marble dining room table sat in the middle of the room, with Polaroids and paper scattered about, and sketches of himself on the walls.

Until he started painting, he had only a passing interest in visual art. He liked the impressionists—Degas, Renoir, maybe Monet—but was never one to hang out in museums or check out an exhibit. As a child, his mother Marilyn—also an artist—encouraged him to draw. He also had the forces of T.C. Steele and other impressionist painters from The Hoosier Group inspiring him from his recording studio's Belmont locale. The desire to paint came seemingly out of nowhere; his instinct said, "Just try." He did, and like music, he took to it easily and completely. He had no formal training, no studied technique. But his works combine elements of folk art and impressionism, with bucketfuls of emotion leaping off the canvas.

His first attempts were quite large...the size of a closet door. He didn't want to paint with a brush because he wanted to use big, broad stokes. Recording artist Paul Simon saw one of John's first creations, an extra-large rendition of an Indian woman with blue lips and swirls of color all through and around her. John admits it was awful. "Simon's standing there," John recalled to *SPIN* magazine, "and I say, 'Well, what do you think, man?' And he says...'I didn't know they made canvases that big.' I just fell down laughing. He had to say *something*."

He got better, and the images got smaller. He started painting his interpretations of family, friends and landscapes. His self-portraits almost always show him with a sullen expression, with deep lines on his face and sometimes a cigarette dangling from his mouth. Paintings such as "The Gates of Hell," with its vicious canines and sullen family, rich with imagery and dark colors point to German expressionists, though he probably didn't think of that at the time. He painted more than 80 pieces in the six months after *Big Daddy* came out. He had no intention of selling them, and he didn't give a wit if people liked them or not. He painted purely for himself and said it's the one thing in his life that he really enjoyed. He's as proud of his paintings as any song he's ever written. He likens painting to music, in that he walks up to the canvas with no idea what he's going to paint, then expresses his unique creativity through brush or blade, without inhibition—completely in the moment—

playing with colors and figures until he decides it's finished. Then he puts it aside and starts another one.

Sometimes in the middle of painting, random thoughts come to mind: love and happiness, there's no value in love and happiness. It's a worthless commodity today. He mulled over these thoughts, put down the paintbrush and picked up the black Gibson sitting on a stand nearby. Those ideas become a song. He took such detours at least a dozen or so times during his self-imposed hiatus from the music business.

Because he paints purely for pleasure, he rarely exhibits his work. The Indianapolis Art League sponsored one of his first shows at the Churchman-Fehsenfeld Gallery from April 12, 1990 through May 13, 1990. He later turned his hobby into a highly publicized charitable venture to support VH-1's Save the Music Foundation. But first, he wanted to do more good works in his own back yard.

Though he swore himself off touring for the time being, he held true to his commitment to Farm Aid. The organization's fourth concert, held April 7, 1990, in Indianapolis became one of the most memorable due in part to John's efforts. The concert sold out in 90 minutes and brought more than 70 artists together with farmers and environmental and consumer advocates. Farm Aid IV's message: The well being of our land, food and water supply depends on a network of family farmers who care about how our food is grown. The Nashville Network televised the event and CBS aired a two-hour highlight to an additional 10 million viewers. Bonnie Raitt; Crosby, Stills & Nash; Garth Brooks; and many others contributed to the show's phenomenal success, but one performance in particular—Sir Elton John—brought down the house with his last-minute moving performance. John recruited Elton John, who happened to be in town visiting Ryan White, a young boy stricken with the AIDS virus through a blood transfusion. At the time, his illness shocked the public into the reality that this disease can hit anyone, even a healthy, heterosexual middle-class American kid. Elton called up John and asked if he would also come and see the boy before he died. He went to the hospital with Elton and mentioned that Farm Aid was the next day. John asked if he wanted to play. Elton agreed, and in a flurry of activity, the Farm Aid crew found him a piano, set it up on stage and he gave one of the most moving performances in Farm Aid history.

Elton performed "Candle in the Wind" as a tribute to White, while nearly all of the 45,000 people in the Hoosier Dome sang along with candles or lighters in hand. White died the next day.

Also around 1990, John noticed that the circa-1851 home in which Mark Ripley and family used to live in Seymour was for sale. He promptly purchased the historic treasure and offered to lease it to the Southern Indiana Center for the Arts (SICA) for $1 every two years after he finished using it as the production headquarters for his film, *Falling from Grace*. SICA gave Indiana artists a place to display and present their work, as well as a place to hold reasonably priced pottery, drawing and painting classes. The center reserved one room for John's work, which comprised about six paintings. When works sold, the center received 30 percent of the profits (several thousand dollars in revenue). The center now contains the only public display of his private collection, and is the only place to purchase prints. While John, as the landlord, finances the home's repairs, fans through the years have spearheaded efforts to erect a "Minutes to Memories Garden," and have raised funds for potter's wheels and electrical work.

Seymour heated up during the summer of 1990, and not just from the weather. Everyone knew everyone in this tiny town, so when "outsiders" arrived, the locals paid attention. The rumor mill buzzed with activity when John and crew started filming *Falling from Grace*, based on his original *Ridin' the Cage* script, heavily reworked by *Lonesome Dove* scribe Larry McMurtry. Using the working title *Souvenirs*, the initial schedule called for a 38-day shoot, all in Indiana. Production coordinators hired an estimated 90 percent of their extras and crew from the area, which meant a nice boost for economic development, as well as a lot of fodder for gossip. Police officers picked up extra shifts as security guards, local townspeople earned their 15 minutes of fame as extras and the local Holiday Inn booked a few more reservations. The Seymour airport and Elks Lodge both served as shoot locations, and the historic home soon to belong to Southern Indiana Center for the Arts served as ground zero. The group stayed so quiet, many residents didn't even know they were there; until, of course, people started talkin'. Mariel Hemingway, who played Bud Parks's wife Alice (aka "that California girl"), was spotted near the hotel; someone else thought they saw co-star/Indiana native Claude Akins, but they weren't sure. A John sighting isn't that unusual, him being the Seymour native with parents who have lived in the same house nearby for more than 20 years. He is, however, still a big local attraction. Vacationers often make a detour to Seymour and ask where his old house is. And everyone in town either remembers him from school, has a friend or relative that does, has lived near his parents, served him a cheeseburger or has some other random connection. When he or Larry Crane, who appears in the film as Ramey, Bud Parks' brother, stop in Robinson's Fish to eat lunch, it's not such a big deal. But when Mariel Hemingway checks in to the Holiday Inn, it's a very big deal.

John's tour manager, Harry Sandler, produced the film with Richard Mellencamp on hand as associate producer and Fay Greene as line producer. They and other principals operated under John's newly formed production company, appropriately titled Little b Pictures (for Little Bastard, natch). John's affiliation with one of the most powerful music and film agencies in the world, CAA (and its head, Mike Ovitz), ensured that the film would finally come to pass after years "in development."

The story contains McMurtry's recurring themes of guilt, redemption and a fruitless quest to recapture the past, conveyed through colorful, wry dialog. The story resembles John's own life in myriad ways, right down to the character names, although he strongly declared that the story is no more autobiographical than *A Streetcar Named Desire* is to actor Marlon Brando, who played the brutish Stanley Kowalski.

Set in Doak City, a small town somewhere near Indianapolis, the drama stars famous country singer Bud Parks (played by Mellencamp; thankfully no longer named "Dud" as in *Ridin' the Cage*), who returns home from California with his knockout wife (Hemingway) and daughter to celebrate his grandfather's 84th birthday. Once home, the film moves from conversation to conversation as Bud faces the deep-seeded family issues that resurface upon his return. He confronts his hard-edged, wealthy father, "Speck" Parks (Claude Akins) and is re-introduced to his high school sweetheart, P.J. (Kay Lenz), now married to his brother, Parker. The plot tangles when Bud regresses into the self-destructive habits that for years lied dormant in his own life. He rekindles an affair with P.J., only to find out she's also having an affair with his father! "It's a typical Larry McMurtry conspiracy of dunces," John told the *Herald Times*. Bud's wife later discovers the affair and leaves Bud to hit rock bottom in his backwards hick town.

Larry Crane plays Bud's half-brother, Ramey, and took a week of acting lessons and grew a full beard for the occasion. According to the *Herald Times*, Crane landed the role by accident when he read a part during John's screen test and performed well enough to catch the attention of the film's casting agents. Crane's character isn't the sharpest tool in the shed, and utters such winning lines as, "I spent my whole life trying to be like you," he says to Bud, "and you come home and start acting like me."

Bud struggles to shake the negative behavior patterns that he picked up from his parents. He desperately wants to break the cycle, but hasn't yet and continues to make the same mistakes over and over. Bud has everything he ever wanted: fame, fortune, a beautiful wife, but throws it all away for the lonely life he subconsciously thinks he deserves. "Bud's odyssey is also Mellencamp's tortured self-examination," proposes Bob Guccione, Jr., in a *SPIN* magazine feature, offering insight into the deeper parallels between John's on- and off-screen persona. "Bud's hick town fantasies, that he can step from the heavens of pop stardom and fit in with the common folk, are Mellencamp's self doubts, too. By freaky coincidence, Mellencamp is Bud's secret sharer—both men fear they can't go home again, that they don't belong there or anywhere and that stardom has doomed them to eternal isolation and loneliness."

Both the external and internal similarities between the character and the actor/director allowed John to give a more authentic performance, though it still took some time to ease into the role. "You can tell what scenes were shot early and what scenes were shot late because he got really good," says booking agent Rob Light. "There are some brilliant scenes of acting where you can see that he was learning his craft." He doesn't perform any music in the film, deciding instead to let the story subsist on its own.

As with acting, John's personal experience also helped him as a director. He likens the job to touring with a band: both involve a large crew and talent, and both point to him as a key decision maker. As a director, he employs a light touch and lets the film unfold at a leisurely pace. At times, however, the dialog-driven movie moved *too* leisurely, and not all of the actors played their roles as superbly as Hemingway and Akins, both of whom received standout reviews.

Certain scenes, such as an intended climactic moment in a hospital room, lack the emotive resonance needed to carry them across to the viewer. Other action scenes lack context. When Bud gets dragged behind a truck in a cage (hence the movie's original title), viewers are left to figure out why someone would subject themselves to such a thing.

The soundtrack, however, was spot-on with a full house of talented folk, rock and country songwriters and performers contributing to the cause. Again, John kept a low profile. Larry McMurtry's son James re-entered his radar as part of The Buzzin' Cousins, an all-star one-off band comprised of McMurtry, John Prine, Dwight Yoakam, Joe Ely and John. They recorded "Sweet Suzanne" for the soundtrack, which would go on to earn a "Vocal Event of the Year" Award from the Country Music Association. Prine, who also appears in the movie, delivers a tune, as does Nanci Griffith, Yoakam, Janis Ian, Larry Rollins (who performs the title track) and Crane. Lisa Germano laid down two instrumental tracks, including the opening "Bud's Theme." John contributes two of the 13 songs. Ross Hogarth engineered some of these songs at Belmont Mall, and engineer Jay Healy worked on other portions of the soundtrack, all under the production supervision of John and Mike Wanchic. PolyGram released the *Falling from Grace* soundtrack on January 1, 1991, though the film wouldn't come out until much later. During the interim, John came out of his self-imposed hiatus to record another album. After two years away from the relentless touring and recording cycle, he felt rejuvenated enough to begin again. He knew how he wanted to reinvent himself this time around, and looked forward to working on a fresh canvas. But before he called the band into Belmont Mall's rehearsal space to talk song ideas, he had a few business issues to tend to.

CHAPTER EIGHT

WHATEVER, WHENEVER

A few months before John began work on *Whenever We Wanted*, his eleventh studio album, he called a band meeting at Belmont Mall. He assembled his core crew—Mike Wanchic, Larry Crane, Kenny Aronoff and Toby Myers—and awarded them all hefty six-figure bonuses.

The bonus was John's way of saying thank you for all of the hard work they had given him over the previous decade. Without them, he probably wouldn't have sold several million albums, earned multiple Grammy nominations, achieved 15 Top 20 singles and earned millions of dollars for himself and his record label. The bonus also helped offset the lack of work they had received from John during his two-year hiatus.

An article in the *Indianapolis Star* reported that John passed out checks at the band meeting, although a letter submitted to the paper by Larry Crane claims that no money was exchanged, only promises. Here's where the trouble starts. Some of the band members started asking questions about the arrangement: What are the parameters of this bonus? What exactly does it mean? Larry Crane, who spent the past two years developing a solo career, spoke up for the group. He asked John to put all of the specifics in writing. "During the meeting described in the [*Star*] article, there were no checks presented or kudos or pats on the back. John simply outlined financial details of the upcoming album and tour. At that point, speaking for the band, I said that we wanted things in writing this time, given John's history of promises followed by excuses. We did not want our futures based on the whims of this person (who had just taken two years off to paint pictures)."

The *Star* reports that Crane asked John to double the amount of their bonus, but no other sources confirm that claim. John, according to sources who asked to remain off the record, became very defensive behind his sunglasses and permanent cloud of cigarette smoke. He called his longtime bandmates ungrateful, inconsiderate assholes and fired all of them.

Within a month, John re-hired Wanchic, Aronoff and Myers, but restructured the bonus arrangement so that they would receive $250,000, and the remaining $250,000 became an advance against their salary for the next two years; thus, chopping their bonus in half. Crane, however, did not get invited back into the band. He had been at John's side since high school and developed a signature guitar sound with the group, but that history didn't mean squat now. He crossed the line with John and paid the consequences.

Friend Tim Elsner offers that Crane's desire to forge a solo career may have aggravated the situation. "Larry got together a band and was playing out regionally," recalls Elsner. "He had recognition factor because he was John's lead guitar player. So he was doing well, and started to see the possibility that he could be 'the guy with his ass to the band.' He was mulling over the idea when John started gearing back up again. He was really tossed as to whether he wanted to come back and be part of John's band as second banana or do something on his own. After John and the band had this disagreement, everybody else cooled down and decided to come back. But in Larry's mind, the decision was made for him to try and do something on his own."

John knew that Crane had wanted his own record deal badly, told the press that he didn't understand why he needed to leave the band to do it. He referred to fiddle player Lisa Germano, still with the band, who recorded and released *On the Way Down from the Moon Palace* on her own Major Bill label in 1991, then signed with Capitol Records to release *Happiness* in 1993, while still on board as John's fiddle/violin player.

In hindsight, Myers recalls, John said that had he known the bonus would cause such problems, he would have just paid his band a retainer during his lengthy break. "Had he done that, people wouldn't have had to scramble all the time to do other sessions," says Myers. "My situation was easy because I wasn't a parent. I was used to those days with Roadmaster and having no money at all. So when I started making money with John, I felt like the richest guy on the planet! When John said, 'You've got the summer off,' I said 'Thank God!' but the other guys might say, 'Oh God, now what?!' The money issue upset the apple cart. The difference between what went on outside the band between 1982 and 1992 is off the scale! But that's not to say we didn't make some smokin' records after that."

Crane's replacement, David Grissom, "conscripted" after his winning contributions to *Big Daddy*, added much of the fire to those smokin' records.

Grissom cultivated his aggressive, spontaneous six-string work from such diverse influences as Roy Buchanan, Albert King, B.B. King and Pat Metheny; developed it during his Joe Ely stint; and polished it up on *Big Daddy*. He impressed the album's "big daddy" enough to earn a full-time spot with the band, and he subsequently impressed the hell out of them with his melding of rock, country and blues. Accordionist John Cascella told the *Herald Times* that "when he starts soloing, I really have to concentrate on my part because I just want to stop and listen." Aronoff, now deemed "America's answer to Charlie Watts" by *Rolling Stone*, was thrilled to reconnect with Grissom on a professional and personal level. They had a musical bond as tight if not tighter than their Streamwinner days, which surely helped the guitarist acclimate to his new role.

The newly configured group arrived at Belmont Mall to record *Whenever We Wanted* enthusiastic about recording together, but tentative after the loss of Crane. Despite her success as a solo artist, Germano even looked forward to re-joining the group that had helped her come into her own. She had gained confidence and respect from the group, both as a person and as an artist. On this album, John gave Germano and John Cascella supporting roles, opting to revisit his affection for the electric guitar. He did this partly to honor his commitment to not stay in the same place for too long, secondly to buck the current trends. When *Scarecrow* came out, pop music didn't offer many fiddles and accordions. Now, he heard them everywhere, which meant it was time for something different. "There's no acoustic guitar, next to no accordion, no violin—none of the stuff that was on *The Lonesome Jubilee*," Grissom told *Guitar Player*. Basically it's humbucking pickups and Marshalls turned all the way up. It's really stripped down, not much overdubbing and we moved the drums into a smaller room, so there's not that huge room sound, not all that air around it. The guitars have been moved up to where the drums were on the last two albums. With *The Lonesome Jubilee*, John felt he'd dug pretty deep into a particular well."

His stripped-down sound would certainly morph in the absence of Crane's signature handiwork, and the vibe around the studio felt different, as well, as if the little brother had moved away to college. Singer Crystal Taliefero had also departed and began a stint with Joe Satriani. Jenny Douglas-McRae, a New York native who had worked with everyone from Keith Sweat to Donny Osmond, took her place for the coinciding tour to begin in early 1992.

Pre-production and recording for *Whenever We Wanted* began in early summer 1991. The band worked through the material without John, then with, piecing together a more electrified sound than the textured Americana of his previous two albums. Grissom didn't know what to expect on his first day on the job, but was pleasantly surprised when John gave him the freedom to let his improv skills take hold. He cranked out power chords, country and Celtic-influenced guitar runs and slippery vibrato with equal aplomb, ultimately helping to win back the admiration of longtime fans who worried that their favorite artist had gotten too old or too serious to rock.

The lyrical theme for this album falls from the same tree as *Falling from Grace*, which was due to hit theaters in February 1992, about a month after the launch of John's 150-date world tour. Both took a long a look at carrying on traditions, whether they're healthy or not. John's cynicism takes hold on "Love and Happiness," which points once again to our world's decidedly unloving tendencies. "They're tearing down walls/In the name of peace/And they're killing each other in the Middle East," he sings, noting there's not much value left in love nor happiness. In John's world, love and happiness are overrated. "Here's the thing about happiness," he told the *Herald Times*. "I just don't think we were put on this earth to be happy. I think that's some kind of bill of goods they sold us as young people and I've said it in my songs, over and over. I think we're put on this earth to work hard and challenge ourselves emotionally, intellectually and physically, whatever your endeavor is. To learn and experience as much as we can, and if you can laugh out loud once a day...that's happiness."

"I Ain't Ever Satisfied" and "Last Chance" focus on inner struggles, continuing themes of emotional pain introduced on *Big Daddy*.

> *I feel nothing I feel no pain*
> *I feel no joy nor hurt inside*
> *I only have myself to blame*
> *If I see that the worlds passed me by*

While the album has its somber moments, he balances these words with more banal wordsmithing, such as "Again Tonight," about a woman who confuses sex for love, and the hot and bothered "Get a Leg Up," a tryst that could have easily sat next to "Hurts So Good." "'Get a Leg Up'" was me trying to do exactly what people said of me," John told *Billboard*. "You want a pop song? Here it is—a lighthearted song about sex and excess. You thought I grew up, but guess what? I didn't. [*Laughs*]" He intentionally wrote the song in a sophomoric fashion for those who expected another *somber* little ditty.

With Jay Healy manning Belmont Mall's Trident recording console, and jazz trumpeter Pharez Whitted laying down some smooth horn parts, John and band wrapped up the album in June 1991. He took the rest of the summer off to visit Justice and Teddi Jo in South Carolina, where they lived with their mother near Hilton Head, not far from John's vacation home. He regrets putting his career ahead of them for so many years, but makes the most of whatever time he has with them now. Michelle, now 19 and a new wife, remained in Indiana to care for her baby, Elexis Suzanne Peach, born August 25, 1989. This made John, a man who also married and became a parent in his teens, a grandfather at age 37.

He said goodbye to Teddi Jo and Justice at summer's end to begin preparations for his next album's release. One of the first tasks included a photo shoot for the album cover and a video shoot for *Whenever We Wanted*'s lead-off single, "Get a Leg Up." Among video, camera and lighting directors, he met his co-stars, including a stunning blonde draped in a dark satin sheet. One of Elite Modeling Agency's brightest stars, Elaine Irwin flew to Indiana to appear in both shoots, although she would soon play a starring role in someone's life. As Irwin posed for both photographers and video directors, her presence radiated far stronger than any of John's paintings scattered about the room. Within this chaotic environment, there wasn't time or opportunity for conversation, and the recording artist barking out orders didn't seem up for friendly chitchat. Irwin flew back to New York, John stayed in Indiana and both of them resumed their hectic work schedules with only a fleeting thought of the charismatic person they had just met.

Whenever We Wanted, issued October 8, 1991—the day after his fortieth birthday—marked the long overdue emergence of *John Mellencamp* dba John Mellencamp—the Cougar permanently erased from his professional name. As with *The Lonesome Jubilee* and certainly *Big Daddy*, his songwriting came from an honest place, with no pretenses and no attention to trends; which usually drifted far from John's blue-collar rock leanings. Even the album artwork, which features images of several of his paintings on both the front cover and inside booklet, revealed another layer of the man behind the songs. He painted more than 400 pieces during his hiatus and through practice he had significantly refined his technique, though the dark colors, broad strokes and looks of despair remained unchanged.

When the album hit retail on the stroke of midnight, he would compete with Guns N Roses, Public Enemy and the Red Hot Chili Peppers for attention. In the early '90s, alternative rock began infiltrating into mainstream culture; Nirvana and the explosion of grunge would seal the deal a few years later. Would John Mellencamp, a 40-year-old "veteran" who delivered roots-oriented rock for the masses for more than a decade, remain relevant among consumers who embraced hard-hitting rap, sleaze metal and punk/funk played by streakers wearing socks?

Considering John hadn't toured or put out an album for almost three years and his new release, despite its reunion with the electric guitar, didn't contain a "Jack and Diane"-level hit, the industry wondered if he still had an audience. He didn't waste time pondering that question; instead, PolyGram/Mercury sent him on an aggressive promotional campaign that began with a "coming out" performance to introduce the new album, as well as his new guitarist, David Grissom, at the historic Carnegie Hall in New York City.

Held September 17, 1991, John's first concert in more than three-and-a-half years sold out just hours after it was announced. Fans filled the 2,800-seat performance hall for a two-part show that stretched the limits of the venue's pristine acoustics with its amplified guitar riffs and thunderous rhythms. *New York Times* critic Jon Pareles noted that John's lyrics were "unintelligible," but "that didn't bother a crowd that was overjoyed to see its favorite rowdy again." He devoted the first set to the new album, the second set to previous hits such as "Lonely Ol' Night," "Pink Houses" and "R.O.C.K. in the U.S.A." During the encore, John brought up a male fan on stage for his 15 seconds of fame. "Not a pretty girl, the standard gambit," Pareles writes. "Mr. Mellencamp handed over the microphone, and the [male] fan belted a verse…and the fan, not Mr. Mellencamp, cued the band for its last crashing note."

Earlier, John had thought about the captivating woman he had met during the "Get a Leg Up" shoot. He invited her to the show, but alas, she was out of the country on a job. Another time, perhaps.

To build on the buzz created after his Carnegie Hall show, retail outlets throughout the U.S. released the album at the stroke of midnight. Guns N Roses warranted a similar promotion a few months earlier for their *Use Your Illusion* Pt. 1 and 2 discs. Especially in Bloomington, record stores planned for a late-night opening, some of them jumping the gun to host special listening parties earlier in the night.

Another piece of the marketing puzzle included a whirlwind radio tour that hit more than 1,000 stations in 45 cities in about 40 days. The promotional tour comprised of on-air performances and interviews and began about a week before *Whenever We Wanted* was released. In order to reach the most listeners, they played many of these gigs during morning or afternoon drive time. John admitted that it was one of the most arduous tours he had ever done in his life. "We would get in one town and be on the radio at 6:30 A.M.," he told *Billboard*, "get on an airplane, be in a different town on the radio at drive time in the afternoon and then fly somewhere else and be on the late show that night."

The tour came to a temporary halt on October 17, 1991 when John collapsed from exhaustion after a show in Seattle. He took a rest in a local hospital and doctors later attributed the problem to "too much coffee, stress and not enough breakfast." John thought it was an anxiety attack, much like the one he suffered after his 1980 American Music Awards performance. Through the years, he learned how to prevent them, but this time he didn't have the energy to fight it off.

The hard work and stress paid off, at least, as *Whenever We Wanted* reached

Number 17 on *Billboard*'s Top 200 album chart, and hit Platinum status within months. The tease of a single, "Get a Leg Up," climbed to Number One on the Mainstream Rock chart and Number 14 on the Hot 100; its follow-up, "Again Tonight," also topped the rock charts but only made it to Number 36 on the Hot 100.

He had barely unpacked his bags from the radio tour when John and band regrouped at Belmont Mall to rehearse for the forthcoming world tour, to begin January 7, 1992, in Savannah and continue for nearly two years, hitting cities across the U.S., Canada, Australia, Japan and Europe.

Early 1992 proved another peak year for John's career. Days after his three-hour Savannah show, the Recording Academy nominated John for a Grammy Award for "Best Rock Vocal Performance, Solo" for *Whenever We Wanted*. In addition, the Nordoff-Robbins Center awarded him the prestigious Silver Clef Award during a gala dinner for his involvement with musical therapy for handicapped and autistic children. He had spent some of his free time spearheading fundraisers, attending charity events and interacting with the children, much to their delight. Considering his own troubles with spina bifida in his infancy, he made an especially empathetic volunteer, and Nordoff-Robbins rewarded his efforts with their highest music-industry patron award.

A month into the Whenever We Wanted Tour, *Falling from Grace* hit theaters in mid-February, although its soundtrack earned better reviews than the film. When John toured his way back to New York, he again invited Elaine Irwin to the concert. She happened to be in town and free that night, so she and a few of friends attended the show and met her new friend for dinner afterwards. Finally, Elaine and John had time for a real conversation, and they clicked in a big way. But John had a tour to resume and Elaine had a busy career herself, so they settled for regular telephone conversations until his next New York stop. Gradually and naturally, they fell in love. They took whatever opportunities they could to see each other, depending on their mutual travel and work schedules. When Elaine flew to Los Angeles to visit him later in the tour, she never left. "I knew it was serious when I had to go out and buy more clothes," she says from their home not far outside of Bloomington. "Now here I am, still on that date!"

Their courtship also led to good fortune for Toby Myers, who met the love of his life, Roberta Chirko, through Elaine. After John and Elaine officially became a couple in 1992, Myers says it was "at least two months before he would let me talk to her!" When he finally did, he asked her if she knew Chirko. He didn't tell her that he had a long-term crush on the woman after seeing her on the cover of *Vogue, Elle* and other fashion magazines. "God yes!" replied Irwin. Not only did she know Chirko, they used to be roommates in New York, when they were both "baby models." "You've got to call her," Myers pleaded. She did, and put her in touch with Myers. After a series of telephone conversations while Myers toured Europe with John and band, they arranged a blind date. "My hair was bright red at the time, and when Elaine described me to Roberta, she thought she was talking about Larry Crane! I knocked on her door and she really didn't know what would be on the other side. Then we met...and it was cool." Cool, indeed. Even though she had a terrible cold when they first met, their blind date evolved into a serious relationship, and Myers sought every opportunity to fly to New York.

As the Whenever We Wanted Tour continued its lengthy journey, John and the band played city after city, having reached Europe by early 1992. Meanwhile, Seymour got itself ready for the *Falling from Grace* premiere, held at the Jackson Park Cinema (Seymour's only movie theater) on February 18, 1992. The VIP reception and screening benefited Southern Indiana Center for the Arts and featured such "celebrity" guests as Larry Crane, Claude Akins (who plays father Speck Parks), Melissa Ann Hackman (John's niece, who plays Bud's daughter), John's brother Joe Mellencamp and Larry Rollins, a country singer from Brownstown, Indiana, who sings on the soundtrack's title song (written by Crane). Fans who opted for the 9 P.M. screening ($20) rather than the $75 per person private affair waited anxiously, hoping their hometown hero would show up, but they weren't surprised when he didn't. Most of the Cinema's patrons had plenty of fun picking out their friends on screen, considering the high volume of local residents hired as extras. The film obviously did well in Indiana, but overall remained a low-key success, although it would ultimately serve as a stepping-stone to future film endeavors for John. Jokingly, John often refers to the film as *Falling Asleep*.

Falling from Grace failed to recoup its $3 million budget. In interviews, John scuffs off its lack of success, stating, "You make a bad movie or you make a bad record? So what? Big fucking deal. They don't take away your birthday for it."

As the film ran its course through theaters nationwide, John also had a world tour to front, and a now-exclusive relationship with Elaine Irwin to nurture, so *Falling from Grace*'s success could have easily dropped down a few notches on the priority list.

Ten weeks after John and Elaine's relationship evolved from casual to serious, he proposed. In March 1992, she attended her first Farm Aid concert; this one, in Irving, Texas. "We smooched all the way from Indiana to Texas," Mellencamp said in the book *Farm Aid: A Song for America*. "The guys in the band kept looking at us and saying, 'Would you stop that?'"

Six affectionate months later, the two married on September 5, 1992 in a private ceremony at Uncle Joe's log cabin. Horse-drawn carriages brought guests to the rustic locale, mainly to ensure the ceremony's privacy. The event marked the third time that John would walk down the matrimonial isle, but the first for 23-year-old Irwin. Despite a 17-year age difference and radically different family lives, the two had much in common. Like John, Irwin grew up in a small town, albeit as an only child just outside of Gilbertsville, Pennsylvania, near Allentown. Her mother and stepfather raised her in a progressive household where they talked politics around the dinner table and junk food wasn't allowed. Though neighbors continually complimented young Irwin on how beautiful she was, her mother praised her for her intelligence, her excellence in sports and her kindness toward others. As a result, she graduated school early, with honors, and had lettered in three sports.

Irwin never intended to become a model, but a New York modeling agent saw something special in the 15-year-old beauty, and Irwin saw an opportunity to travel. She spent her summer vacations living and working in New York (rooming with Roberta Chirko), then commuted to Manhattan during her final year of high school. Upon graduation, she inked a deal with Elite Modeling Agency, moved to Paris and built her career posing for European editions of *Vogue, Elle* and *Marie Claire*, among others. Upon her return to New York, she landed contracts with Victoria's Secret, Ralph Lauren and Versace, and later became one of Pantene's "don't hate me because I'm beautiful" models. In the midst of all of this activity, she got word of the John Mellencamp video and album cover shoot that would change the course of both her personal life and career.

John grew up in a middle American small town among five rowdy siblings, where one might have to yell to be heard at dinnertime and where the vegetable of the day was mashed potatoes with butter and gravy made from animal fat. By the time he met his future wife, he had already experienced the heights of fame and had taken a few hard hits along the way.

Their stories differ, but the underlying no-nonsense values that come from living in a rural environment (not to mention shared political interests and high standards for excellence) certainly helped them understand one another on a deep level. "If you're from a rural or suburban-like setting, your experience is very different than if you'd grown up in an urban environment," she says. "John grew up in a small town and has a big family; I grew up in a small town and have a small family. So it's a very similar experience."

As the lush fall foliage fell to the ground along with Indiana's first dustings of snow, John rounded up his band at Belmont Mall to work through and record his latest batch of songs, many written during and about his relationship with Elaine. This would be his auspicious thirteenth record, and he was well aware that much of his core audience had diminished. Some loyal fans assumed that after 12 albums, the last of which failed to impress, they already owned the essentials—from *American Fool* to *The Lonesome Jubilee*—so they lost interest. But in order for a middle-aged rocker to attract a young audience again, he would have to incorporate some contemporary elements into his classic sound. He always knew what he wanted. This time, he knew he wanted something new.

For guidance, he called in Malcom Burn, producer/musician Daniel Lanois' right-hand man, both of whom were known for their experimental sonics, moody atmospherics and attention to great songcraft. With Lanois in the producer's chair, Burn had engineered and/or mixed such albums as Peter Gabriel's *Us*, Bob Dylan's *Oh Mercy* and the Neville Brothers' *Yellow Moon*, among others. On his own, Burn had worked with Blue Rodeo, Chris Whitley and happened to be Lisa Germano's producer *and* boyfriend. Upon her suggestion, John brought Burn into the fold to assist with "mixing concepts." In other words, come up with some sounds that will make a veteran sound hip again.

"Malcolm came from a very different school of recording," says Germano. "He comes from Lanois' world of atmosphere and sound effects, and John didn't do a whole lot of that. Malcom brought in some of those messier elements. John had to be open to trying some new things. Like John, Malcom was used to doing things the same way, so to be in John's world would be insightful for him, as well."

Germano, John Cascella, Mike Wanchic, Kenny Aronoff, Toby Myers, David Grissom and Pat Peterson gathered at Belmont Mall (redecorated now with nicer furniture and lighting) in the winter of 1992, but not at the same time. Instead of the usual organic recording method with everyone playing together, John opted to record many parts one at a time, with engineer David Leonard building a track instrument by instrument, as was typical on mainstream pop and R&B albums. Much to Aronoff's chagrin, they experimented with drum loops and samples.

Emotional distance separated the band members as much as physical space. They maintained a solid bond, but the warm family feel that they shared on *The Lonesome Jubilee* had diminished a bit. The musicians had less involvement this time in the arrangements; coincidentally, the album had fewer hooks than previous efforts, with more attention pointed toward John's songwriting. He had evolved into a colorful storyteller, with vivid character sketches emerging through detailed verses—a far cry from the simplistic nature of his last album. "Beige to Beige" looks at a world without color, examining the mediocrity of a "world to keep the rabble down." "Case 795 (The Family)" paints a harsh portrait of Tony Jones, who stabbed his wife Alice on their first anniversary. "He left her bleeding/On the floor in the kitchen/With cake on her fingers/And her wedding ring holding./In her hand was a note/That said the wicked must suffer/And he drove off quickly/To his girlfriend's apartment." In the end, who really suffered the most, he asks.

The simplicity of "Sweet Evening Breeze," a tale of unrequited love and a yearning for what could have been, makes a deeper impression than his more

The rough and tumble John of 1982…ready to kick some butt. (Robert Matheu/Retna Ltd.)

John "Cougar" signs with Mercury Records in New York City in July 1979.
(Gary Gershoff/Retna Ltd.)

Another fresh face hits Manhattan.
(Richard Aaron)

Walking the tracks in Bloomington, Indiana in 1982. (Robert Matheu/Retna Ltd.)

John posing in 1982 for the American Fool *photo shoot in Bloomington.* (Robert Matheu/Retna Ltd.)

Soulful eyes that have mesmerized female fans for decades. (Lynn Goldsmith/Corbis)

1985 brings more success John's way. (Fabio Nosotti/Corbis)

John and Mitch Ryder in 1983.
(David McGough/Getty Images)

John in 1982…solitary as ever.
(Lynn Goldsmith/Corbis)

John in the ring. (Richard Aaron)

Everything looks better when you're on stage.
(Bob Leafe/Frank White Photography)

John and his band (top and bottom left) set the stage on fire, as usual. (Lynn Goldsmith/Corbis)

*Playing to a Chicago crowd on
March 24, 1984.*
(Paul Natkin/WireImage.com)

*L-R: John with Neil Young and Willie Nelson during
Farm Aid 1985.*
(Paul Natkin/WireImage.com)

The three amigos — L-R: Neil Young, Willie Nelson, and John — at Farm Aid in 1985. (Bettman/Corbis)

L-R: John, farmers Mrs. & Mr. Rockman, Nelson and Young backstage at Farm Aid. (Corbis)

Closing the decade on stage. (Bob Leafe/Frank White Photography)

John at home in Bloomington and comfortable in his own skin. (Mark Cornelison)

Guitarist Larry Crane (left) with John at Farm Aid in Austin, Texas on September 22, 1995.
(Paul Natkin/WireImage.com)

John with his good friend Timothy White before he died in 2002. (Timothy White Photo)

Looking cool in a crowd, as always.
(Raeanne Rubenstein)

Still cool after all these years. (Kurt Markus)

John onstage at the Hammerstein Ballroom in New York City with the late, great Johnny Cash on April 6, 1999. (Kevin Mazur/WireImage.com)

John and friends in Green Bay, Wisconsin on November 25, 2002. (Paul Natkin/WireImage.com)

Once again at Farm Aid, this time in 2006 at Camden, New Jersey's Tweeter Center.
(Paul Natkin/WireImage.com)

John with wife Elaine and Senator Barack Obama at Tinley Park, Illinois in 2005. (Rick Diamond/WireImage.com)

John kicking back at the Sundance Film Festival in Park City, Utah in 2001. (John Bernstein/WireImage.com)

Former President Bill Clinton thanks John during the Democratic National Convention's Every Vote Counts concert in Washington, D.C., on October 9, 2002. L-R: Actress Lynda Carter, Clinton, Mellencamp and singers Deborah Cox and James Taylor. (Mike Theiler/Getty Images)

John gives this 2002 performance his all at the "Music to My Ears" tribute to honor his friend, the late and legendary music journalist Timothy White. (Kevin Mazur/WireImage.com)

Contemplating life and music. (Mark Cornelison)

John with his beautiful wife Elaine.
(Frank White Photography)

*John prior to the start of game two of the 2006
World Series at Comerica Park in Detroit,
Michigan on October 22, 2006.*
(Mike Ehrmann/WireImage.com)

John at The Bridge School Benefit. (Jay Blakesberg)

A quiet moment during soundcheck. (Mark Cornelison)

John Mellencamp: Born in a small town. (Kurt Markus)

socially conscious works. In hindsight, he's admitted that his attitude of indifference toward his career lingered with this album, and the pain over his divorce from Vicky Granucci and separation from his children still bit when he wrote these songs. Between changes in his personal life and issues with PolyGram, the fire that he had during the *The Lonesome Jubilee* era had dwindled to a mere glowing ember, which is partly why this album takes on a more somber tone.

That said, the band came through with some stellar performances, as Myers recalls. "When Lisa sang her background part on 'Beige to Beige,' she had this really dim light on her, but the studio was totally black. All you could see was Lisa doing this sexy dance while she sang. We just all fell in love with it."

The hushed mood of that moment falls right in line with the album's poetic intent. "The songs were good, with beautiful melodies," John emphasized to *Billboard*. "There was gospel, with the Sounds of Blackness [singing] on the single version of 'When Jesus Left Birmingham.' And the verses of the song 'Human Wheels' were from George Green's eulogy at his grandfather's funeral, and I wrote the chorus." When Green read him the speech, John replied, "Great, after you're done I want to use it as a song!"

The passing of the instruments continued to an extent. Myers for example, played bass on all but one track; laid down a guitar hook on "Suzanne" and "two-fingered a keyboard part...and all this between sandwiches," he reports in the album's liner notes. Grissom added mandolin and bass parts, along with acoustic, electric and baritone guitar, Aronoff unleashed an army of percussion instruments and Germano toyed around with a penny whistle and zither, a stringed instrument the sits on the lap or on a table often used in folk music.

Though John refers to *Human Wheels* as "the best record he's ever made," the album took many months to make, with one of the highest expense reports in many years. The band worked from morning to night with engineer David Leonard patiently capturing it all on tape. Occasionally Burn would offer up sonic suggestions, as well as add keyboard, synthesizer and guitar parts. He added his "mixing concepts" after everyone had left. "He'd stay at night and goof around with mixes on the board and then play them for us in the morning," says Leonard. "So the mixing was a collaboration between he and I."

Burn received production credit on this album, and so did Leonard and Wanchic. The album's problematic inception had much to do with internal conflicts and tragedies that arose during the recording process. Aronoff, now regarded as arguably the one of greatest rock drummers to ever grace a session, continually accrued thousands of frequent flyer miles jetting to New York, L.A., Nashville and beyond for near-constant session work. If he didn't see John for several months because he was booked on a session or on the road with another act, John would give him the finger. And mean it. By this time, Aronoff had built up his client roster to such an extent that he could really leave the band at anytime, but his loyalty kept him on board as John's drummer.

Germano, no longer the agoraphobic young woman who struggled through the Scarecrow Tour, felt confident about her writing and playing, both in John's band and outside of it. Her DIY solo album, *On the Way Down from the Moon Palace*, had earned her favorable attention, particularly from Capitol Records, who gave her a record deal. Her playing had become fearless, and song ideas came forth in waves; as a Mellencamp newbie, she often felt too intimidated to share ideas. Now, she offered up so many, her bandmates jokingly taped her mouth shut—they even drew lips on the tape—in the studio. The band still liked to cut up and kid around with each other, and many nights, as Leonard wrapped up a rough mix and Burn lounged on the sofa, John often joked around, too. "He's a very charming, entertaining guy when he's just sitting around telling stories," Leonard recalls. "A lot of times he'd say, 'Leonard! If I wasn't paying you we'd go out on the lake and go waterskiing.' He loved his Lake [Monroe], and he loved his football."

But in the midst of recording, when John attempted to create the tension that he tended to feed off of, his efforts sometimes backfired. "There was one fight where John just couldn't get any of us angry!," says Germano. "It was like, 'You guys aren't taking this seriously.' He brought us into the studio and really yelled at us: 'All of you guys can do your own thing, but you wouldn't have gotten anywhere without me.' I thought, 'This is bullshit. You open doors and it's up to us if we go through them.' I was the only one that stood up. I was shaking, but I said, 'John, I'm here because I want to be here. I'm not here because I feel I owe you something, and if you don't want me here, I can go. I would hate to go, but I will.' I was real clear, and I left. I was shaking in the hallway. Kenny and Toby said, 'We're so proud of you that you spoke up.' It was this last-ditch effort of John's to feel like we owed him something and to feel threatened. But the beauty of it was, when I stood up for myself, everybody else stood up for themselves. So John cooled down, and when we came back after dinner, we just went forward. There was no discussion. I think he had to lose his temper, but then realized that it's not going to work on us this time. Once you've been fired and rehired, you can't really be threatened with the fear of being fired. He's lost his power at that point. You learn to be a strong person by being fucked with like that."

It's not hard to forget and move on after a fight, but the album and everyone in the band later suffered a debilitating blow that wasn't as easy to recover from. On November 14, 1992, they recorded "When Jesus Left Birmingham." They were thrilled because the track turned out beautifully. At the end of the night everyone parted ways with their usual "see you tomorrows," but accordionist John Cascella never came back. In his car, probably on his way home, the 45-year-old musician died of a heart attack. "He felt a problem, pulled over into the median, called someone and died," says Myers. "That was rough. It was really a blow, because boy did we need that guy. His accordion was so vital. It was a defining deal. After Cascella died, things became different."

With the loss of Cascella, a wonderful person as well as an enormously talented musician, the essence of John's band—the synergy that made them the hottest rock band of the mid-'80s to early '90s—crumbled for good. The signature fiddle/accordion sound that Cascella helped create could never happen again. A significant regime change was on the horizon.

In hindsight, John told *Billboard*, "The only shining light in the whole process was Elaine Irwin. She was in the studio every second, and she was almost the producer of the record. I couldn't have made it without her. She kept everything together, herding everybody back into the room where we were supposed to be."

Mercury released *Human Wheels* on September 3, 1993 to positive reviews, but no hits. The single, "When Jesus Left Birmingham" caused a stir, though not due to radio airplay. The video featured a child dressed as an angel in whiteface, others in blackface, and a succession of images featuring Nazi symbols, drug needles and a marijuana bong. The video intended to portray the degradation of our society, "the solid values that in some respects we once had, that we no longer rely upon. A society falling apart, with nothing to hold on to," as reported by his then-publicist, Jodi Miller. MTV's Standards and Practices Department, however, deemed the video unacceptable. To keep the peace with the all-powerful music video network, PolyGram's creative department heavily edited the video to blur out faces and obscure many of its offensive scenes. MTV then aired the video, which now looked like a news clip with criminals' faces blacked out, which only caused viewers to wonder what they were missing and why.

John didn't tour for *Human Wheels*. Instead, he marched right back into the studio to work on more songs.

First up was a cover of the Big Joe Williams tune "Baby Please Don't Go," to be featured in the 1994 film *Blue Chips* shot in Bloomington. The film stars Nick Nolte as a university basketball coach and features sports celebs such as Larry Bird, Shaquille O'Neal and Indiana University basketball coach Bob Knight. John, being the Indiana native and basketball fan that he is, made a fitting choice to provide music for the film.

For added guitar muscle on the track, John recruited Andy York, the young gun from Hearts and Minds that had recorded with Mike Wanchic five years earlier at Belmont Mall. John remembered York, and brought him in for this track, possibly as a test run. "It couldn't have gone any better," York recalls.

"There was a high degree of mirth in the control room; we were all having a great time."

In December 1994, John had plans to record some new material in the "think fast, make mistakes" philosophy of *Uh-Huh*. Again, he pared down the lineup to its core: Mike Wanchic added some lap steel parts and backing vocals, but mainly sat in the co-producer's chair; Kenny Aronoff handled drums and percussion; and Toby Myers, Lisa Germano and Pat Peterson played on only a portion of the tracks. David Grissom was initially part of that lineup, but he opted out of the deal. According to a 1998 *Austin Chronicle* feature, John's manager at the time, Ron Weisner, offered him less money and warned him that things would be different. "It was definitely a sign," he said. "I called him back and said, 'I can't do that.' He said, 'Fine, we'll just get another guitar player.' I haven't talked to John since."

There were signs of trouble even before that fateful telephone call. Grissom, not a man to back down to anyone, even John, had crossed the proverbial line with his boss. One day in the studio, when John was in full-on "Little Bastard" mode, he directed his sharp words toward Grissom, who, like the rest of the band, was only trying to do his best. The altercation ended with John telling Grissom, 'Well, if you're man enough then why don't you come in here.' Rather than ignore him or give in, Grissom set his guitar down and walked toward the control room, not intending to fight, but certainly aiming to challenge the temperamental artist. Their relationship changed dramatically at that point. According to one source, "If you cross that line and his ego gets severed, he takes it personally and he never forgets it. *Never.*"

"It was intense. There were incredibly great times and incredibly terrible times," Grissom told the *Austin Chronicle* of his three-year tenure. "The chemistry within the band was great, but it was my also my first experience being in a situation where somebody would actually mentally abuse me. [Mellencamp] was an intense character and it was hard-core. [Joe] Ely spoiled me. With Joe it was his band, but never once did he do anything to say, 'You'll do what I say.' We were all in it together—like brothers. With John, it was clear that he was paying and I'd do whatever he wanted me to do or I could get the hell out." In the end, he opted to get the hell out.

They called back York to replace him, and quickly went to work on *Dance Naked*. They recorded and mixed the album in 14 days—faster than any other record to date. John had a couple of reasons for churning out the album so quickly and delivering it less than a year after *Human Wheels*.

PolyGram admittedly dropped the ball on *Human Wheels*. A series of upper management changes that began with the departure of CEO Dick Asher in 1989 and continued to Alain Levy, who moved up from executive vice president to president/CEO in 1991, trickled down to affect the sales of not only John's albums, but much of the roster. Initially, the label argued that the album didn't "fit the format." John's music hasn't fit a format in years; arguably, if ever, but that hasn't stopped him from selling millions of records. Irritated by the comment and exhausted from the troublesome *Human Wheels* recording process, John wanted to record another album from the gut. He wrote a batch of pointedly radio-friendly songs, but didn't play them for the band until the day of the session, bypassing the rehearsal/pre-production stage completely. "John would bring in the song in the morning and say, 'Here's what I got,' and then we'd go out and cut it," recalls Andy York of his first album project with John's band. "Sometimes we cut two tracks a day. It was intense, and everybody was really focused. It was an exciting time for me, because it was my first time working with John, and I wasn't used to how fast you could work. It was a challenge to keep up and come up with original ideas—exhilarating, really."

John intended to keep the music sparse. He recorded basic tracks with only Aronoff and York in the studio, bringing in guitarist Jimmy Ryser (Grissom's replacement), Lisa Germano and Pat Peterson later. More than half of the nine songs didn't even have bass guitar, an idea Toby Myers took particular offense to. "I was so mad about that I couldn't stand it!" he says. "I took the hardest physical labor job I could find on the days I knew they were cutting tracks. I just didn't understand it. With Cascella gone, and this record having no bass guitar, I didn't know where [my place] was. I spent a lot of time with Roberta in New York around that time and wrote a lot of music."

Inside Belmont Mall, the atmosphere was predictably intense, intimate and alive with restless energy. Initially, John had planned a three-disc anthology for PolyGram, tentatively titled *Nothing Like We Planned*. In the spirit of its title, things really didn't go as planned—the nine new songs John wrote felt too good to bury among dozens of old songs. They felt fresh. And with some new blood and more room to breathe, it felt like a new beginning. "Let's be a rock 'n' roll band again," John told the group. No arguments there. "With *Dance Naked* we were livin' it," he told *SPIN* magazine. "There weren't any long, heady discussions about what needed to happen—everybody just went in and played. Which is what I think this is about. It's about the feeling."

With no plan outside of John's raw acoustic guitar/vocal demos, the songs took on a life of their own. If they veered too far off course, John and Mike Wanchic found a way to steer things back on track. "Another Sunny Day 12/25," for example, began as a slow, haunting ballad—an "expression of stoic faith" as Anthony DeCurtis described in a *Rolling Stone* article. As the day progressed, John's bandmates gave the song a makeover, contributing arrangement ideas and layering the song together piece by piece: percussion (including a Charles Chips can), followed by keyboards, a zither and the requisite background vocals and guitar solos. "At one point, the proceedings get so confused that a take of the chorus that Mellencamp wants to keep gets erased," DeCurtis describes. "He bets Germano and guitarist Jimmy Ryser $50 each that the part could be found. When Germano walks in after dinner, Mellencamp takes out a $100 bill, rips it in two and hands half to her and half to Ryser. Everyone laughs, but the message is clear that Mellencamp, who doesn't like to lose or be proven wrong, isn't happy with the way things are."

At one point, he called in Germano's beau, Malcom Burn, one of the co-producers on *Human Wheels*, for guidance. In his usual manner, the request came over the telephone lines as, "Malcolm! What are you doing man?! We're making a fucking record. Get your ass out here. We need your vibe." He wants to make sure it doesn't sound too overproduced. He doesn't want a Pink Floyd record. He wants a John Mellencamp record, albeit with some new twists. In the end, John stripped "Another Sunny Day" of most of its accoutrements. They had over-thought that one, and once John realized this, he adjusted the arrangement to more closely reflect its original form.

The album's only discernable hit, a cover of Van Morrison's "Wild Night" was just the sort of happy accident he hoped for. *Billboard* editor-in-chief Timothy White had turned John on to Me'Shell Ndegéocello's landmark debut, *Plantation Lullabyes*. Impressed by her talent as both a vocalist and bass player, and intrigued by her soulful grooves, he invited her to come out to Indiana and record.

Born in Germany but raised in Virginia, Ndegéocello took an avid interest in music at a young age. In the 1980s, she wanted her MTV just like most young teenagers, and became a closet fan John's music in the days of "Pink Houses." She knew all of his hits. She even mailed off about 15 postcards to the "Paint the Mother Pink" contest.

Armed with some musical ideas of her own, she left the bustle of New York City for Belmont Mall. But again, the session took a left turn. "I made the sudden decision to jam on Van Morrison's "Wild Night" on the drive over from my house to the studio, because it was a nice little rhythm of the kind I wanted to get to on this new record, and I thought it would be a nice way to refresh everybody's memory," John told *Billboard*. "We started playing it and ended up recording it."

In the studio, Ndegéocello came up with spontaneous ideas just like everyone else. Even though she had never heard the Morrison song before, she sat down and immediately played the bass line to "Wild Night," which became the song's primary groove.

Ndegéocello recalled the unpretentiousness of working in John's world, a world where instead of sparkling mineral water and gourmet catered meals, the musicians walked into the kitchen and made their own peanut butter and jelly sandwiches, or, even worse, satiated late-night hunger pangs with gut-bombs from

White Castle. One night, for kicks, they shaved Aronoff's purposely bald head.

Partway through the *Dance Naked* sessions, John fired Aronoff, his drummer of 15 years, after he missed three days of recording to play on a Hank Williams, Jr. session. Irritated that Aronoff had such a heavy workload outside of his band, John re-stated that he wanted a drummer who could fully commit to the band, and didn't think that Aronoff was that guy anymore. "It would be easy for me to get a session drummer, but I don't want one of those—and I guess in the case of Kenny, I don't want one in the band," John told *SPIN* magazine. "I wouldn't think it would be that challenging for him, but Kenny really has a desire to be a big session-man. And I think that desire is more important to him than being in this band. That's what it boils down to."

As if to prove that maybe Aronoff wasn't one of the greatest rock drummers of all time, he replaced him with a 19-year-old *intern*. Michael Dupke, an Indiana University School of Music student (like Aronoff), got college credit for playing on a couple of songs before John reconsidered his decision.

"John called and said, 'Why don't you come on over? I want to take a look at your schedule.' That was the first time he'd ever said anything like that to me. He's still got an aggressive edge, and at any moment that shit can come back. But he's mellowed a bit."

"Oh fuck it, we can make this work—we have for years," John admitted. "Why am I being so demanding? And Kenny, why are you being so reckless?" Maybe John's hard head was softening a bit. He reconciled with Aronoff, and when Germano announced that she needed a hiatus to promote her new album, *Happiness*, he gave her his blessing and considered her still a part of the band, even though he would have to find another fiddle player for the next tour. "If you work for John, you really need to be at his disposal," says Germano. "With my own record deal and my own creative life, at that point, I couldn't really do that, and he understood."

He had also expanded his musical horizons to incorporate dance remixes, beginning with a bonus track on *Whenever We Wanted*—a "London Club Mix" of "Love and Happiness" by Ralph Jezzard that didn't quite work, as well as a "Dance Naked" remix that ended up on a "Wild Night" CD single. New York DJ/producer/remixer Junior Vasquez also produced a remix for "Love and Happiness," with better results. Just as he gradually worked in fiddle, dobro and accordion a decade earlier, he had started incorporating loops, samples and other very un-Mellencamp sounds.

The downer mood he had felt for the last few years started to lift, mostly due to the positive presence of Elaine Mellencamp. Her optimistic outlook tempers John's cynicism, while her confidence and inner strength prove a good match for his combative side. On April 27, 1994 Elaine gave birth to Hud Mellencamp, her first child and John's first boy. Obviously, John chose the name, taken from his favorite character in his favorite movie.

PolyGram released *Dance Naked* on June 21, 1994. However, Mercury Records, PolyGram's parent company, cut back promotion on John's music, with president Ed Eckstein, who headed the label until 1995, even going as far as to state: "John Mellencamp is not our future, he's our past." But he had a more powerful ally in PolyGram head Alain Levy. John's tenure with the label meant something to Levy, and he worked the phones himself to help propel *Dance Naked* to Number 13 on *Billboard*'s album chart, and the single "Wild Night" to Number Three on the pop chart and Number One on the AC chart for a lengthy 42 weeks. The coinciding video quickly went into high rotation on VH-1 and MTV and became one of the most-played videos in VH-1's history. Not only did the video show a more with-it side of John, it also showed the public NdegéOcello's brighter side. They knew her three-time Grammy-nominated song "If That's Your Boyfriend (He Wasn't Last Night)," and from photographs and videos that showed a serious artist singing about serious gender and race issues. In the "Wild Night" video, they saw her smile for the first time.

With *Dance Naked*'s release, John rallied up the troops for a 35-city North American tour that would run through October 1994. Mindy Jostyn sat in for Germano, and York prepped for his first stint on the road with the group. As they wound their way through the U.S., "Wild Night" made its way up the charts. The crowds swelled. New fans came around, lured by "Wild Night's" prominent VH-1 exposure. John maintained his high energy onstage and off, singing and smoking at a frantic pace.

Two weeks after "Wild Night" peaked and less than half way into the tour, John woke up at 3 A.M. with what he thought was the flu. He stayed in his bed at the rented home in Wantagh, New York, where John, Elaine and Hud were staying. They had two shows booked at an outdoor venue called Jones Beach, which is near the Hamptons, and the Mellencamp family had planned to take a short family vacation that week. Unfortunately, John and band arrived to a dreary, rainy day that offered no potential for frolicking on the beach. The nasty weather exacerbated John's chills and overall sour mood, and he retreated to his temporary home to try to recoup. As the day wore on, he still felt terrible and for the first, and one of the only, times of his career, John cancelled a show. After a full day and night of bedrest, John felt well enough to continue the tour. When they had a week off, John decided to play it safe and scheduled a checkup with his Bloomington physician. "The guy says, 'Looks like you had a heart attack—when do you think you had it?' I couldn't imagine," John recalled earlier. "He said, 'Well, did you feel like you got the flu or something? That was it.'" He didn't know it when he was resting in New York, but one artery in his heart had closed off 100 percent. "Neither of us anticipated that as an option," recalls Elaine Mellencamp. "He was young, and we were naive and uneducated as to what would be symptomatic of a heart attack, and it wasn't on the horizon as an option."

The doctors advised that John could continue the tour, as he obviously felt okay, but the shock of the news—heart attack—gave him enough motivation to choose his health over work. "It just pissed me off so much: I'm not gonna be able to correct my diet or stop smoking on the road, or stop being stressed out getting on airplanes every day and walking onstage. If I want to make these changes, I need to stay home."

As much as he hated to let down his fans, he cancelled the rest of the tour. "At that time I just thought my life was over, thinking that if you have heart disease, you just stay home," he said.

He stayed home for 18 months, and for the first time in decades, he did not work. Taking time off in the past meant spending time on side projects—producing, painting, directing films. This time it *really* meant time off—no songwriting, no talking to others about music and certainly no recording. He watched television for the first time in decades. At first, the 42-year-old spent a many an idle hour beating himself up over his poor eating habits: too many stops at the fast-food drive-through window, too much soda and way too many cigarettes, sometimes up to three packs a day. For years, doctors had told him he had high cholesterol. They warned him of the risk of heart disease and advised medication. He turned it town every time.

Now that he faced a life-threatening illness, he knew he was paying dearly for past mistakes. The thought of a shorted life combined with the ample free time propelled him into a depression. "It was terrible to realize at 42 that you're so vulnerable," he said. "When you first hear that you've had a heart attack you think I'm dead. It's just a matter of time. 'What do I got doc, 10 more days?'" To make matters worse, his longtime friend and frequent co-writer, George Green, also suffered a heart attack not long after John.

To pull himself out of the dumps, John read everything he could on heart disease, and Elaine did the same. "I felt helpless," she says. "I knew that I could offer my support and empathy, but I chose to be more proactive. I spent a lot of time and effort to really be an expert in the area as best I could. For John, if he wanted to commiserate with someone, at least I was coming from a knowledgeable point. And it was therapeutic for me, as well. The more you know about things, the less scary they are."

He cut out the junk food, sodas and red meat. "My new motto is, if it tastes good, spit it out," he said. He also started exercising regularly, something that he hadn't done in years, aside from the occasional flag football or basketball game. He did get a vigorous workout onstage, which probably saved him from a more serious case of heart disease.

He did not, however, cut out smoking, although he did cut down to 10, sometimes five, cigarettes a day. And he switched brands, from a regular filtered cigarette to the more natural (if there is such a thing) American Spirit. Over time, he improved his cholesterol levels through a healthy diet, regular exercise and fewer cigarettes, and as a bonus, the positive lifestyle changes led to a more relaxed version of John Mellencamp. "In a funny way, my heart attack made life a little easier," he said. "I don't get mad like I used to. I used to have no filter—in the head, out the mouth. Say anything to anybody."

His bandmates breathed a sigh of relief at this change. "He had a...lighter approach," says Pat Peterson, who was in Vancouver when the heart attack happened, unaware that their tour was about to be canceled. "He doesn't have to grab or bark. He chooses those times now. He has to get into a higher intensity about things [to perform], and he chooses that. But I still don't think that it peaks as high. He used to go into some real good peaks about expressing what he needed, wanted and what was going on with him. After [the heart attack], it took on another phase."

As devastating as it was, the heart attack served as a blessing in many ways, including his tempered temper. He had time to take stock of his life, and again, questioned whether or not he wanted to stay in the music business. Of course he stayed, but considering life on the road partly contributed to poor health, he wondered whether or not he could tour, and whether he really even wanted to. He thought about his "young boy days" before the record deal, before the arenas, when he was just a singer in a cover band, hitting bars around the Midwest college towns. That was fun. If he embarked on a similar club junket now, would it still hold the same appeal?

CHAPTER NINE

HAPPY LITTLE BASTARD

H oping to reignite his fire for playing music, John formed Pearl Doggy, which included himself and his band. Instead of hitting arenas, they played 1,000-seat clubs in small cities within a short drive from home. They didn't promote the tour, really; word of mouth gave them all the publicity they needed. In Grand Rapids, Michigan, for example, about 50 people shivered in frigid December weather outside of the Orbit Room the afternoon of the show. By 5 P.M., the crowd had swelled to 400. By the time the doors opened, a sellout crowd wrapped itself around the block. How often does one get to hear John Mellencamp in a small club, his fans enthused. Judging by the number of bootlegs and hard-to-find ticket stubs still floating around eBay, the show did not disappoint.

John had a blast touring around in the green minivan on long weekends, and it stoked his fire enough to decide to make another album. He didn't dive into that endeavor right away though. Life made sure of it, in fact. In between Pearl Doggy jaunts and songwriting spurts, he kept an eye on Elaine who was pregnant with their second child. On April 24, 1995, they welcomed Speck Wildhorse Mellencamp into the world, their second boy. They named him after John's grandfather, another key character in John's life.

It would take a pretty sweet offer for John to break away from his wife and new baby Speck, and the grand opening celebrations for the Rock and Roll Hall of Fame in Cleveland fit the bill. On September 2, 1995, he made the relatively short commute across the Heartland to participate in a monumental concert starring Bruce Springsteen, Bob Dylan, Al Green, Jerry Lee Lewis,

Aretha Franklin, Johnny Cash, Lou Reed and others. Longtime friend and supporter Jann Wenner, *Rolling Stone* founder and a founding member of the Rock and Roll Hall of Fame Foundation, cheered him on when John sidled up to Martha Reeves to sing "Dancing in the Street." Her vocal group Martha and the Vandellas would be inducted into the Hall eight years later, along with his east coast musical colleague, The Boss.

A month later, Farm Aid celebrated its tenth anniversary with a concert in Louisville, Kentucky. A crowd of 47,000 descended upon Cardinal Stadium on October 1, 1995, to hear such diverse acts as Supersuckers, Hootie and the Blowfish, BlackHawk, John Conlee and Steve Earle, along with John and fellow founders Willie Nelson and Neil Young. Dave Matthews joined the crew for the first time this year, recruited by John. Matthews would ultimately become such a strong supporter of the organization that Nelson would ask him to serve on the board in 2001 (which he did), making him the "fourth face" of Farm Aid.

At the end of the event, members of John's band treated the audience to a once-in-a-lifetime performance. Toby Myers married his sweetheart, Roberta Chirko, right there on the Farm Aid stage. A band of Indians, friends of Willie Nelson's, presided over the ceremony. "He did it on a dare," recalls Mike Wanchic. "John said, 'Why don't you guys get married onstage?' Toby said, 'We can't do that; we don't have a judge.' So he got on the phone and got a judge. They got married in front of 40,000 people. We had plenty of witnesses on that one!"

When John returned to Indiana to begin planning the next album, he had to take into account the industry's radically different musical landscape. Many of the "dinosaurs" of rock had watered their music down to fit into the adult contemporary market. Grunge gave way to the more commercially acceptable "post-grunge," with middle-of-the-road rock and hard rock bands such as Bush, Silverchair, Candlebox and Collective Soul, as well as the synthetic beats and bleeps of Kula Shaker, Beck and Radiohead taking over the airwaves. Established acts such as John Mellencamp, Journey, Rod Stewart and Eric Clapton found their place outside of pop radio. Also around 1996, record sales began their steady descent due to the rise of the Internet and MP3 downloads, which begat vicious piracy wars. Needless to say, labels had less money to spend, and they funneled most of it to a few commercial pop acts that ruled the top of the charts.

John, in an effort to hopefully glean some more marketing muscle from PolyGram/Mercury, wanted a fresh sound and a fresh start. Again. First off, he had a talk with his band, many of whom struggled to find balance between working for their taskmaster boss, John, and managing their respective solo careers. He sensed their wane in commitment and didn't want to continue unless he had their full attention and enthusiasm.

"I sat down with Mike [Wanchic] and Toby [Myers] and said, look guys, don't even come to make this record with the attitude that's been around the last couple years because if you do I'll kick your ass out of the studio," Mellencamp said earlier. At this point, Wanchic had 20 years of sweat equity invested in this group and held dual roles as guitarist and co-producer. Even if he did get the boot, he wouldn't budge.

Myers mulled over the situation. "For some reason, I think I was still mad about John not using bass guitar on *Dance Naked*, but when we had the production meeting to make *Mr. Happy Go Lucky*, I told John that I didn't feel like cutting a record right now. He said, 'Well okay. Go home, and when you feel like cutting a record come back. I couldn't believe he didn't fire me for that. Three weeks later he called and said, 'Myers! I think you'd better get over here because if you don't you're going to have to look for a new job.' I went over [to Belmont Mall] and cut the rest of the record. It was an absolute gas!"

Germano's solo career had kicked into high gear, and she had her fourth album to promote. She opted to let go of her spot in John's band, but he left the door open for her to come back.

Aronoff gave John's words serious thought. He had played with nearly hundreds of artists as both a session and live drummer. By this point, his phone rang so often with work, there was no doubt he could fly solo. Hell, he had full drum sets and cartage companies at the ready in New York, L.A. and Nashville, so that he could fly into town at a moment's notice for double-scale session work. He was a rock drummer at heart, and he had a hard time saying no to all of the live and studio work. Over time, John had an increasingly difficult time booking his own drummer, which caused numerous conflicts between the two. The final straw came when John had to perform at a special PolyGram showcase in Hong Kong. Aronoff was touring with Bob Seger, who coincidentally had two days off. Aronoff flew to Hong Kong, got off the plane, walked right into rehearsal, went back to the hotel, came back, played the show, had a car waiting for him at the backstage entrance, sped to the airport, hopped on another plane and arrived within an hour of Seger's concert at the Silverdome in his hometown of Detroit. That was way too much pressure for the overbooked drummer, and not fair to either of his clients. It became painfully clear that he had to make a choice, so, at the end of this record, Aronoff decided to leave John's band to continue his career as a top-flight session drummer. As valuable as he was to the group, John felt a bit of relief at the opportunity to find another drummer who could give 110 percent to the band.

In Germano's place, John brought in Jimmy Ryser. Mindy Jostyn—who played fiddle, guitar and harmonica during the Dance Naked Tour—did not rejoin the group. While Ryser played on much of *Mr. Happy Go Lucky*, they brought in violin specialist, Miriam Sturm, to add a special introduction. Like

Aronoff, Sturm graduated from Indiana University's renowned School of Music. She assumed after graduation that she would go on to a career in the orchestra or symphony, but a couple of musical detours radically altered the course of her career.

Sturm had played with John's band before, a few one-off dates here and there, and in 1996, at the Hong Kong showcase. They knew her from her previous band, an Eastern music-influenced trio called Eclectricity. Sturm suspects that Aronoff and Wanchic caught a few Eclectricity shows in the Bloomington clubs, and word of the trio's wild gypsy music-playing violinist caught John's ear. By the time *Mr. Happy Go Lucky* came around, she had also composed and/or performed music for more than two dozen plays in both her home base of Chicago as well as New York.

She thought the Hong Kong date would be a one-time deal, but not long after their return to the states, John called her again to compose an overture for John's forthcoming album. He's been calling her ever since.

"The album was basically in the can when he called and said, 'Hey Miriam. I would love to have an overture like they used to have [in stage productions],'" she said. "'I'd like you to quote all 10 songs, just do it all strings like *Eleanor Rigby*-ish kinda, and I'd like it to come in under two minutes.' So I quoted all 10 songs in one minute 55 seconds. The overture is intended to tip a hat to all the songs that are on the album. It was a really unusual idea, but a really cool device."

Another newcomer, Moe Z, added some zest with his upbeat spirit and fresh loops and keyboard riffs. He arrived to Bloomington via L.A., where he was part of an exploding west coast rap scene that included Tupac Shakur, Heavy D and LL Cool J, among others. So how did a street-smart hip-hop artist from southern California end up tied to John Mellencamp? Connections, baby. Moe Z's publisher held an office across the hall from the latest in a string of men to take on the challenge of managing John, Alan Kovak of the Left Bank Organization. Kovak stepped across the hall to ask for Dr. Dre's number, because John wanted to bring him on board to do some drum programming. Instead of handing him Dr. Dre's digits, he gave him Moe Z's number instead.

Shortly after, Moe Z found himself in the comparatively slow-moving, quiet town of Bloomington and on his way to Belmont Mall. John kept their relationship no-pressure, at first. "If this doesn't work out, no big deal," he said to the rapper/multi-instrumentalist. Moe took a different attitude.

"I told John when I first met him we were going to make history!" Moe Z reports on his website. "He said, 'Moe slow down, I don't know about that.' 'John, mark my words' is what I told him."

John took a similar low-key approach with Junior Vasquez, the New York DJ and producer who remixed "Love and Happiness" in 1992. "I told him,

'Look, I don't have any expectations. If this doesn't work, it'll just be a couple days wasted," John said in an interview with *SPIN*. "After a while he came to me and said, 'John, I don't feel like I'm doing anything. You guys have been together so long.' I said, 'Just hang around a few more days.' And inside a week, he was just one of the guys." In Vasquez, he saw someone who could contribute new ideas as well as deliver the sounds he liked from other records, but didn't quite know how to replicate. "I don't have a firm grasp of using computers, loops, programs and the type of rhythm that goes into the urban sound," he admitted. "So when Junior came in, he was like a non-musician band member who could come up with different rhythms and sounds than we ordinarily use."

"This was our first real foray of loops and urban sounds in our recording process," says Andy York. "Then we added our guitars, keyboards, mellotron and other instruments. The psychedelic aspect of this album was really fun. It was our Summer of Love phase. We watched the making of *Sgt. Pepper* during one of the pre-production meetings. It was a nice juxtaposition of urban, rhythmic loops and mid- to late-'60s pop sounds."

In contrast to on-the-fly *Dance Naked*, the band spent a great deal of time on pre-production for *Mr. Happy Go Lucky*. John and the band worked out a "game plan," which was to meet for a couple of weeks each month to work on new songs. When they had an album's worth ready to go, they would move to the studio to record with their various guest musicians. "John had a bunch of songs and kept writing more," says York, "so we spent a good deal of time and effort on this record. We worked over a period of a year."

As they acclimated to small-town living, Moe Z and Vasquez played integral roles in the album's success. Plus, they were both a heck of a lot of fun to be around, which lightened the mood in the studio. After he found a way to adapt his style to John's traditional recording methods, Vasquez made his presence known by adding rhythmic textures and sonics that filled out the album's bass undercurrent, without turning John's classic roots rock into techno dance material. Vasquez generally works "from the loop up," he said earlier, "and here I am dealing with this acoustic folk song. Then Kenny goes out and plays these big overheads and drums and it's like, 'Where can I take it from there?' I think John's main focus was to get a stronger bottom."

While Vasquez focused on rounding out the bottom end with percussion and drum loops, Moe Z filled in the gaps between the stringed instruments with additional loops, programmed drum parts and keyboard riffs. The stylistic difference between John's sound and his initially threw Moe Z for a loop, so to speak. "I thought, 'How am I supposed to loop this?" he said. "And then it finally came along."

Experimenting with various loops and samples, he compiled keyboard and background vocal arrangements on "This May Not Be the End of the World," a John/George Green co-write with John's basic sound at its core, but spiced up with psychedelic funk-inspired synth parts, processed drum sounds and other effects. Toby Myers wrote one of the most atypical Mellencamp songs on the album, "Emotional Love," penned while the rest of the band worked on *Dance Naked*.

One of the first times he's used a song penned by a band member, "Emotional Love" marries soulful background vocals and danceable beats into one of the album's catchier tunes, while songs such as "Life Is Hard," with its urban beats, embodies a prominent Vasquez influence with hip-shaking results. Conversely, the album's strongest hit, "Key West Intermezzo (I Saw You First)" calls to mind traces of *Scarecrow*, albeit on a tropical vacation. Released in August 1996, the single made it up to Number 14 on *Billboard's* pop chart. "People, happily, were up for hearing a romantic rock song," John supposed.

Lyrically, the material follows John's well-worn territory of insightful observations of real-life America, but with contemporary twists that match the atmospheric music. In "Jerry," he sings about a 37-year-old skate rat with six kids who "sees the world through a 10-year-old boy's eyes." Jerry struggles with the concept of maturity. Growing up leads to growing old and then to dying, right? "Jerry is basically just our conscience," John told *Performing Songwriter.* "That's who Jerry is, he was my conscience. It's not really some guy. It is some guy right outside your window or on your shoulder [*Laughs*]. I don't know if anybody got that, but that's who Jerry was to me."

Other characters include Bobie Doll and Big Jim Picato, who love to kick back and give advice on "It's Just Another Day." For most of his adult life, slackers have fascinated John. He fell into that category as a young adult, but since his vision took hold, he hasn't stopped working. While shooting music videos in Savannah, he marveled at the men kicking back with a beer in their hand.

"I've always been interested in people who were able to live a kind of freeform lifestyle," he told *Performing Songwriter.* I always thought that I would live that way but, of course, I don't. But I sometimes vacation on these islands, and you see these guys sitting at the tiki hut everyday and you wonder, "How in the world do they get by doing this?" They don't have any jobs and they just sit in the tiki hut drinking and smoking. They're there every day. They appear to be living the life of Riley. Who really knows what's going on underneath, but the appearance is that these guys have it made. They don't work, they don't want to— just like the songs says [*Laughs*]. They've been able to get by somehow. Then I look at my own life and it's kind of like, I'm on the phone every day doing this music business stuff. Sometimes you feel like, "Well, maybe I did miss the boat here. Perhaps what they said is true, that less is more."

"The Full Catastrophe," with its dobro and chanting and real drums matched with programmed sounds, most closely resembles John's initial vision for the album, which was "to take as urban a beat as we could and put it with the most '40s blues we could find," he said. "In the '80s, if you wanted to be taken seriously, you had to put a violin on your record. I think by using new technology, we've shown that rap songs and little folk songs have more in common than people think."

Beginning with the title, the album takes a sardonic yet playful tone. The name itself even came from a sly remark: John walked into the studio one day with a sterner than usual look on his face, and one of the band members said, "Look out, here comes Mr. Happy Go Lucky."

John seems as though he enjoyed himself this time while pushing himself and his band to the limit. The album cover expands on the whimsical, satirical tone of its contents. Images of Jesus and the devil assume the background while John sits in the foreground dressed in pure white pants and tank, holding a half-asleep Hud who's dressed in white bottoms and matching clown makeup. Justice Mellencamp stands to John's right dressed as a ballerina in white with clown makeup. A small dog stands to their side, also adorned in black and white clown garb. In contrast, skulls and crossbones decorate the perimeter of the cover.

His most ambitious album in many years, the songs on *Mr. Happy Go Lucky*, released September 10, 1996, "squarely face the fact that he's 44 years old, with thoughts about life beyond the next dance and the next come-on," writes *New York Times* critic Jon Pareles. "Mellencamp has realized that his old musical reflexes don't go with his new perspective. But without letting go of his 1960's roots, he has found a way to make peace with the present."

As a sweet reward for his labor, "Key West Intermezzo (I Saw You First)" was nominated for a 1997 Grammy Award for Best Male Pop Vocal Performance. "Just Another Day" was nominated for a 1998 Grammy for Best Male Rock Vocal Performance. Neither garnered a win; in fact, despite several nominations, he only had one trophy—for *American Fool*.

Aronoff said goodbye to his family of 16 years after this album wrapped, and with a string of promotional appearances on the way, John had to find a replacement. Replacing Aronoff's renowned power and passion was *not* going to be easy. "I auditioned at least 20 drummers," says Mike Wanchic. "And these weren't just random drummers. They were Tesla's drummer, Bette Midler's drummer, Loverboy's drummer—known drummers, and they came from all over the country."

They auditioned some of the industry's finest skinsmen, but hadn't found anyone close to Aronoff, nor had they found a drummer who's personality clicked with the rest of the band. Wanchic then got a call from Dane Clark. He had played a bit on the *Falling from Grace* soundtrack (although John doesn't remember this). He was an A-list studio drummer around the Bloomington area and often bumped into Aronoff in the hallways of Indiana and Nashville studios. He played in a band with Toby Myers years before, so he had his foot a little father in the door than most. "Please let me audition," he said on the phone to Wanchic. Fine, he thought. Why not give him a shot. When Clark showed up to audition, he smoked all of the "known" drummers who had already taken their turn. And even better, he lived "right up the road," says Wanchic, which meant a level of relating and bonding with the band that an L.A. or New York musician just wouldn't have.

Clark recalls playing a couple of songs at the audition, during which time John made a comment that Clark's hair looked better now that he had gotten it cut. "I said, 'Well, great! I'll shave my whole body if you want, I don't care!' [*Laughs*]. I made the guys laugh, and made everybody feel comfortable, and I think that was part of [getting the job]. You've got to have somebody that's good, but you've also got to be able to sit eyeball to eyeball with them."

Much like Myers' initiation into the band, Clark's first gigs with the band included a VH-1 *Backyard Barbeque* taping live at Niagara Falls, followed by a *Late Show with David Letterman* appearance, days after getting hired. No pressure, right?

Compared to the 10-day recording of *Dance Naked*, John and band spent a long time on *Mr. Happy Go Lucky*. Out of concern for his health, John first opted not to tour with this album. But since it had such high sales out of the gate, he changed his mind.

The Mr. Happy Go Lucky Tour kicked off March 3, 1997, with a four-night run at Bloomington's Indiana University Auditorium. It then continued through a small number of larger cities such as Boston, Chicago, Minneapolis, Detroit and Indianapolis through the end of April. With Indy band The Why Store tapped as an opening act, the tour earned reviews on par with the album; not only for the performance, but for the venues played. Instead of hitting super-sized arenas—not a favorite of John's anyway—the band hit smaller, 2,000- to 5,000-seat theaters for three- and four-night residencies, most of them sellouts. "...people of our age group want to go see rock shows—but not in arenas and be treated like cattle," Mellencamp told the *Herald Times*. "They want to walk into a nice small theater and not be treated like shit."

Unfortunately, playing the smaller-size venues, even with multiple night residencies, led to higher ticket prices, with Bloomington fans paying up to $75 a head. Some loudly protested the high cost, yet three of the four shows sold out the day tickets went on sale. His decision to play in a more intimate setting would pave the way for other top-draw acts—most notably Bruce Springsteen—to organize similar theater tours.

VH-1 viewers confirmed that, yes, they wanted to see John on a smaller stage. During a February 8 promotion called "Tickets First," viewers purchased 30,000 seats for the upcoming tour in two hours. The network deemed it their most successful "Tickets First" promotion yet. U2 followed Mellencamp's lead and sold 40,000 seats through the promotion.

To prepare for the tour, the group rehearsed the new album, as well as many of John's previous hits and rarities, three different ways. They learned to play them exactly like the album, they learned a looser "live" version and they learned an updated version, revamped for 1997.

"We're rethinking the old material and playing the songs in a new and different way," violinist Miriam Sturm said to the *Herald Times*. "They're still recognizable. But we've found out that there is more than one way to play 'Pink Houses' or 'Jack and Diane.'"

Continuing the theme of combining past and present, John wanted to hear vintage organ—Hammond B3, Wurlitzer—in some of his songs. To educate 28-year-old Moe Z to what he was looking for, he played him the Young Rascals and Bob Dylan (*a la Highway 61 Revisited*). Moe Z immediately incorporated those traditional sounds into John's repertoire and then added a few embellishments of his own. The tried and true "Jack and Diane" found themselves in a new relationship under the new lineup. Gone was the unforgettable drum solo that Kenny Aronoff added just before the bridge went away. In its place, Moe Z raps about how "life goes on...but I don't feel like living." For the original, John hadn't yet incorporated fiddle into his work. But now, he had Sturm deliver a rollicking string part to follow Moe Z's rap. A strange combination, but it worked.

With internists Dr. Larry Rink and Dr. Carter Henrich's approval and with John's new personal chef (who made sure he ate healthy meals—no junk, no fast food and certainly no Big Red) in tow—John and band embarked on their relatively short U.S. tour, armed with an elaborate stage setup designed to mimic the album cover's warped carnival theme.

When the lights dimmed and the curtain rose, John, guitarists Mike Wanchic and Andy York, bassist Toby Myers and Mirium Sturm approached the front of the stage. Keyboardist Moe Z, drummer Dane Clark and vocalist/percussionist Pat Peterson then took their places on three round platforms decorated in patriotic red, white and blue; Clark in the middle, Moe Z and Peterson to either side.

John kicked off the performances with "Small Town," followed by a lengthy set of older hits and songs from his new album. Moe Z added his improvisational rapping to "Jack and Diane," and Peterson assumed the role of Me'Shell Ndegéocello for "Wild Night." When she wasn't working out her powerful pipes, Peterson danced with as much energy as she had in the *Uh-Huh* days. The frontman sounded as strong, if not stronger than ever, his voice reaping the rewards of a healthier diet and regular exercise. Female compatriot Sturm's expert violin playing floated through most of the tracks, gelling the old and the new into one seamless performance.

John's newly configured lineup proved more than adept at delivering the high-energy, high-flash performance John Mellencamp was known for. Musical theater, one former band member called it, meaning the band was expected to deliver exactly like the record, or exactly as planned, no in-the-moment solos or musical explorations allowed.

His fans ate it up. Even with tickets priced up to $100, most of his shows sold out. His three-night residency in Minneapolis alone grossed $659,746 according to a report in *Rolling Stone*, and the tour itself would become one of the biggest sellers of that year.

The theater tour was winding down when John decided that maybe he should keep this good thing going a while longer. Contradicting his negative thoughts about large venues and arenas, he decided to play a string of amphitheaters and sheds. This summer leg kicked off May 29 at Phoenix's Desert Sky Amphitheater and continued through July 1, where he fittingly closed the tour at Deer Creek, outside of Indianapolis. Again, he utilized VH-1's "Tickets First," which yielded him thousands of advance sales.

After surviving a heart attack, whipping a new band into shape and securing his place in a new musical playing field, John's career had had hit a solid stride, and his relationship with wife Elaine made life all the sweeter. John's band sensed his renewed enthusiasm, which brought back some of the good family vibes that had started to fade. Bass player Toby Myers, however, would carry bittersweet memories from this tour. He loved playing in John's band and had a blast on the road, but his father died during this tour, and after that, he had a hard time feeling excited about anything.

"Boy it fucked me up," he says of the loss. "I slid into a depression that was tough to get out of." When the tour ended, he knew he had to do something that would bring him joy. He remembered how much fun he had playing in bars and wondered if it would hold the same thrill 25 year later. To find out, he joined Jimmy Ryser, David Grissom's replacement on *Dance Naked*, to form Daisy Chain. They played the bars around Bloomington, lugged their own gear and played for a fraction of a fraction of a Mellencamp gig. The club owners and patrons, however, treated Myers like a rock star. "Ladies and Gentlemen, Daisy Chain...with Toby Myers!" He loved it. It was nice to be treated like a main course instead of a side dish. The ego boost helped lessen the pain of losing his Dad, but left him in conflict with his career. When John came a callin' to cut another record, he struggled to get himself to the sessions. "I just didn't want to be a part of that big-ass level of rock anymore," he says. "I lost my Dad; I kind of lost my way."

CHAPTER TEN

MERCURY BLUES

S ince signing with Mercury/PolyGram two decades prior, John maintained a love/hate relationship with the label. They gave him the means to release his records, but they battled almost constantly over everything from content ("I don't hear a single!") to lack of marketing and promotional support to money: the usual arguments between artist and record company. In 1997, he surprised PolyGram executives by announcing his departure. He told the press that it was not due to any real negligence on their part, but more a case of a dysfunctional marriage that had run its course. "I've been there 22 years, which is amazing," he said in an interview with *Billboard*. "But I've never known another life, so to be leaving there is downright thrilling." He had admitted more than once that for years, the label had more of an interest in the bottom line and its stockholders than the music, and felt a continual pressure to maintain his position as one of their top-selling artists, a demand that can kill the creative spirit in weaker men.

He felt confident he could get another deal, but with so much history behind him, wondered if he could find the arrangement he really wanted. He wanted a label that understood how to market to the large baby boomer generation, as opposed to just kids. "I think it's ridiculous to try to sell [my] records to teenagers, because teenagers don't buy my records...I want to sell to people my own age, because that's the way I write songs."

Before he went on to find a label in line with his thinking, he had to honor his contractual obligations with PolyGram, which meant another two albums. He started off with a greatest-hits collection, *The Best That I Could Do*, issued on November 18, 1997. He chose 13 classics, including "vintage" tunes such as "Ain't Even Done With the Night" and "I Need a Lover," as well as ubiquitous favorites such as "Jack and Diane," "Hurts So Good," "Paper in Fire"and "Check It Out," among others. Only problem was, he had more hits than one CD could hold, leaving many fans to ask, "But what about...and why not..." "I was supposed to deliver a greatest hits in 1985 as far as my contract goes, but I kept putting it off for 10 years!" John said. "But they really wanted it for this Christmas, and I said, 'Okay.' To be perfectly frank, I wasn't very good at picking [tracks], and had actually left off 'Paper in Fire'! I've been fortunate to have had a lot of hit records. 'Human Wheels' doesn't qualify as a hit record, but it's really the best single I've ever had." He ended the semi-retrospective with one new track, a cover of British rock singer Terry Reid's "Without Expression." "As a young guy, I was really drawn to vocalists because I was in a cover band in high school," John said, "and it never dawned on me to write a song, because what could you do with it when you could be doing 'Honky Tonk Woman'? So I was drawn to people like Terry Reid and Paul Rodgers and Michael Fennelly of Crabby Appleton."

The decision to add the Reid song came at the last minute, which meant John had to arrange a recording session, fast. The band shuffled their schedules to accommodate while John searched for an engineer. He didn't have time to wait for someone to fly in from L.A., New York or Nashville. He needed to find someone locally who knew their stuff. Wanchic suggested a young engineer named Paul Mahern, who had engineered several projects at his Echo Park Studios. Mahern had moved to Bloomington from Indianapolis only three years prior and had developed a good reputation in a short time. He got the gig, recorded the song and left without any major drama. So all went well.

Billboard editor-in-chief Timothy White wrote eloquent, expertly researched liner notes for one of John's final PolyGram releases. John had met the premier music journalist years before when White, then senior editor at *Rolling Stone*, interviewed the musician for an in-depth feature. White worked hard on the piece; as usual, he dug deep in his research and took an honest, respectful approach. He called John after the issue published to see what he thought of the article. John hated it! He then proceeded to point out what he didn't say, didn't mean and what White may have taken out of context. White was obviously troubled, and as a man with a deep passion for music, history and truth, wanted to set the record straight. "They started a friendship and Tim, as a writer, through his curiosity, wanted to understand John better," says Elaine Mellencamp. "The creative process brought them together."

John fulfilled his PolyGram commitment with *Rough Harvest*, a collection of subtly re-arranged acoustic versions of what John deemed some of his favorite songs, including gems such as "Jackie Brown," "When Jesus Left Birmingham,"

"Rain on the Scarecrow" and "Minutes to Memories," among others. He added a few covers, ones that have meaning for him almost as personal as the songs he penned himself: The Drifters' "Under the Boardwalk," the traditional blues song "In My Time of Dying" and Bob Dylan's "Farewell Angelina."

Mercury came up with the idea for this "unplugged" album, and to their surprise, John approved. "It was very easy for me," he said. "Actually, every song I ever wrote I wrote on acoustic guitar first. That's pretty much how the songs sound before I put electricity to them."

They recorded live-to-tape for a more natural sound—no endless vocal overdubs or time spent noodling on guitar. They didn't spend weeks on rehearsal, either, though John's choice in cover songs calls to mind what the band might play "to re-center themselves when the world around them seems a tad out of kilter," according to Timothy White, who also wrote this album's liner notes.

When the band assembled, instruments in hand, Myers brought with him an upright bass. "The only one I could find was made of aluminum," he says. He didn't know if the rare model (only a handful of aluminum basses exist) would work for the session. Turned out, it had just the right tone. "Myers, that's the bass sound I've been looking for as long as you've been in the band," John said to him. He cut the entire record on that aluminum bass.

The band had played these songs hundreds of times before, but this time, they had to feel like starting from scratch. "Forget anything you know about the song. Let's start from square one," he instructed his band. "Let's go in a completely different direction."

The versions that appear on *Rough Harvest* more closely resemble their folkier acoustic origins. "It's a very organic, quiet and simpler record—more about the feeling being conveyed than the intricacies of the melody and beat," John said.

The new version features harmony vocals by Janas Hoyt, the star guest artist of *Rough Harvest*. Singer and songwriter for the Bloomington-based Mary Janes, Hoyt provides soaring accents to eight of the 11 songs recorded for *Rough Harvest*. "Even though I front a band, one of my favorite things to do is sing harmony," said Hoyt to the *Indianapolis Star*. "There's something very spiritual about it. And I really enjoy singing with John's voice. Our voices have a nice rapport." Before engineer Paul Mahern invited Hoyt to join the *Rough Harvest* sessions, she had never met Mellencamp. "I was a little nervous," she said. "When John introduced himself, he said, 'You get two chances. You better make it good because whatever you do is going on this record.' I thought that was an interesting way to inspire an artist. It was like a dare." Hoyt met the challenge, and said the sessions were a low-key delight. "It was all very off-the-cuff," Hoyt said. "Because of that, the band seemed happy and relaxed. It was a very creative session. It was amazing to watch John as a producer, sitting on the couch making calls on how the record was put together."

Each of the songs' intimate qualities came forward in the tracks, making the album somewhat of a gift for loyal fans who listened close enough to each album to pick up on the more subtle elements. Though PolyGram wouldn't release the album until August 17,1999 (they recorded the tracks in 1997), it served as a nice way to close John's lengthy tenure with the label.

Building on this period of regime changing, John left his longtime booking agency CAA to sign with William Morris. In 1995, CAA head Mike Ovitz—a key leader in the film and television industry—left to become president of Walt Disney Company, a move that shook not only the powerhouse agency itself, but Hollywood as a whole. At the time, John had some film ideas he wanted to pursue; hence his move to William Morris, another leader in that field. The arrangement lasted about a year before he returned to CAA and longtime friend/agent/supporter John Sykes.

At the same time, he took a look at his management structure: Left Bank Management's Alan Kovak with Harry Sandler for personal management. Sandler excelled as a tour manager, and because he and John had a reasonably friendly relationship, often acted as a liaison between John and Left Bank. John treated all of his managers "like hell," which partly explains why he had gone through five of them in his career. In 1998, he bumped into music industry heavyweight Randy Hoffman at New York's Hit Factory studio. Hoffman had gotten his start at Champion Entertainment, owned by Tommy Mattola, who managed John in the mid-'80s. Back then, Hoffman was a young upstart; now, he managed pop superstar Mariah Carey, who was on Columbia, coincidentally run by Sony Music Entertainment CEO Mattola. "I always felt akin to the old Champion Entertainment company," John told *Billboard*, "even though I treated them like hell, because I knew they always worked hard on the records." John signed with Hoffman Entertainment in 1998, where he remains today.

With that deal nailed down, it's no surprise that John's next label home was Columbia Records, who signed him to a four-album worldwide deal in April 1998. Label president Donny Lenner, a longtime fan of John's, gave him the deal he had hoped for. But more importantly, the label had enthusiasm for his music. When Lenner shared his vision for John's next album—a vision based on the records he had grown up on—John delivered, and thus named his album simply, *John Mellencamp*, a statement of the times as much as the *John Cougar* record issued 20 years before.

While John prepared to record his first album for Columbia, his fan club bustled about Seymour to organize the second annual Mellenfest, a weekend-long homage filled with story trading, memorabilia purchasing and sightseeing trips to Uncle Joe's Rok-Sey Roller Rink (featured in his "Small Town" video, and where John's teenage band Crepe Soul played), the Southern Indiana Center for the Arts (which he helped fund and featured works from him and his mother Marilyn) and John's childhood neighborhood. They asked for an in-person appearance, and hoped and prayed it would happen this year. He was on vacation for the inaugural Mellenfest, and therefore couldn't attend. If he didn't show up this year, performances from the Bobby Clark Band, Rusty Bladen and former Mellencamp studio band member Jimmy Ryser would have to suffice. But to the uncontained delight of 350 avid fans, John *did* make an appearance this year. His short set included an acoustic version of The Serfs "Early Bird Café," and two new songs from his forthcoming album. He stuck around to sign autographs, take pictures with fans and interact with event organizers, which included members of his official fan club, Minutes to Memories; the Human Wheels Internet discussion list; and his webmaster, Tony Buechler. Buechler and co. who donated proceeds from the event—which totaled about $1,000—to Farm Aid. They presented the check to John backstage after the 1998 concert in October. After a landmark year of Mellenizing, the event took a hiatus, promising to return in 2000.

John expounded upon the off-the-cuff recording style used on *Rough Harvest* for his first album of original material in five years. He had a strong batch of songs to play for the band and a clear vision: to return to the acoustic roots that he had nurtured in the mid-'80s.

Andy York and Dane Clark recorded the basic tracks live. Toby Myers, still enthralled by the aluminum upright, overdubbed his parts later so that the drums wouldn't bleed into his mic. John called back Paul Mahern, the engineer who passed the test during the "Without Expression" session. This was his first full album project with John, and he hadn't fully learned John's way of communicating. "He wanted the acoustic guitar to really sound like an old Stones recording, like on *Let It Bleed*," says Mahern. "And it took me a lot of playing around with different microphones and preamps to figure that out." He had a hard time finding the "dirty" guitar sound John wanted until he handed him a copy of that Stones album. "That sounds horrible!" the young engineer said to John. "Yeah! *That's* what I want it to sound like!"

One week into the sessions, John fired the entire band *and* his engineer. "I'm not gonna make this record," he grumbled. The band took it in stride and went home without much worry. They had been through this before. Mahern, however, freaked. He had just cleared more than a month of his schedule for this session, and now he's *fired*?! He went home and immediately began looking for other work, but a few days later, John called everyone back, but not before Mike Wanchic, Andy York and Mahern had a long talk about the record. "John was like a father to his band and everyone wanted to please him," says engineer David Thoener, who tracked several songs and mixed the album. "We all had a great respect for his vision and would always listen to his thoughts and ideas and try not to only meet his vision, but hopefully exceed it and take it to a level beyond his vision to create something even better."

Rejuvenated and reassembled at Belmont Mall, John and band secluded themselves for an intense period of recording. Their "old school" methods meant playing a track over until it was right, then going back and shaping the track during the overdub phase. Many vocalists hold back during the tracking sessions, singing what's called a "scratch vocal," which serves as a placeholder and a guide for the band. The vocalist will then replace the scratch vocal with his master takes later. As with many of his albums, John sang in the studio as if the first take were the only take, going back later to re-do certain parts (or on occasion, an entire performance) that he knows can be better. This way of working gives the recording sessions more of a live feel and maintains an authenticity that can be heard on the final recording.

Moe Z had the rare opportunity to co-write with John, a distinction officially held by only one other band member: Toby Myers, who penned "Emotional Love." "We were recording [*Rough Harvest*] and John says, 'Man why don't you write a song for me,'" Moe Z said. He messed around with samples, drum beats and other elements, when "all of a sudden I made a little pattern. I started dancing around the room with a little tape recorder and I got the melody and the words to it." That became the backbone for "Break Me Off Some."

Several weeks into the project, John brought in engineer David Thoener to sit in the engineer's seat with Mahern. He wasn't completely confident about some of Mahern's decisions, but instead of taking him off the project, he decided to bring in a more experienced engineer that could not only offer some support to the fatigued engineer, but also share tips that would help Mahern in the long run. "I looked at the recording set up, made some changes in mic choices and placement and EQ adjustments and we continued like a team," says Thoener.

With the basic tracks complete, the band brought in Sturm and guest Lisa Germano to add respective violin parts. Andy York threw in some Indian instruments, Pat Peterson added her signature powerful backing vocals and former Guns 'N Roses axe-slinger and fellow Indianan, Izzy Stradlin, laid down guitar parts on "Miss Missy."

In the control room, Mahern and Thoener continued to work together through the mixing process, with Thoener asking Mahern for feedback, and Mahern learning invaluable lessons from a seasoned engineer.

Mastered by the legendary Bob Ludwig, John's eponymous Columbia debut hit stores on October 6, 1998—one day before his forty-seventh birthday—to mostly positive reviews and, more importantly, ample enthusiasm from his new record label. As a self-titled album, the release symbolized a veteran artist starting anew. But instead of trying to adopt late-'90s trends, which had little to do with his own rootsy style, he stuck with what he does best: singable, acoustic-based rock, with heavy attention to melody and intelligent songcraft. He wrote the lead single, "Your Life Is Now," with longtime partner George Green. Having both overcome heart disease, they wrote the song with their life-threatening illnesses in mind. Like many of John's tunes, the song offers hope to the disillusioned and reminds us that now is the time to do what's right. "I believe you could change your mind and change our lives," he sings. "It's quite crafty," a *Billboard* singles review states of "Your Life Is Now," "how a soft, choir-like backing vocal rises in the arrangement, while a whirling, churchy organ quietly seeps into the deft guitar/violin interplay." While his music remains insidiously catchy, there are some complex musical nuances at work underneath.

Prior to the album's release, John admitted that he was so happy with this record and his new label's support, he didn't care how well it sold; which is good, considering the album ultimately wasn't one of his strongest sellers. Rather than soaring to Platinum status, he sold close to half a million over the course of several months. However, only a select few performers see million-plus sales these days, not many of them middle-of-the-road rock. "Who my age is selling the amount of records they used to?" he asked the *Indianapolis Star*. "What did Tom Petty's last album sell? Half a million. R.E.M.? Half a million. John Mellencamp? Half a million. It's just the way it is for people our age." These days, seven-figure album sales are reserved for the princes of hip-hop, cute teen-agers and self-absorbed metal acts. "It's either your time or it's not. I'm definitely not in the 'It's your time' business."

The record marked a new beginning for John, as well as a new life path for his longtime bass player, Toby Myers. Shortly after finishing the record, his wife, Roberta, found out she was pregnant. "I can remember John missing stuff, and Larry and Mike, too, with their kids," says Myers. "I thought, well damn man, I got to do 10 years with Pure Funk and Roadmasters, and 18 with John, that's 28 years in a row of recording and touring. I think I'm done. I had just turned 50, my Dad was gone, I was ready to see what would happen if I just stayed home for a few years. I sure had one hell of a time with those guys though." Myers currently plays in a band with Moe Z, and gets to attend every one of his son's baseball games, football practices; heck, even the PTA meetings. "Not to say that you can't be a good parent and a good musician at the same time," Myers counters, "But I didn't know if I had that covered."

He gave John ample notice to find a new bass player, and even recommended an excellent replacement in John Gunnell, an Indianapolis-based groove-master who had just come off the road with Ted Nugent. In small-town fashion, "Johnny G" had played in a band years before that opened for Roadmasters. He had also known Dane Clark for many years, so when he showed up to audition, he saw a couple of familiar faces. John hired someone else, at first, but about a month later, Gunnell got the call. That other bass player didn't work out, and would he want the job? Of course! As is tradition with the Mellencamp band, he got thrown into the fire with his debut gig on *The Late Show with David Letterman*. "Only in front of 20 million of your closest friends!" he jokes.

With the music trends leaning more toward Kid Rock than heartland rock, Columbia had to find new ways to promote their "career" artist. They focused much of their marketing muscle on VH-1. "Your Life Is Now" made it into heavy rotation about a month before the album's release. The video network then named him "Artist of the Month" for November 1998, during which time they featured him on their VH-1 *Storytellers* series.

The popular hour-long program gives viewers a sneak peek into the stories behind the songs, with artists trading off live performances with commentary on the song's inspiration. Taped at the Rivera Theater in Chicago in front of a select group of VH-1 contest winners, fan club members and requisite record label and VH-1 staff, along with Elaine Mellencamp, friend/journalist Tim White, friend/VH-1 head John Sykes and songwriting partner George Green—only the second *Storytellers* episode to originate outside of New York—John and band performed standards such as "Small Town," "Pink Houses," "Pop Singer" and a more beat-driven version of "Jack and Diane," with Moe Z playing some of the guitar riffs on keyboard. In between, he talked about the songs and answered questions from the fans.

They filmed the episode the day after the media campaign began for *Mellencamp: Paintings and Reflections*, a book featuring some of John's finest oil paintings, released November 1, 1998. Publisher HarperCollins gave John a $30,000 advance to compile the book, which he in turn donated to VH-1's Save the Music Foundation. "A thousand people in the world deserve to have an art book more than me," the notoriously self-effacing artist told *Billboard*, claiming he didn't want people to think he was being too "uppity" by publishing an art book. Because of VH-1's established relationships with music retailers, the foundation could take advantage of special pricing, which allowed them to purchase nearly $60,000 worth of musical instruments for Chicago-area schools, which John personally delivered. He then stuck around to talk with the students about music, then held a press conference to talk about the importance of Save the Music's mission: music education in schools. As a parent, a supporter of Indiana schools and of the Nordoff-Robbins Center's work in music therapy, John remains a strong advocate for arts education. "He's one of the first artists I came to for Save the Music," says VH-1 CEO John

Sykes. "I asked him if he would go to a school and talk to the kids, and he said absolutely. He's loyal as the day is long. If he believes that someone is doing the right thing, he will fight tooth and nail to support that."

Though he had exhibited his work on occasion throughout the Midwest, the 9x12, 160-page book introduced this "other" creative side to many of his fans for the first time, showing them the dark figures and bold lines developed during his hiatus between *The Lonesome Jubilee* and *Big Daddy*. Once again, Tim White contributed fine prose for the book's introduction.

The promotional blitz for the new John Mellencamp and his new album forged on through the end of the year, with performances on the *Late Show with David Letterman*, the Rosie O'Donnell Show, Canada's MuchMusic and Canadian TV talk show *Open Mike with Mike Bullard*, in addition to regular appearances on VH-1 and MTV. He played a City of Hope cancer hospital benefit with Elvis Costello, Stevie Nicks, James Taylor, Don Henley, Shawn Colvin and country artists BR5-49, Anita Cochran and Deana Carter. They all played songs by one-hit wonders for a prime $500 ticket.

Not long after most of the world rang in the last year of the 20th century, John and a 60-person video crew braced snowy 15-degree weather for about 14 hours as they trekked to the Monroe County courthouse square in Bloomington to shoot the video for "I'm Not Running Anymore," the second single from John's self-titled release. Considering the album's back-to-basics approach (albeit with loops and samples instead of fiddles) and the single's lyrical theme (John wrote the song about his wife Elaine and their two sons), Columbia reps decided to shoot the video in John's hometown, with its regular Saturday morning activities going on in the background.

"The whole idea was to let John do a performance in his hometown. The video will feature images and close-ups of John displayed through multiple boxes, and these boxes will collectively compose John as a person and small town father," video producer David Glean told the *Indiana Daily Student*. "It's been beautiful to do in the snow, and all of these images together make this all about John." The soil upon which his family raised him is as much a part of him as his identities as a songwriter, a husband and a father. To shoot a video that claims that it's "all about John" would have to involve his community, his external family. It's central to his music, it's central to his life.

Rumors began swirling in early 1999 about a short U.S. tour. Shortly after the album's release, John and band played a show at the Bowery Ballroom in New York City, a semi-promotional event held for contest winners and label staff, to be broadcast live on the syndicated radio portal Album Network. The 70-minute show received excellent reviews, with critics stating that a goateed Mellencamp was in fine form and high spirits.

The one-off gig didn't immediately yield a tour; the Rural Electrification

Tour kicked off in April 1999 and continued across the U.S. through July, with alternative roots rockers Sun Volt as the opening act. Little by little, tour manager Harry Sandler added more junkets, stretching the tour through the end of 1999.

While the large-venue tour fared well, each show selling about 13,000 seats, a few special events loomed large on John's calendar. On Saturday, October 23, President Clinton and First Lady Hillary Rodham Clinton hosted "A Concert of the Century," a private event broadcast live on VH-1 in an effort to raise awareness to the network's Save the Music program. A lineup that included Garth Brooks, Eric Clapton, Sheryl Crow, Lenny Kravitz, 'N Sync, John Fogerty and, of course, John Mellencamp performed that afternoon with the White House as their backdrop and celebrities such as Angela Bassett, Robert DeNiro, Calista Fockhart, Gwyneth Paltrow, Sarah Jessica Parker, Keri Russell, Meryl Streep and Kevin Spacey introducing each act. Melissa Etheridge and B.B. King received a standing ovation for their rendition of "When Love Comes to Town," Brooks got attention for his all-American medley and John raised eyebrows with his closing performance of "This Land Is Our Land" with Mike Wanchic, Andy York, Miriam Sturm and Susan Tedeschi as his backing band, and a high school choir and the rest of the afternoon's performers joining in. He didn't realize, or maybe just didn't care, that his old Gibson Dove had "Fuck Fascism" scrawled on the front, a slogan he had carved the night before taping an MTV *Unplugged* performance a few years before. For MTV, he consented to cover the "U" with a "Censorship is UnAmerican" button, but this time, the four-letter word bared itself fully for the whole world to see, especially Bill and Hillary Clinton, who sat in the front row. The White House got a flood of calls complaining about the slogan, but Clinton let it slide.

The Rural Electrification Tour stretched on through December, with last-minute bookings added in Sunrise, FL; Greenville, South Carolina; and Cincinnati, Ohio. Fourteen-year-old blues rocker Shannon Curfman opened the December dates. By the end of the year, the initial 40-date tour had doubled to more than 80 shows. John and band had only a short break before New Year's Eve, when they pulled out all the stops for a holiday "blowout" performance at the Conseco Fieldhouse in Indianapolis. Rumors of an acoustic theater tour continued to swirl; no confirmations yet, but the idea would tie in well with his recently released acoustic-based *Rough Harvest*, his final album under his contract with PolyGram/Mercury. The album's relaxed, acoustic tracks had received mostly favorable reviews, although John himself bristled a bit upon hearing the album's two bonus tracks (which many reviewers advised listeners to skip): A 1985 cover of The Drifters' "Under the Boardwalk" and a live version of his hit single "Wild Night." "I'm dismayed by the record company's decision," John told the *Indianapolis Star*. "They're always looking for some way to bastardize the work you're doing." Adding insult to injury, PolyGram/Mercury released "Under the Boardwalk," a version that sounds out of step with the rest of *Rough Harvest*, as the debut single. Their decision to add the bonus tracks, and their song choice, just further confirms that John made the right decision in leaving the label.

Guests who "partied like it's 1999" with John Mellencamp in Indy paid anywhere from $25 for a nose-bleed seat to $200 for a VIP ticket that included a pre- and post-reception in the Pacers' locker room and practice court. Fan club members were informed that no, neither John nor his band were planning on attending these before and after-parties, and no, not even the priciest ticket would get you backstage. It would get you pasta and salad bars, Asian stir fry, cheese trays, free beer and wine and DJ entertainment before the show, a John Mellencamp midnight toast (his headlining set would stretch past the witching hour), and desserts, munchies and champagne post-concert. The concert lasted until at least 1:30 A.M.—a perfect way to ring in the new Millennium. After a hectic year that included two album releases, a stretched-out concert tour and a slew of promotional shows and special events—not to mention having a new home built that resulted in a messy lawsuit—John gave word to his band that he would take about four months off. He told his manager he wanted to write, and he didn't want to talk to anyone. It was time to reflect, renew and be still for a while so that his next creative vision could surface, allowing him to formulate his next plan of attack.

CHAPTER ELEVEN

VISION AND CONNECTION

B y the time the 1990s came to a close, John had been living in the same house since 1981. The spacious structure located just outside of Bloomington, not far from Lake Monroe, held memories of marriages, divorces, children, grandchildren and more than a few redecorations and renovations. Once he and Elaine married, they bought a vacation home together on Hilton Head, South Carolina, but continued to live in John's already very lived-in home. In 1996, they purchased 56 acres of land on Lake Monroe, an area John has loved and visited often, for most of his life. He had always dreamed of living along its calm waters, and finally, he would see it happen. Initially they thought of building a cozy vacation cabin, but over time the idea evolved into a 10,000-square-foot estate, one that would symbolize their life together, and their future as a family.

Building this "dream home" took many, many more months than planned, and many more problems. They hired local contractor Tim Eldredge, who reportedly "stole" more than $100,000 from the Mellencamps. He was ultimately charged with five counts of forgery and one count of theft, and released on bond after a trial in March 1999. Problems included everything from poor construction, choosing shoddy materials and myriad other problems that resulted in more than one attempt at building and rebuilding. After years of problems, the Mellencamps say they had no choice but to sue.

With all of that drama put to rest, John and Elaine had an impressive finished structure and hired Atlanta-based designers Fred Dilger and Monique Gibson to finish the job. The home is huge, but comfortable, with a mix of

Elaine's affinity for eclectic and John's more traditional tastes melding together within each room. A Burmese bed rests with antique textiles in the master bedroom, a clawfoot bathtub adorns the spacious bathroom and a sturdy family-style wooden table takes center stage in the kitchen. Huge windows open to scenic views of Lake Monroe, shedding ample natural light in every room. Out back, a divided barn contains a basketball court on one side, John's art studio and gym on another. A sweeping terrace overlooking the lake sets off the swimming pool.

This is where John spent the first few months of 2000. He secluded himself from the music industry bustle in order to write some new material, be a father to Hud and Speck (who have a blast playing in the woods and on the basketball court) and enjoy time with Elaine in a relationship that he says still feels like a honeymoon even after eight years. He also spent time conversing with horror novelist Stephen King about collaborating on a stage musical, to be titled *The Ghost Brothers of Darkland County*. The two came together via their mutual CAA agents. "John came to us with the idea for the story," says booking agent Rob Light. "He had the music written, and was looking for someone to write the book. He said, 'This would be the perfect vehicle for Stephen King.' I brought Stephen King's agent into the room, we put the two of them together and it happened. Stephen's a rock junkie, and John's a natural storyteller, so it was a good fit." The story is about two brothers, both in their late teens/early 20s, who "dislike each other immensely," John told *Billboard*. "The father takes them to the family vacation place, a cabin that the boys hadn't been to since they were kids. What has happened is that the father had two older brothers who hated each other and killed each other in that cabin," he continued. "There's a confederacy of ghosts who also live in this house. The older [dead] brothers are there, and they speak to the audience and they sing to the audience. That's all I want to say, except through this family vacation, many things are learned about the family, and many interesting songs are sung."

As of spring 2007, the book and music are both complete, discussions with directors and investors are taking place. "Broadway moves at its own speed," says Light, so a date for production is still being determined.

As the weather warmed up enough for the Mellencamps to actually take a dip in their inviting swimming pool, John received an invitation to give the commencement address on May 6, 2000, for the 171st graduating class of Indiana University. At the same time, the school presented him with an honorary doctorate of musical arts degree. Not only had John become one of Bloomington's most successful exports, but he generously supported the school through the years, donating a portion of his concert proceeds from two recent events to the IU Student Foundation for a scholarship fund. Even more notably, he donated $1.5 million to help fund the school's four-year-old indoor practice facility, which they named the Mellencamp Pavilion in his honor. He also donates his time as a member of the President's Circle, the Hoosier Hundred and the IU Alumni Association. Combined with his tremendous contributions to music, as well as his affinity for IU grads (Kenny Aronoff and Miriam Sturm are both alumni), the doctorate seemed a fitting reward. Luckily, the IU faculty asked John early enough so that he could make a firm, definite commitment to attend. The students asked for him, and by golly, they got him.

Memorial Stadium filled with young 20-somethings in black caps and gowns, some bleary eyed from the previous night's partying, along with family and friends for the 10 A.M. commencement. John wore a cap and gown himself as he walked on stage, but after a perfunctory 'Hi, how ya' doing?" he took them off. Too damn hot. His speech was simple and straightforward—no lofty philosophical statements, no grandiose musings as typical of the yawn-inducing graduation ceremonies. Instead, he spoke their language. With only a few four-letter words peppering his speech, he reinforced his own secret to sustaining a successful career: having a vision and staying connected. Instead of preaching to the new grads, he spoke from his own experience and shared some of the core beliefs that make him John Mellencamp. In regards to his "paint fast, make mistakes" philosophy, he admitted some of his mistakes were "so laughable, it's ridiculous." "I've never given up, and I've never given in," he continued, noting that he's lost many times but always "enjoyed the fight much more than the victory." "Your family and friends are the best things you'll ever know, he said, paraphrasing one of his own songs and assuring the class that they can still rely on their support system. He closed his talk by advising the students to enjoy this life because it's all we've got, and reminded them to "exploit your opportunities and never give up. And always, always, above anything else, always be honest and never kiss ass." Spoken like a true Mellencamp.

Later that month, he left his cozy refuge for Rochester, New York, where he spent two months filming *After Image*, a low-budget ($1.4 million) film directed by Bob Manganelli, a 1983 graduate of Rochester Institute of Technology.

The murder mystery/romance, which also starred actress Louise Fletcher and Terrylene, featured John in the role of crime scene photographer Joe McCormack who left his own home to stay with his aunt (Fletcher) and her deaf assistant (Terrylene). John had to learn sign language to play the part. He studied daily with an instructor for two weeks prior to filming. The film debuted at Sundance in January 2001 and Cannes in May, with John's image prominently featured, although none of his music.

While John exercised his acting abilities in Rochester, the Warner Bros. film *A Perfect Storm* made its theatrical debut, with John's song "Yours Forever" closing the epic ocean disaster tale. Collaborating with renowned composer

James Horner, John had to compile three melodies prevalent throughout the film and translate those melodies from violin to voice, while also penning lyrics to fit the film's intense theme. He turned to George Green to co-write, while Mike Wanchic co-produced the track, recorded at Belmont Mall with John's tried-and-true band. "In writing the lyrics I based 50 percent on the film and 50 percent on the real people on which the film is based," he said. While some critics snub the closing track as marketing-driven pop, he survived this storm with "dignity intact," as one reviewer commented.

As the summer got blistery hot, John decided that he had enough material compiled to record another album. But as he had told the press at the start of the New Year, he wanted to move out of the comfort zone of Belmont Mall, where he'd recorded every album since 1985's *Scarecrow*. "I'm tired of making rock records," he told the *Associated Press*. "I want to make a different kind of record. I want to work with some people who will make other people say, 'Why is he working with this person?'"

This time, John's idea of trying something different meant returning to the same sandy soil where he worked on some of his first few post-DeFries albums. But this time, John, accompanied by his core lineup of guitarist/co-producer Mike Wanchic, Andy York, Dane Clark, Miriam Sturm, John Gunnell, Moe Z and Pat Peterson made the pilgrimage to southern Florida, bypassing by Criteria Recording and ending up at the Florida Keys. In June 2000, when the temperature threatened to soar past 100 degrees with full-on humidity, they set up a mobile recording studio inside an abandoned hurricane shelter in Islamorada, "Sportfishing capital of the world."

Aside from the business ties of making records in Miami, shooting videos and playing numerous concerts throughout the state, John holds a certain affinity for the steamy Gulf coast. One of his favorite playwrights, Tennessee Williams, wrote much of his best work in Florida, and John himself used the Sunshine State as the setting for "Key West Intermezzo (I Saw You First)." In Florida, they call the rural white folks "crackers," a now-derogatory term that used to mean whites of Celtic descent, usually settling in south Florida from Alabama, Georgia and the Carolinas, drawn by its abundant farming and fishing resources. John, although of German descent, can identify with the "crackers" that get looked down upon by the upperclass white folk.

They found idyllic refuge in charming Islamorada, which is filled with boutiques and art galleries and nature trails, all surrounded by clear blue seas brimming with shrimp, tuna, dolphin and sailfish, making it a favorite spot for fishermen, divers and snorkelers alike. The band stayed at an 18-acre resort property called The Moorings, situated on one of the largest white sandy beaches in southern Florida. Tourists came to kayak, swim and windsurf; this crew came to work.

John said he wanted to make a "different" kind of record. With *Cuttin' Heads*, he did. The album's earthy blend of roots rock started off sounding about as laid back as if the band had perched themselves on an Islamorada cottage front porch and turned on the tape machine. And maybe they did! The title track lets us know, via York's Keith Richard-esque guitar riffs, that yes, this is a rock record, but the elements that follow—some obvious, some subtle—point to so much more. There's an almost Appalachian-sounding folk romp on "Women Seem"; upbeat, pure pop melodies and backing vocals on "Peaceful World"; and a mix of acoustic guitar, bass and fiddle running through blues, funk and folk spread throughout the album.

John and band came up with simple arrangements, because John didn't want "anything else to muddle up the melody," he told *Rolling Stone*. "We have some really talented guys and women in the band and they can really play their instruments. You see, that's the difference between us now and, say, 20 years ago. We're fighting the impulse to play like accomplished musicians." He credits one of those musicians, Andy York, as a driving force in *Cuttin' Heads*. "The two of us really made this record," John explained in the album's press materials. "Andy played instruments he didn't even know he could play—pedal steel, bass on half the tracks. It was out of necessity—because it was either me or him. Once we were done with drums and basic tracks [which included John's phenomenal touring band, as well as session superstars like drummer Steve Jordan and bassist Willie Weeks] "it was me on acoustic guitar and Andy would follow along. That's how we came up with the arrangements."

But in front of these deceptively upbeat, straightforward melodies and singable choruses, John writes some of his most powerful and eye-opening verses to date. The title track tackles racism and inter-racial marriage in the Deep South. "Peaceful World" builds on that theme, affirming that "racism lives in the U.S. today," and "I don't want my kids being brought up this way/Hatred to each other is not okay." When he sings "everything is cool as can be in a peaceful world," he does so with more than a hint of sarcasm.

"When people ask why I'd think to even write something like "Peaceful World," I say, "Hey, as far back as 'Now More Than Ever,' I sang, 'Now more than ever, the world needs love, not just a slogan'," John told *Billboard*. "That argument has been out there since the early '90s, and I argued since August 2000 that "Peaceful World" had mass appeal and should be on *Cuttin' Heads*."

"Crazy Island" makes an even fiercer attack on our country, with its "strip malls a growin'/And your handguns and your heresies/Don't hold no responsibility/In this land of easy millions." Other tracks continue the search for peace and happiness in an often tumultuous world, while others, such as "The Same Way I Do," "Women Seem" and the good-natured "Worn Out Nervous Condition," refreshingly talk romance, not politics. The change of scenery and recording environment served them well. John tentatively titled the album *Kiss My Mule*.

In between the June and October sessions in Florida, John decided to have some fun and do a little something special for his fans in the process.

Accompanied by a spartan band that included Sturm (on a few dates, with Chicago-based Merritt Lear subbing on fiddle and mandolin), Indiana-based Mike Flynn on accordion and Mike Wanchic (on most dates), he performed a series of nine impromptu sets that he dubbed the Good Samaritan Tour.

He initially intended the short road trip as a family vacation, but before long, it morphed into a tour that included unannounced spots in Philadelphia, Boston, Pittsburgh, Cleveland, Chicago, Atlanta, Cincinnati and Nashville, concluding with Woodfield Lawn on the IU campus in Bloomington.

"The idea is to be able to just walk out on the street corner like I did 30 years ago with a guitar and just stand there and play," he told *Rolling Stone*. "I call it the Good Samaritan Tour 'cuz we're not gonna charge anything. It's just for the fun of it and if people are having fun with it that day then I'll run with it and if they're not, then I'll just get in the truck and go on. It's like we're really and truly doing the traveling minstrel thing. Although I have to say it's not exactly Jack Kerouac, but, this as close as we can come today."

They usually didn't find a location in each city until the night before. They didn't promote the show, but word generally got out fast among fans. In Chicago, the crowd around the downtown plaza swelled to 25,000, with office workers peeking out of nearby skyscrapers in attempt at a bird's-eye view. The sets John played with his impromptu combo resembled more of a late-night jam session than John's usual highly produced concert performance. He played only a few originals, leaning instead toward cover songs he enjoys to play, including tunes by Woody Guthrie, Bob Dylan, the Rolling Stones and Leadbelly. Flynn and Lear hadn't rehearsed these songs; instead, they just jumped in as best they could.

Though there were only nine of them, the Good Samaritan concerts were a huge success in terms of bringing joy to his fans. At the same time though, he brought a little joy back into he and Wanchic's musical lives, as well as an opportunity of a lifetime for two young string players.

After the October sessions for *Kiss My Mule*, John gave the band the winter off. He had no plans to tour yet, and John presumably wanted some time to live with the tracks. Which he did.

It's not unusual to hear "Pink Houses," "Jack and Diane" or "Cherry Bomb" in just about every public space with a speaker system: the grocery store, the drug store, the local gym, maybe even the bank. But when President-elect George W. Bush decided to use "R.O.C.K. in the U.S.A." at a campaign event, it struck some people as odd. Is this the same artist who turned down former President Reagan's request for "Pink Houses"? And because of his involvement in Farm Aid, as well as the social consciousness of his lyrics, much of the public knows, or at least assumes, the liberal leanings of a man who loves his country, but doesn't love a lot of its citizens' actions. A younger John Mellencamp may have loudly protested the President-to-be's song choice. But today, he kept his cool. "I think that it is good that he likes the song, as an 11-year-old girl I once talked to did," he says. "I don't think that anybody that knows me would think I have the same position as this man. I'm on the other end of the spectrum. But I really think that music is intended to be enjoyed by everybody and I'm sure that is a good thing. And I think it's great that there is a place where these guys can have an opinion and appear to be changing the Republican Party stance, which I think is the main reason to use that song. I think that party needs a new face on it. I think that both parties could use a new face. Quite clearly I'm a liberal. I don't see any sense in being silly about it. It's entertainment. It's a song."

The more John listened to his Moorings tracks, the more they didn't sit well with him. He's always held fast to his vision, and now, he felt the songs didn't clearly represent what he wanted to say with his twenty-first record. He started re-thinking, and then decided to re-cut. Not expecting this change of plans, some of his band had committed to other projects and couldn't make the sessions. He brought in Willie Weeks, who played on a few of John's earlier records, beginning with *Uh-Huh*, to play bass in lieu of John Gunnell, and Steve Jordan nailed some of the drum tracks. The most significant change came when Mike Wanchic had to let his longtime partner go ahead without him. "I had another record [to produce] on the books," he recalls. "The contracts were signed, and then John decided to go back into the studio. I'm his primary bounce-off guy. I know what he likes and doesn't like, how far he can push before it becomes counter-productive, and I wasn't going to be there."

At that point, they had finished most of the recording, but John still needed that "bounce-off" guy who could offer an honest opinion, as well as someone to mix the record. John looked down the very short list of trusted people who could fill such a role. Don Gehman, whom he hadn't worked with since *The Lonesome Jubilee* still topped the list, despite their separation more than 15 years ago. While Gehman surely had to address any lingering wounds afflicted from years of getting buttons pushed, John recalled Gehman's honesty and patience, and knew he would rather work with a "known commodity" than deal with a complete outsider. "One thing that's very scary to us is to bring in an unknown commodity," says Wanchic of their close-knit circle. The band and the people that work closely with them were like family, similar to the Mellencamp clan itself: They stuck together, did what they pleased, didn't give a wit what others thought and didn't much trust those outside the circle. John pulled Don back in, while Paul Mahern sat at the ready behind the console.

During the *John Mellencamp* album, Mahern got to learn from one of the industry's premier engineers, David Thoener. For this record, he picked up even more valuable skills by working alongside one of Thoener's mentors, Don Gehman.

"Don has a really good grasp of what John sounds like, and once he came in, the vocal sessions were really different," says Mahern. "It's not about being correct or in time or in tune, it's much more about attitude. I noticed that we would keep different takes than we would have if Gehman hadn't been there. Plus, there was a really good dynamic because he and John had worked together when they were both younger. He wasn't intimidated by John, and John can be really intimidating."

They re-cut the tracks at Belmont Mall beginning in March 2001. John brought in his same core band from Miami, along with Kenny Childers, who added some additional acoustic guitar and accordion parts. He also hired two new backing vocalists—Jenn Cristy and Courtney Kaiser—to add some embellishments in the studio and later accompany them on tour. Moe Z remarked that Kaiser, whom they nicknamed "Pee Wee," "belted out the lyrics of each and every song as if it might be the last time she sings." Cristy shared that passion, but up until joining John's band, the overachiever showed exceptional promise as both a professional musician and swimmer. The Indiana University senior had just done a bang-up job in the swimming competitions at the Big 10 Championships. A week later, the school invited her to sing the national anthem at an IU men's basketball game so that they could honor her achievements. John, the rabid IU basketball fan he is, heard Cristy's performance and was intrigued enough to approach her after the game. He had an album to finish and a tour coming up, he explained, and would she be interested in joining them? He gave her a day or so to "sleep on it."

Not that she could sleep after receiving the offer of a lifetime. She had excelled in music since childhood, beginning with piano lessons at age four, flute at age 10 and vocals and percussion beginning in high school—all scheduled around many hours of swimming lessons and competitions. She excelled in athletics but loved music, but never knew how to develop a career as a performer—until now. Obviously she accepted John's offer, and shortly after, found herself spending 12-plus hour days at Belmont Mall. Even though she had only a supporting role in the band, she took in as much as she could. "I figured, if this is the only thing I do with my music career," she says, "I'm going to do as much as I can!"

She and Kaiser brought a youthful energy to the Mellencamp fold. They didn't grow up on Dylan or Guthrie. Actually, they hadn't heard much of their music at all, which meant listening to '60s folk and rock became as much a part of her homework assignment as taking up piano lessons again.

John spiced up the Indiana sessions by bringing in a number of guest artists. Trisha Yearwood came up to Belmont to add her powerful vocals to "Deep Blue Heart," one of the album's standout tracks. "She showed up and for some reason John was running late," says Mahern. "We were probably there for about an hour before they showed up, so I went ahead and got sounds and found the microphone she wanted to sing into. I knew what lines John wanted her to sing, so we cut her vocals before they got there, and it was great—the first thing that came out of her mouth was amazing. We put it together, and when John showed up he said, 'Oh, that's great.' Maybe we fixed one line or something, but her [first take] was effortless, and what she was naturally doing was just the right thing."

Rapper Chuck D gave an equally powerful performance on the title track, a song that evolved out of a conversation that John and Pat Peterson had in Florida. They were listening to a popular rap/hip-hop song and Peterson expressed her distaste in the song's offensive lyrics. The song made frequent use of the n-word, and she felt that the derogatory term had gotten so overused that it had become slang, and a word that the white kids think is okay—which is not okay.

The lovely India.Arie came in later, also to Indiana (no shuttling Pro Tools files back and forth with anyone) to record her embellishments to "Peaceful World."

Despite their diversity in musical styles, all of these guests shared an admiration for John's music. Yearwood voiced her opinion most publicly; she often sang "Small Town" in concert. Chuck D. confided to *Rolling Stone* that "Anywhere you go in America, you're going to hear a John Mellencamp song." Drummer Steve Jordan agrees, noting, "John grew up hearing black music in the Midwest. He played it in his own bands, and you hear his appreciation and understanding of it in all his great rock songs, like 'Pink Houses' and 'Cuttin' Heads.' Any musician who works with John, whether it's me or Chuck, gets into John's music, because he's got the melodies and the lyrics you want to hear. He's got the songs, just like everybody else who's great in popular music and who didn't care about the boundaries—like Jimi Hendrix, who had to leave America and go to England to be himself. John makes American music, music for all of us and that's why I think *Cuttin' Heads* may be his best work ever."

John even took the official title from some of rock's founding fathers—the early blues players. "Cuttin' heads is what the old blues guys used to do to each other," he told *Rolling Stone*. "On a weekend or a hot summer night, they would get on a street corner and start playing. And down the block would be another blues guy playing for change, and whoever drew the crowd would be the winner and they called it cuttin' heads. Robert Johnson was the king of cuttin' heads. He always cut everybody's head 'cause when Robert Johnson showed up, everybody was [saying], 'Fuck that guy! We quit. He's gonna get the crowd.'" John hoped to cut a few proverbial heads with this album. He knew how to get the crowd, only now he had to find ways to keep them.

It had been some 25 years since a young John Mellencamp saw the cover of his first album, *Chestnut Street Incident*, emblazoned with his unwanted epithet, Johnny Cougar. He and his band had evolved from playing to crowds of two bartenders to arenas seating tens of thousands and the man himself has matured from an immature kid who chased women, sang cover songs and lived the rock 'n' roll lifestyle, to a skillful storyteller and socially conscious spokesman for American farmers and the working class. He was a man who openly took a stand against racism and overblown corporate America.

He embarked on his next tour in late July 2001 with his new album slotted for an October 16, 2001 release. He tapped AAA radio-friendly rock band The Wallflowers (led by Bob Dylan's son, Jakob) to open the 27-city jaunt. He planned for a stripped-down tour, although stripped-down for John still meant three backing vocalists and a full band delivering a high energy, pitch-perfect stage show, but no pyrotechnics, no elaborate props or fancy video displays. He envisioned an all-black stage, much like the dark nightclubs he played years ago. They would kick off the tour at San Diego State University, then continue north, through Canada, before making their way across the east coast to their two-night concluding performances at Indianapolis' Verizon Wireless Ampitheater.

Their set included 64 songs. The band delivered their expected spot-on performance, John sang as well as ever and new additions Cristy and Kaiser added new energy on stage. Cristy accompanied violinist Miriam Sturm on flute, then switched to tambourine to interact with drummer Dane Clark, played percussion in tandem with Kaiser and sang and danced alongside the frontman. Offstage, Kaiser and Cristy palled around together or met up with Moe Z, who later joined Cristy's band when she launched a solo career. The rest of the band caught up on the events of one another's husbands, wives and children, told and/or listened to off-color (or just plain bad) jokes. Elaine Mellencamp often packed up Hud and Speck to meet John in various cities across the U.S., and as a family they sampled "funnel cakes and roller coasters from coast to coast," she says. Elaine tries to make the boys' mini-vacations both fun *and* educational, so much so that even at ages six and seven, the two boys voluntarily sought out museums and other attractions in whatever town they visited. "Everything's about experiencing as much as you can in life, and that's what we try to do," says Elaine. It takes a bit of effort on both of their parts to accommodate one another's busy schedules, but the benefits of a balanced, healthy relationship are certainly worth it.

Toward the beginning of September 2001, with "Peaceful World" already on the airwaves," John spent a week in New York hitting the major morning and late-night talk shows, including a live performance for the *Today* show on September 7. At week's end, John, Elaine and their boys flew from Manhattan to Montreal, where he would play his next show. They looked out over the New York City skyline, and noticed the World Trade Center's Twin Towers shooting up amongst the steel of the city. How lucky, Elaine told John and the kids, that they could see such a remarkable sight from an airplane window. Not everyone gets to do that.

John and the band played the show in Montreal, then received word the next morning that they would not fly across the Canadian border that day, and neither would anyone else, because at 8:46 A.M., EST, Al Qaeda hijackers crashed two planes into WTC's North and South Towers, both of which collapsed, killing thousands of innocent people. For the first time since his 1994 heart attack, John cancelled a performance (in Hartford, Connecticut), this time under the most horrific conditions imaginable. In addition to the attacks in New York City, another hijacked plane hit the Pentagon outside Washington D.C., and a fourth plane crashed into a field in Pennsylvania. For the first time in U.S. history, the administration halted all flights at our nation's airports. The U.S. military is placed on high alert, and New York City firefighters and policemen make their absolute best attempt to rescue as many victims as possible.

Separated from their loved ones, some of the band members wanted to stop the tour altogether and just go home. But they couldn't go home. They couldn't go anywhere. Once given permission by U.S. authorities, they soldiered on (it's the Mellencamp way), which in the midst of the worst tragedy in U.S. history, turned out to be a blessing not only for them, but for thousands of Americans. They were cleared to fly on September 13, which allowed them to make it to their next booked performance; fittingly, in our country's birthplace—Boston. They were one of the first major acts to play in the U.S. after the attacks, and while they initially wondered if anyone would come out at all, the Tweeter Center concert turned out to be one of the most memorable of their careers.

"To see the energy in the people—the American flag, the patriotism, the want and desire for us to be there—was so memorable," says John Gunnell. "It's burned in my memory forever. It was absolutely fantastic. I remember looking at the people in the first two rows, and seeing the sense of patriotism on their face."

The band returned to a very different Manhattan a month and a half after the attacks to perform in The Concert for New York City, the massive, now-historic affair that took place at Madison Square Garden on October 20, 2001. Over the course of nearly six hours, New York firefighters, police officers, survivors, families and fans all came together to witness unparalleled performances from event organizer Sir Paul McCartney, as well as David Bowie, Eric Clapton, Destiny's Child, Billy Joel and James Taylor and many, many more, all of whom donated their time to one highly worthy cause: to lift the spirits of the people of New York. Jenn Cristy, new to this high level of musical performance, calls it the "most rewarding musical experience of her life." "Everybody was a rock star that night," she says, recalling that firefighters, backup singers and lead singers all got equal respect. "When The Who went on, you felt the whole ground start shaking!" Cristy didn't know who The Who was before that night, but her boss sure did, way back from 20 years prior as their warm-up act.

Cuttin' Heads hit stores about a month after the September 11 attacks, and its single "Peaceful World," became an anthem of hope, its verses ironically fitting despite the fact that John wrote them more than a year before. The single shot up to Number 11 on the Adult Top 40 chart, the closest he'd come to Top 10 since "Key West Intermezzo (I Saw You First)" in 1996. The album peaked at Number 15 on the *Billboard* 200 chart and hit Number Six on the Top Internet Albums chart.

As the year closed, John would receive two of the music industry's highest honors, one marking his achievements over the past year, the other celebrating the scope of his entire career. In December 2001, the Recording Academy announced their nominees for the forthcoming Grammy Awards. John earned one nomination for "Best Male Rock Vocal Performance." This year, just like every other year, he didn't attend the Awards ceremony, and like every other year since 1982, he didn't win.

"The members of NARAS [Recording Academy] vote for the Grammy's, and who are the members of NARAS? The record companies, the trendsetters," states Mike Wanchic, emphasizing John's desire to stay true to his vision rather than follow the trends, as well as his indifference toward playing the "game." If he'd have schmoozed a little more, maybe he'd have more trophies, but accumulating hardware sits closer to the bottom of his priority list. "We've really just tried to make our career real, just going out to the garage where we *still* rehearse; coming up with songs; going into the studio by ourselves and recording them; putting them out there; honestly going out and playing the songs live; and making an honest career out of it. Not too many whistles and bells, not a lot of hairspray. That's worked out well for us."

Throughout his career, John has insisted that the public judge him by his music, and to a lesser extent his painting, rather than his wardrobe, his celebrity friends or how many times his picture ends up in a tabloid. For someone who's lived most of his adult life in the public eye, he doesn't scramble for the spotlight, doesn't take compliments well and takes little credit for his creative achievements and many of his good deeds. He's brought countless dollars to Farm Aid, but doesn't make a fuss over it. "Many times we'll hear about a group or a company that he is doing a show for, and all of a sudden we get a donation [from them] directed to us by John," says Farm Aid executive director Carolyn Mugar. "He doesn't even call to tell us, because he doesn't want credit for this stuff."

Much of his music has been omnipresent (who doesn't know the chorus to "Hurts So Good" or "Jack and Diane"?) in American culture, and he was one of the first contemporary rock artists to meld traditional acoustic instruments with electric guitar, bass and drums into what people would now call Americana. But by and large, John has been mostly unrecognized for his accomplishments until 2001, when *Billboard* magazine presented John with its highest honor, the Century Award for distinguished creative achievement. At the insistence of editor-in-chief Timothy White, *Billboard* established the award in 1992 as a means to "acknowledge the uncommon excellence of one artist's still-unfolding body of work. Moreover, the award focuses on those singular musicians who have not been accorded the degree of serious regard their achievements deserve."

White deemed John "arguably the most important roots-rocker of his generation" and stated that his is "rock music that tells the truth on both its composer and the culture he's observing." The Award also recognizes the fact that "all of his bands have been integrated, and all his finest recordings have openly acknowledged the meld of gospel/blues/R&B strains with European-derived song lines, band forms and parlor ballads; this mix is the crucible of the American musical experience."

This roller-coaster of a year, John's fiftieth, closed on a high note, with John attending the *Billboard* Music Awards at Las Vegas' MGM Grand Garden Arena in December to accept his hand-crafted award. Jeweler/sculptor Tina Marie Zippo-Evans carved John's award from hardwood using a hammer that once belonged to his grandfather, Speck. This award, more than any other, meant something to John.

CHAPTER TWELVE

SAYING GOODBYE

With *Cuttin' Heads* now certified Gold, in the spring of 2002, John's fans received word of another tour, this one dubbed the Summer Work Tour. Kicking off in Burgettstown, Pennsylvania, just outside of Pittsburgh in July 2002, the tour would pick up where the 2001 dates left off, continuing initially through August, although they would add more dates through the end of the year.

Before the tour commenced, however, John announced his decision to leave Columbia Records. Just walked in and told them. They parted amicably, though he later admitted that he got sick of arguing about the content of his albums—they didn't have to like them, he argued. They just had to sell them. But they disagreed about "Peaceful World" specifically; the label wondered why he couldn't have just made all of the words as, well, peaceful as the chorus? Because that's not the way the song came out. Goodbye, Columbia. Also, with the industry in transition (aka, ruled by the "Mickey Mouse Club" of tween pop artists) he thought it best to explore other options. He had his painting and he had a stage musical in development with blockbuster horror novelist Stephen King. Almost as soon as he gave Columbia his walking papers, other record labels began courting him. But he told them that for the time being, he wanted to focus on things he hadn't done before, which is the way he's always preferred it.

All projects came to a halt when less than a month later, he received word that one of his closest friends and strongest business allies, *Billboard* chief Timothy White had died of a heart attack at age 50. The news shocked the entire music community and left many devastated, especially his wife, Judy, and twin 10-year-old boys (one of them autistic). John, a man who lets only a chosen few into his close circle of friends, took the news very hard. "It was so unexpected," says Elaine Mellencamp. "No one expected that Tim was going to leave for work one day and not come back. Going back to John's own heart attack, it resonated with him on a very personal level, and they were very close. He's still missed."

White served as John's sounding board, the one he shared his ideas and songs with almost daily. He knew he would get an honest opinion from White and trusted him for his conscience and sound judgment. He also appreciated how attentively White listened to his music. "Tim would notice the subtle nuances in John's music that most people would miss," says Elaine.

Though it began out of a journalist-artist relationship, their friendship extended beyond their business lives. Their families vacationed together, and their kids became close friends. When White passed away, John was one of the pallbearers at Tim's funeral. Warner Bros. publicity head Bob Merlis, a friend and colleague of White's who had also followed John's career since hearing him at the Whisky back in 1976, flew to Boston on short notice to attend the funeral. He also attended White's interment, where John sang "Amazing Grace," joined by Miriam Sturm.

Not long after that day, Merlis signed on as John's publicist. He'll never claim to be the sounding board that Tim was, but their mutual love of the man brought them together. Merlis soon had his work cut out for him, too, as John quickly set about helping to organize a benefit concert for White's family, to be held in Boston on October 7, 2002. Celebs such as James Taylor, Sheryl Crow, Sting, Don Henley, Billy Joel and Roger Waters voluntarily flew to Boston on their own dime to play the first concert, then to Madison Square Garden in New York the next night for the second event. When John took the stage, he played one of White's favorite songs: Robert Johnson's "Stones in My Passway." The concert closed with an all-star rendering of the gospel number "This Train Is Bound for Glory" bidding their friend farewell.

"It was a very therapeutic thing for everyone involved," Elaine Mellencamp says of the concerts. Even today, the Mellencamps welcome White's boys to their Indiana home, where they can play football and goof off with computers and video games with Hud and Speck. "It's good for them to stay in touch with Tim's friends to give them a different perspective of their Dad. Plus, it's nice for us, too."

During rehearsals for the Summer Work Tour, John noticed that his vibrant backup singer, Jenn Cristy, lacked her usual verve. She wasn't smoking cigarettes (John, of course, would notice this), she didn't join in on the usual post-rehearsal beer and she seemed a little more reserved than usual. John pulled her aside. "What's going on? You're being grumpy." She tried to deny that anything was wrong, but after more prodding, she broke down. "I'm pregnant!" she told him. Oh. They discussed her situation, and he asked if she would be okay to tour. She thought she would be fine, especially once her appetite came back.

She made it through six shows before it became clear she would not be fine to finish the tour. She didn't have her usual boundless energy, making it difficult to finish their intense two-hour performance. Again, he pulled Cristy aside to talk, but this time they mutually agreed that she should quit the tour. She went back to Indiana to spend the rest of her pregnancy at home with her fiancé and family, leaving Moe Z and the others to take up the slack on stage. When they arrived to the Verizon Wireless Music Center in Noblesville, Indiana, on July 12, they invited her to join them on stage during an acoustic rendition of "Small Town." She accepted, and she and her now-husband turned it into a prelude to their honeymoon. "We drove up the night of our wedding day," Cristy recalls. "It was really nice to get such a great warm welcoming."

In the summer of 2002, John really put the "work" into the Summer Work Tour. He threw Andy York, his reliably ambidextrous guitarist, a curveball when he said he wanted to perform some material with a slide guitar *a la* Robert Johnson. York accepted the challenge, and promptly armed himself with a Robert Johnson songbook, CDs, videotape and the all-important National steel guitar, and then "pretty much sequestered myself in my room for about six weeks," he recalls. He learned how to play "Stones in My Passway" first, which they played at the 2002 Farm Aid and at White's benefit concerts.

To his surprise, John got a call from Columbia's then-president Don Lenner, who asked him to record an entire album of early folk, blues, country and gospel. He wondered if he owed them another album. He wondered if this might be his last album ever. Either way, it felt like the right thing to do. It was actually an idea that had crossed his mind during the making of *John Mellencamp*, a time when he tuned out most music save for Johnson, Woody Guthrie and Hank Williams. He had already begun deeply researching material during the past year, and at this point, he began to dig deeper. Trouble is, the deeper you dig, the more you discover.

He sifted through hundreds, maybe thousands, of songs—American roots treasures covering delta, Texas and west coast blues, country and folk. He found so many good ones, he had a hard time narrowing the list down to an album's worth of material. He came close, then called in the troops to the Belmont Mall rehearsal studio.

Mike Wanchic, Andy York, Dane Clark and John convened at the first sign of 2003 to "test drive" John's song list; some didn't work, but the ones that did purred like a classic Mustang. Fellow Bloomington native Hoagy Carmichael

("Baltimore Oriole"), Woody Guthrie ("Johnny Hart"), Lucinda Williams ("Lafayette"), Philly group Dickie Doo and the Don'ts ("Teardrops Will Fall") and Skeeter Davis ("The End of the World") were all represented, their songs worked and reworked by John and band until they became their own. Once they had the songs' basic structures nailed down, they called in for backup; namely, John Gunnell, Miriam Sturm, Toby Myers and their new accordion player, Mike Ramos. Again, they worked long hours for many days rehearsing the material, working up each song until it sparkled with their warm energy. John wanted himself and his band to have a "stage-ready level" of the material, meaning that they could play them to near-perfection at the drop of a hat. In this case, "stage-ready level" also meant "studio ready," as John wanted to record them as a band would have in the early '60s—run it through from top to bottom. If you screw up, move on to take two. In those days, technology did not allow for easy fixes. "We'll fix it in the mix" was not an option.

Further emphasizing the music's original state, John wanted to record live-to-tape using vintage tape machines and microphones. To pull this off efficiently and expertly, he needed an engineer that was well versed in these "old school" methods of recording, and of the analog tape machines and tube microphones he wanted to use. Almost unanimously, band members recommended Ray Kennedy, a Nashville-based producer/engineer best known for his longtime partnership with Steve Earle, but also the mastermind behind albums by Billy Joe Shaver, Lucinda Williams, David Allen Coe and Jack Ingram, among others. His studio, Room and Board, had earned an equally stellar reputation for its extensive collection of tube microphones and vintage equipment—exactly what John wanted.

During their initial conversations about the album and the recording environs, Kennedy immediately deduced that some modifications would be in order. "As we got closer [to the recording dates] I said, 'John, if you really want to commit to making an analog record, we should put 16-track heads on your tape machine," Kennedy recalls. "The 16-track heads will sound way better."

They brought over the 16-track headstack from Wanchic's studio, Echo Park, for John's Otari MX-80 machine. Kennedy then filled his Hyundai Santa Fe SUV to the roof with gear from Room and Board, including vintage microphones, old mic preamps, drums, guitars and guitar amps. To bypass the mediocre sound of Belmont Mall's Trident console, Kennedy brought racks of classic API mic pre's and EQs. He also brought up Telefunken KM56 and V76 microphones for the acoustic guitar, mandolin, and violin, and a precious RCA ribbon mic for Clark's drums. (Clark used Kennedy's Slingerland set for these sessions.)

Kennedy arrived a day early to set up all of his gear, then on day one of the *Trouble No More* sessions, he arrived hours before the band to further test and troubleshoot the equipment. When the band showed up promptly, instruments in tow, Kennedy positioned Clark and Myers in the main room; York, Wanchic and, when required, Sturm, in their own isolation booths; accordion player Ramos in a back room; and John in his own vocal booth. When the band started to play the first song, Kennedy opened up the doors just a bit so that each instrument's sound would naturally bleed into one another, which helped to create the live sound they wanted. The band recorded almost every song in one or two takes, three max. As usual, John sang his vocals live and fixed very little after the fact. "He may have fixed a couple words here and there, but not much," says Kennedy.

Most days, they recorded a song, then took a break while Kennedy mixed the song to half-inch tape. After listening back to their work, they promptly moved on to the next song. The whole album took only a week to record, with the band usually recording three songs a day. "There's a consistent sound to the record when you put it on; it's timeless sounding," says Kennedy. "Because it's pretty much all live performances, it shows off quite well that it's a *real* record—there's not a lot of messing around."

The atmosphere usually stayed as relaxed as the songs themselves. Periodically, Elaine Mellencamp would drop by with Hud and Speck so they could visit with their Dad and spend time in the studio, which they loved to do. Sometimes Elaine brought her camera, which resulted in the black and white shots featured on the inside booklet.

"Over the years, I noticed that John really hated having his picture taken," she recalls. "I'd taken lots of pictures of the boys, because that's natural for a mom. Gradually I became very fond of using the camera, and have some experience on the other side of one. But being in front of the camera does not feel natural for John, so I thought I could easily make him more comfortable. It's just your family." Mrs. Mellencamp also has full VIP access 24/7, and is equally welcomed by the band, so to have her observing the sessions with camera in hand felt natural for everyone.

They had a more difficult time ignoring the video cameras. John wanted to document the *Trouble No More* sessions, and contacted Ron Osgood, a telecommunications professor at Indiana University, to ask if he would be interested in making this a "hands on" project for his students. It took a bit of planning on the professor's part to get enough students involved so that they could properly capture the 12-hour a day, five-days-a-week sessions, but they pulled it off exceptionally well. Their efforts resulted in an accompanying *Trouble No More* DVD with cinematography, graphics, post-production, writing, directing and, of course, filming, all handled by IU students. For the most part, the band, Kennedy and crew tried to pretend they weren't there, and when tense situations occurred, such as an argument between Kennedy and John, for example, the students didn't back away from the camera.

The only real time to goof off came at the end of the day, after Kennedy had mixed the final song for the day. Then he could kick back with John and others from the band, who would tell stories, bad jokes and discuss the day's work. The kitchen served as the best listening station. If it sounded good in the kitchen, they knew they had "the mix."

Columbia released *Trouble No More* on June 3, 2003, with "Teardrops Will Fall" as its first single. But the song that got the most attention was "To Washington," released in March 2003 as a free download on *JohnMellencamp.com*. It's a traditional song, originally written in 1903, and later updated by the Carter Family and then Woody Guthrie as "Baltimore to Washington." The artists modified the lyrics from generation to generation, but the overall theme—political protest—remained intact. John's version questions President George W. Bush's motives at waging war against Iraq: "So a new man in the White House with a familiar name/Said he had some fresh ideas, but it's worse now since he came/From Texas to Washington and he wants to fight with many/And he says it's not for oil/He sent out the National Guard / To police the world." When they recorded the song, it didn't really occur to John that there would be a problem. He's recorded "socially scathing" songs before, but in our post-9/11 fear-based society, it hit a nerve on both the left and right ends of the spectrum.

Columbia, of course, asked him not to put it on the record, but they knew his response before they even asked. They feared he would experience the same harsh treatment as the Dixie Chicks, who made an anti-George W. Bush comment not long before, which resulted in death threats, a number of country radio stations refused to play their songs and certain organizations held bonfires to burn their CDs. John laughed at the idea that anyone would call *him*, Mr. Heartland rock himself, un-American. But sure enough, a public that had supported him for decades called John, one of the most pro-American artists of his generation, just that. Radio listeners fumed about "To Washington." "When the song first came out I was in the car one day and we were driving to the airport and I had my kids with me and a radio station was playing 'To Washington' and having callers call in," John told *Salon.com*. "Some guy comes on and says, "I don't know who I hate the most, John Mellencamp or Osama bin Laden." My kids heard that and my nine-year-old said, "Dad, are they talking about you? Why are people mad at you?"

Heated responses flooded his website when he initially asked for comments about the song. But time passed, and in just a few short months, people's reactions cooled, as some of them started to question the war themselves.

John insisted that "To Washington" was not a protest or anti-war song, merely a statement of the times. Maybe so, but his political beliefs come through loud and clear when he refers to our previous eight years of "peace and prosperity." He's said that his politics haven't changed much in the past 20 years, even though the country's surely have. He inherited his liberal leanings from his parents, who were both active in Jackson County politics. His mother campaigned for Bobby Kennedy and John grew up "surrounded by Democrats."

On the road, he started projecting the Albert Einstein quote, "You cannot simultaneously prevent and prepare for war" behind the stage. In October 2003, he and Elaine expressed their views in depth in an open letter published on *CommonDreams.org*:

"Who is to say what is or isn't 'patriotic'? Do the flags that wave from every minivan really offer any support? Where is the support for the thousands of service men and women who return to the states to see their benefits cut, their health problems ignored, their jobs gone and their families living in poverty? How are they repaid for their efforts; for risking or losing their lives? So far, dismally.

"This nation was founded to enable freedom and diversity of opinion, and many lives have been lost to secure that liberty. Paradoxically, some still resist the open mindedness that is the very foundation of this country." It's time for a change.

CHAPTER THIRTEEN

THE CAMPAIGN TRAIL
TOWARD FREEDOM'S ROAD

John didn't formally tour in support of *Trouble No More*. Instead, he played a few select dates—most notably an April 9 tribute concert celebrating Farm Aid partner Willie Nelson's seventieth birthday—took on a few short-term projects and focused some attention on his musical with Stephen King. In April, he teamed with country artist Travis Tritt to record the duet "What Say You," to appear on Tritt's forthcoming album, *My Honky Tonk History*. Aside from recording a good song, the union further emphasized John's influence on both rock and country. Acts such as Sheryl Crow and Hootie and the Blowfish cite John's folk-rock-country hybrid as an influence as much as roots and country acts such as Tritt, Keith Urban and Kenny Chesney, the later of whom performed with John on an episode of *CMT Crossroads* in 2003. Chesney, who often closed his set with "Jack and Diane," was just another East Tennessee kid in pajamas watching John perform on the 1983 AMA Awards, but his music stuck with Chesney. He remained a fan and his music, while deeply rooted in country traditions, has a rebellious edge that could call to mind some of John's earlier work. "Everybody rose to the occasion really well," says Dane Clark of the *Crossroads* performance. "John did great on Kenny's stuff, and Kenny couldn't have been a nicer guy. He obviously knew John's songs, and it was fun to hear John put his own stamp on Kenny's songs, kind of roughen them up a little bit."

Musically, the pairing with Tritt also fit, and "What Say You" quickly climbed toward the top of *Billboard*'s country singles chart. Politically, however, they made an odd couple. Just a few months later, Tritt would play during the

Republican National Convention, while John played seriously for the other team. But their deeper values and musical commonalities trumped any party differences. "I've admired his music for so many years," Tritt told *Rolling Stone*. "I also admire his integrity. Very much like me, he has resisted all outside pressures to change his music or let anybody tell him what his music should be. And the fact that I thought our voices would work well together, even though we have different political viewpoints, really illustrates what this song is about."

Also in April, John performed with comedian Tom Dreeson as part of Bob Costas' charity event for the Cardinal Clennon Children's Hospital, which packed the Fox Theatre in St. Louis and raised more than $550,000 for the Bob Costas Cancer Center. He and Costas have been friends since the early '90s, when he appeared on the sportscaster's *Later* show. The night before the benefit, Costas took John to the NCAA tournament games at the Edward Jones Dome. John, who's traveled to the city to catch Indiana University games, was thrilled to be his date for the night.

The year rolled on with John recording a cover of the folk song "Wreck of the Old 97" for the compilation CD *The Rose & the Briar: Death, Love and Liberty in the American Ballad* (a companion disc to the book of the same name, written by Sean Wilentz and Greil Marcus) and "The World Don't Bother Me None," exclusively for the Disney documentary *America's Heart and Soul*, which opened July 2 in limited U.S. release.

As the summer closed, John decided to hit the campaign trail as part of the groundbreaking pro-Kerry Vote for Change Tour that hit key cities up to election day.

John was down in the Florida Keys working on *Cuttin' Heads* when the 2000 elections hit, and admittedly, he didn't give the whole ordeal much thought. But four years and more than enough anti-American jabs later, he saw things differently. He saw a country plagued by fear, and politicians playing off of that fear. That's not right, he thought, and it's time to at least *try* to do something about it. For the first time in his life, the Indiana native felt like a stranger in a strange land, and that's not right, either.

In July, he performed as part of a star-studded fundraiser for Senators John Kerry and John Edwards at Radio City Music Hall in New York City and raised a reported $7.5 million. Supporters put down $1,000 per ticket to hear John perform "The Texas Bandito," an original ditty that expressed his disapproval of the current administration. He followed that with the comparatively tame "Pink Houses." Other acts on the bill that night included the Dave Matthews Band, Jon Bon Jovi, Wyclef Jean, Mary J. Blige and John Fogerty. John then led the house through "This Land Is Your Land," with Matthews, Fogerty and Bon Jovi taking over lead vocals on the subsequent verses. Kerry strapped on a guitar and strummed along, while Edwards and Bon Jovi shared a mike. The "Bush bash," as naysayers called it, was produced by some old friends of Mellencamp's: Infinity Broadcasting chairman and CEO John Sykes, Miramax films co-chairman Harvey Weinstein and *Rolling Stone* editor/publisher Jann S. Wenner.

From there, he returned to his home state for additional performances in conjunction with the Democratic National Convention, with John and Elaine both receiving publicity for their participation. "Small Town" and "Your Life Is Now" were used as theme songs for vice presidential candidate John Edwards. For fun, he and Elaine would sneak out periodically and stick a Kerry-Edwards sign in their Republican neighbors' front yards. By the next morning though, those blue signs were gone.

But the main event of John's campaign efforts occurred on October 1, 2004, when the Vote for Change Tour kicked off for its two-week run, to hit 33 cities in 11 swing states, including Florida, Ohio, Pennsylvania, Michigan, Iowa, Wisconsin, Missouri, Minnesota, Virginia, Arizona, Washington, New Jersey (this one added at Bruce Springsteen's request, after he learned that Kerry and Bush were running a close race) and concluding with a concert at MCI Center in Washington D.C. Artists such as Springsteen, Dave Matthews, Pearl Jam, R.E.M., Kenneth "Babyface" Edmonds, John and the Dixie Chicks all went out guns-a-blazing during this music/politics combo; they strongly urged fans to vote on November 2, 2004; specifically, for Democrat John Kerry. "I'm here to support change, freedom and democracy for all of us," John told the D.C. crowd, "not just the rich of us." Then, he launched into "Pink Houses."

"Vote for Change is a historic undertaking in a number of respects," *Rolling Stone* reported. "It is a milestone in grass-roots campaigning, a whistle-stop invasion of the most deadlocked states in the presidential race by the biggest names in music. It is certainly the most logistically complex rock tour ever mounted: six separate bills hitting select cities in one state on the same night. And Vote for Change marks the first time that many of the artists—including Matthews, R.E.M., Pearl Jam, the Dixie Chicks and, most prominently, Springsteen—have ever publicly stumped for a presidential candidate."

The Vote for Change concert tour raised a reported $15 million for America Coming Together, a group organizing get-out-the-vote drives for Democrats, and identified 300,000 potential new members for the political action committee associated with *MoveOn.org*, an online liberal advocacy group. The concerts attracted pockets of protesters in nearly every city, along with swelling crowds of supporters. In the end, Kerry lost the election, but the efforts of these artists raised some important issues that would keep the fight going for the next four years.

During the Vote for Change Tour, John played five dates with fellow

Indiana native Kenny "Babyface" Edmonds. Apparently, the two had a good rapport, as John would tap the super-producer/artist/songwriter to produce two new songs for his *Words and Music* retrospective, issued in the midst of the Vote for Change whirlwind on October 19, 2004.

With 21 studio albums and 22 Top 10 songs to his credit, John certainly deserved, and had the material for, a proper greatest hits collection. The 1997 release, *The Best That I Could Do*, only covered his personal favorites up to 1988. This one would cover the entire gamut, beginning with seminal tunes such as "This Time" and "I Need a Lover," up to freshly written songs such as "Walk Tall" and "Thank You."

John and band (Rick Lawson stepped in for Dane Clark; Reggie Hamilton in lieu of John Gunnell) recorded the two new songs at Belmont Mall with Babyface adding his expertise at his own facility, Brandon's Way in Los Angeles. Paul Mahern assumed engineering duties in Indiana, with Jon Gass handling the bulk of the mixing in L.A. They recorded the song in their usual performance-driven style, although Babyface brought the more layered, Pro Tools-centric methods commonly used on R&B tracks to the process. John observed Edmonds stacking about 40 vocal tracks for backgrounds harmonies onto "Walk Tall." "I couldn't do that in 10 years," he told *Rolling Stone*.

As he wrote the song, John kept the philosophies of Woody Guthrie in mind. With so many outside forces putting out messages of fear and anger these days, when he got the inspiration to write an inspirational song, he took it.

"I heard Woody Guthrie say in some kind of documentary that it was important for him to write songs about people and try to make them feel good about themselves," John told CMT. "He said, 'I ain't gonna write no more songs that would make anybody feel bad about themselves.' And I always kind of took that with me as a songwriter."

With "Thank You," he took that idea one step further. "It's another attempt at writing an inspirational song," he said. "It has a lot in common with the feeling of "Pink Houses" or something like that. You know, I've written hundreds of songs, but I only really ever wrote four of 'em. I mean, I write the same four songs 4,000 times. You know, I got about four topics I can deal with, and then anything other than that and I'm lost. I'm not a very good love-song writer. I have one love song on the record ["This Time"], and when it comes on, I want to burn the clothes I have on, because it's so silly."

It's no coincidence considering how much exposure MTV and VH-1 had given him through the years that nearly every song on the album had a video to go with it. The bonus DVD contains five of them: "Crumblin' Down," "R.O.C.K. in the U.S.A.," "Rain on the Scarecrow," "Check It Out" (live) and "Key West Intermezzo (I Saw You First)."

As the album hit retailers, John and his regular band prepared for a slew of promotional appearances, most notably A&E's *Live by Request* concert program, an interactive show that allows viewers to call in, talk to the band and request their favorite songs. Fans from all over the U.S. asked for hits from the various eras of John's career: the John Cougar, John Cougar Mellencamp *and* John Mellencamp years. He performed from Buskirk-Chumley Theater in Bloomington, Indiana, which marked his first performance in the 1920s-era theater. Local Mellenheads were disappointed that they couldn't attend in person, but happily raised a glass during a viewing party held at The City Grille nearby. The *Washington Post* got VIP access to both the rehearsal and performance. Staff writer Sean Daly observed a 53-year-old John Mellencamp lighting up another American Spirit—clearly ignoring the historic space's no-smoking policy. Hud, Speck and Elaine Mellencamp looked on as well, joining a crew of A&E cameramen, audio engineers and miscellaneous executives as John and band ran through "Pink Houses," "Rain on the Scarecrow" and a feedback-riddled "Small Town." As expected, the soundmen caught hell for that one.

On Thanksgiving afternoon, John and his band headed to Ford Field during the Detroit Lions vs. Indianapolis Colts game to play during the halftime show. They performed "R.O.C.K. in the U.S.A." and "Walk Tall," with Kenny "Babyface" Edmonds joining them for the first live televised performance of the new single.

The New Year started with the Words and Music Tour, which would ultimately continue through March 2006. The tour marks one of the lengthiest since Cuttin' Heads, performing some of the Midwest dates with Donovan—one of John's influences—and 37 dates in the summer of 2005 with one of his contemporaries, John Fogerty. The two first crossed paths during Farm Aid in 1995, where John lent Fogerty his band for the day. They most recently connected during the Vote for Change Tour, and share a mutual respect for one another's work.

Rather than appear as an opening act or even a co-headliner, Donovan was billed as a special guest. He took the stage in the middle of the show, with John's band backing him. A harder-rocking side of the folksy balladeer came forward on the tour. He was quite happy to be rocking in the U.S.A. to 7,000 to 10,000 people each night, mostly in sold-out venues.

During rehearsals, John wondered how he'd pull off that very thing, considering some of his more "cartoonish" hits, as he calls them, date back more than 25 years. "We have to go in, and we have to rearrange these songs so that they present themselves in a more grown-up, I guess, way...so that I don't feel silly out there playing them," he told CMT. "You know, I can't go out and just be a jukebox of my material." Been there, done that.

Flashbacks of the 9/11 tragedy came to mind in late August 2005 when

Hurricane Katrina, the deadliest natural disaster in U.S. history, raged through Louisiana and Mississippi. Again the music community leapt to action and a series of large-scale benefit concerts took shape to aid Katrina relief efforts. John was one of dozens of acts, including Green Day, Usher, Dave Matthews Band, Alicia Keys, Ludacris, John Mayer, Neil Young, the Rolling Stones, Kanye West, Kelly Clarkson, Sheryl Crow, Dashboard Confessional, Kid Rock, Melissa Etheridge, Paul McCartney and others to perform at ReAct Now: Music and Relief, a concert event staged simultaneously in Los Angeles, Nashville, New York and Atlanta, and broadcast on MTV, VH-1 and CMT on September 10, 2005. This was only one of many concerts held to benefit Katrina victims, and many more artists donated ticket sales from their regular concerts to the Red Cross while others collected canned goods for donation. Farm Aid activated the Family Farm Disaster Fund to accept donations for families hurt by the hurricane, and, in addition, donated $30,000 to the ravaged Gulf Coast. On September 18, Farm Aid would celebrate its twentieth anniversary with a concert in Tinley Park, Illinois. Though the efforts did offer some relief to the Gulf Coast, it didn't make a dent in the destruction that's still being remedied today.

During the final leg in early 2006, York recalls playing to "just wonderful crowds" in Youngtown, Ohio; Cedar Rapids, Iowa; and South Bend, Indiana (their final show). Disaster, albeit minor compared to the events six months prior, struck again during a free concert at Monument Circle in Indianapolis. The concert—which also featured American Idol winner, Carrie Underwood, as well as Collective Soul, Michelle Branch and R&B singer Chris Brown— was part of the NCAA's Final Four weekend festivities. The April 2, 2006 concert drew more than 80,000 people to downtown Indianapolis to celebrate two Indiana treasures—basketball and John Mellencamp. "There were miles of people as far as the eye could see," says Andy York. As the event concluded, strong storms kicked in, followed by a tornado that shattered windows on the *Indianapolis Star* building and damaged numerous cars, homes and apartment buildings, and injured nine people. "We were in our tour buses, and fortunately we didn't get picked up," says York. "We got out of there all right."

Leading up to the championship weekend and concert, CBS Sports began airing a newly recorded version of "R.O.C.K. in the U.S.A.," as the theme of its NCAA coverage. The new adaptation included references to college teams in the verses and the catchy "R.O.C.K. in the NCAA" chorus. They filmed the spots at Memory Hall gymnasium in Lebanon, Indiana, site of the 1986 movie *Hoosiers*. It's a logical tie, considering John's longtime support of college basketball, especially Indiana University basketball. But what happened to the man who protested high-dollar endorsements and sponsorships? Had John Mellencamp sold out? In a way, yes. The commercial disappointed some of his fans, who felt he should have left well enough alone and not turned one of his catchy hits into a commercial jingle. The year before, he let Chevy use his song "Now More Than Ever" for their Silverado ads. It paid a lot, and not many people know the song, so why not?

To his credit, he's highly selective about the organizations he licenses his music to, only choosing companies and/or organizations that he can personally support. NCAA basketball, he surely supports. And as for Chevy, their homegrown products merit well enough for him to establish an ongoing relationship. At least Chevy's all-American, hard-working image matches John better than, say, the ketchup company that wanted to use "Hurts So Good" back in the '80s.

For the duration of the Words and Music Tour, John and his band kicked off their shows with a newly written song called "Our Country." It was an American anthem, along the lines of "This Land Is Your Land," and even inspired a few fans to pitch John Mellencamp for Governor. (To date, he has no plans to run for political office.) Why not, an *Indianapolis Star* columnist wrote. California elected Arnold Schwarzenegger and while the "Governator" wielded heavy firearms onscreen in the '80s, John fought for the American farmer and social justice through his music and by co-creating Farm Aid. His new song brings his values to light again, as well as the strong feelings he has for "our country." "I can stand beside, things I think are right/I can stand beside, the idea to stand and fight/and I do believe, there's a dream for everyone..."

Former vice president Dan Quayle might take offense if such a campaign really did take place. In July 2006, John played a concert at Harvey's Outdoor Arena in Lake Tahoe. Quayle, in town for a celebrity golf tournament which took place the same weekend, got himself a ticket to the concert, but received much more than he bargained for. John introduced "Walk Tall" with the statement, "This next one is for all the poor people who've been ignored by the current administration..." Quayle, who served under George W.'s father, didn't appreciate the comment and promptly walked out. To rub in his discontent further, Quayle went on to state that John's concert really wasn't very good anyway, and his comment put him over the edge. John didn't take back his words; instead, he commented later: "I wasn't aware that Dan Quayle was at the show the other night but had I known, I certainly wouldn't have changed a word. I still feel there are many people left behind by this administration. Not talking about problems doesn't make them go away. It's kind of telling that he chose to walk out as I was doing a song about tolerance."

When John finished writing "Our Country," he called up Mike Wanchic to express his excitement over the song he just wrote. They soon worked up an arrangement with the band, recorded a rough version at Belmont Mall and commenced playing it live. By the spring of '06, John had enough material written for them to start a new album, but with no record labels ties, they could take their time in the studio. "We have no agenda other than to make a great record," Wanchic said in April 2006. "If it takes us a year, it takes us a year. If it takes two weeks, it takes two weeks. We're not going to be dictated by time; we're going to let the record unfold organically."

That all changed when Chevy contacted John's management company, Hoffman Entertainment, about using the song for their next Silverado campaign, an aggressive plan based around a commercial spot called "Our Country, Our Truck." Chevy planned to kick off the campaign in September 2006 and would continue through 2007. With this bit of news, the loose plans for finishing a new album firmed up dramatically. "We realized if we don't make a record now, we never will," says Wanchic. "We had the attention of the world again. So we said, 'now let's go out and make a great record.'"

For the first time since 2003, John, co-producer/guitarist Wanchic, guitarist/vocalist Andy York, violinist Miriam Sturm, bassist John Gunnell, drummer Dane Clark and new keyboardist Troye Kinnett gathered at Belmont Mall's adjacent rehearsal facility to work out an album's worth of material. John gave the band similar pre-rehearsal homework as with *Scarecrow*, when the band prepped by listening to songs by The Animals and The Troggs. "We tore apart every song from 1966, 1965," Mellencamp told *Billboard*. "We listened to all that music, then we learned it, we listened to it, we examined it: 'How did they do that?' We were inspired by it, we copied it, we stole it. We did everything we could from that era."

John, Wanchic and York agreed that musically, they just wanted to return to their real roots. "John and I grew up listening to the same radio stations, the same DJs, the same roots, R&B and soul music," says Wanchic. "John's a walking encyclopedia of late-'60s rock 'n' roll. He and I and Andy York all know the early Stooges material, Paul Revere and The Raiders, early [Jefferson] Airplane, the Mamas and the Papas, you name it. We decided to go back to the origins of our guitar playing and songwriting, the actual core of our knowledge and apply that to our new songs."

Aside from the basic guitar-bass-drums-keyboards, the only other instruments on the album are Sturm's violin and an occasional flute recorder courtesy of York. They brought in only a handful of microphones and a Pro Tools digital workstation. They worked 12 hours a day, and by the end of the day, they'd have a great song arrangement, one they felt passionate about. "And now," Wanchic continues describing their routine, "you're pretty beat up by the experience, rehearsing this much, arranging, but at the same time, you've got it down. It's under your hands. It feels really good, you've got all your parts right, everybody's on the same page, has the same amount of exhaustion and the same amount of excitement. And everything's pretty relaxed. *That's* when we turned the tape machines on and started running the rehearsals into Pro Tools." Instruments bled into each other, but since it wasn't a master recording, they let them bleed. "We were going to go back and re-cut the record properly, but we went back and listened to all these demos and said, 'What are we doing? This is fantastic! This is exactly what we want—it's loose, it's natural and it's got mistakes (which all of the early records had)." Wanchic usually doesn't listen to John's albums after they're finished, but he listened to this one. It's the first record he's been fired up about in years, and says it's the best thing they've done since *The Lonesome Jubilee*.

John easily found a label to release this new album—UMe/Universal Republic; ironically, the company that owns his PolyGram titles. Released January 23, 2007 as *Freedom's Road*, the album's 10 tracks all hold the anthemic spirit of "Our Country" with content that reports on present-day America with an attitude of hope laced with underlying cynicism. John combines his gritty state-of-the-union address with a musically warm, stripped-down sound culled from those long hours spent in the rehearsal space. Little Big Town, the country group that opened for John during portions of his Words and Music Tour, contribute backing vocals to the lead single. Joan Baez lends her voice to the song "Jim Crow," one of the album's many highlights.

The media attention surrounding John, *Freedom's Road* and, specifically, its debut single, began to snowball in October 2006 when Universal released "Our Country" for digital purchase/download on iTunes, *WalMart.com*, Rhapsody, AOL Music, Napster and select other portals. The song hit the 'Net around the same time that Chevy launched its "Our Country, Our Truck" campaign. The aforementioned commercial, designed to replace their "Like a Rock" anthem of a few years prior (sorry, Bob Seger), featured John's song and a voiceover stating "This is our country, this is our truck." Then we see John Mellencamp perched on top of an antique Chevy. But what stood out even more than lines such as, "I can stand beside ideals I think are right/I can stand beside the need to stand and fight," was the montage of "historic" photos and news footage, including a photo of Rosa Parks sitting on a bus; a brief clip of Martin Luther King, Jr., preaching; Nixon's famous wave from the presidential helicopter upon his 1974 resignation; U.S. troops in Vietnam; and more recent—and most puzzling in terms of their place in the ad—devastating images from the Hurricane Katrina and 9/11 disasters.

The multi-million dollar campaign went into heavy rotation during NBC's *Sunday Night Football in America*, the *Country Music Awards* and the Chevy-sponsored MLB World Series, during which John performed before Game Two of the 2006 World Series in Detroit.

Chevy intended to make a patriotic statement by highlighting the good and the bad from American history. These are our scars, but we have rebuilt.

However, many bristled at the ad's content. It showed a lack of reverence for those that suffered, and Chevy's decision to incorporate such content to sell trucks was just plain wrong, the public argued. The issue of John's own conflicting messages also came to roost—is he for or against corporate greed? This is the guy that sang "Ain't That America" with a hint of sarcasm. Now he's singing "This is America, buy this truck?" What ideals does he stand beside, exactly? "Times have changed," he told *Rolling Stone*. "Dylan's selling his songs. If nobody's playing [Tom] Petty's ["Saving Grace"] record, why the fuck would they play mine?" With that in mind, John asked the folks at Chevy how many times they planned to air this commercial. They assured him the commercial, and his song, would receive more airplay than any of his previous singles to date, and they were right.

Thankfully, Chevy revised the offending commercial to include more wholesome images of kids and dads, no wars or terrorist attacks. As for Chevy's new "like a rock" guy, aligning with a big corporation is just another way to get his music to the masses in an industry that puts little emphasis on 50-something roots rockers. "Quite honestly, the future of music is not coming from record companies anymore," says Wanchic. "Branding is going to be one of the most important things an artist has going for them, be it good or bad. With us, we'll get some radio, but we're not going to get pop radio. That's for the young, now artists."

Christina and Justin may dominate pop radio, but classic rock, AAA (Adult Album Alternative) and country stations have all cleared space for "Our Country" and other *Freedom's Road* tracks. So, yes, he'll get *some* radio. And he'll sell *some* records and *some* concert tickets.

On their previous tour, the 55-year-old midwestern roots rocker turned to Pat Peterson—his backing vocalist for more than 20 years—and asked, "How long can we keep doing this?" Until people stop showing up to hear him, he figures, which doesn't seem likely any time soon. In a January 2007 interview with *Rolling Stone*, he compares his life to that of the mythological Greek king Sisyphus: he gets knocked down again and again, but always finds the strength to stand up, dust himself off and keep rolling that rock up the hill. He may not ever reach the top, but be certain he'll keep pushing. He's invested too much effort over the past 30 years to do anything else but press on.

Whether he asked for the distinction or not, John Mellencamp, through his music, has become an ambassador for small-town America, even though the only thing "small town" about the man anymore is the rural Indiana locale upon which he built his exceedingly large home, its spotlights illuminating the trees along Lake Monroe.

But the music, the man, and the listener intersect in many other ways. He's achieved phenomenal success, but he's also endured innumerable failures and mishaps to get there, and all of us can identify with screwing up somehow. Over the past three decades, the public watched a young man christened Johnny Cougar against his will talk a big game. We also heard his band play countless ill notes, and read the reviews from critics who ripped his first songs to shreds. But he hung in there. As the man and his songwriting matured, we watched him develop a conscience, and saw him stand by the people and issues that mattered most to him, and heard him boldly express his opinions no matter how harsh they sounded. Behind the scenes, he pissed off his friends, he's infuriated his bandmates and made even himself sick of himself, but learned to channel that disgust into timeless verses coupled with melodies so uplifting and hook-laden, they often disguise the dark undertones that color his lyrics. As he continually challenged himself to do things different and better than the album before, he created a large body of work that has made a definitive impression on Americana music and culture, even though he rarely receives credit for such wide-reaching influence.

Love him or loathe him, John Mellencamp has sustained a long and fruitful career by doing exactly what he wants, how he wants, in an industry not necessarily known for longevity. In the process, he's touched the lives of many with music that people can either crack open a keg to, or intimately relate to. His ability to stay true to himself, as well as his unwavering strength, faith and vision, mirror the American spirit and serve as guideposts for some of the most memorable music "our country" can claim.

Selected Discography

EPs
U.S. Male
1978 (Gulcher Records, out of print)

Albums
Chestnut Street Incident
October 1, 1976 (MCA Records)
American Dream / Oh, Pretty Woman/Jailhouse Rock / Dream Killing Town/Supergirl / Chestnut Street / Good Girls / Do You Believe in Magic/Twentieth Century Fox / Chestnut Street Revisited / Sad Lady / Hit the Road Jack / I Need Somebody

The Kid Inside
1982 (Castle Records, recorded for MCA Records, 1977)
Kid Inside / Take What You Want / Cheap Shot / Sidewalk & Streetlights / R. Gang / American Son / Gearhead / Young Genocides / Too Young to Live / Survive

A Biography
1978 (Riva Records, UK; U.S. release, Riva Records, 2005)
Born Reckless / Factory / Night Slumming / Taxi Dancer / I Need a Lover / Alley of the Angels / High C Cherrie / Where the Sidewalk Ends / Let Them Run Your Lives / Goodnight / I Need a Lover (U.K. Single version, on 2005 U.S. re-release)

John Cougar
1979 (Riva Records)
A Little Night Dancin' / Small Paradise / Miami / Great Mid-West / Do You Think That's Fair / I Need a Lover / Welcome to Chinatown / Sugar Marie / Pray for Me / Taxi Dancer

Nothin' Matters and What If It Did?
1980 (Riva Records / Mercury Records)
Hot Night in a Cold Town / Ain't Even Done With the Night / Don't Misunderstand Me / This Time / Make Me Feel / To M.G. (Wherever She May Be) / Tonight / Cry Baby / Wild Angel / Peppermint Twist / Cheap Shot

American Fool
April 1, 1982 (Riva Records / Mercury Records)
Hurts So Good / Jack and Diane / Hand To Hold On To / Danger List / Can You Take It / Thundering Hearts / China Girl / Close Enough / Weakest Moments

Uh-Huh
October 1983 (Riva Records / Mercury Records)
Crumblin' Down / Pink Houses / Authority Song / Warmer Place to Sleep / Jackie O / Play Guitar / Serious Business / Lovin' Mother Fo Ya / Golden Gates

Scarecrow
November 1985 (Riva Records / Mercury Records)
Rain on the Scarecrow / Grandma's Theme / Small Town / Minutes to Memories / Lonely Ol' Night / The Face of the Nation / Justice and Independence '85 / Between a Laugh and a Tear / Rumbleseat / You've Got to Stand for Somethin' / R.O.C.K. in the U.S.A. / The Kind of Fella I Am

The Lonesome Jubilee
August 24, 1987 (Mercury Records)
Paper in Fire / Down and Out in Paradise / Check It Out / The Real Life / Cherry Bomb / We are the People / Empty Hands / Hard Times for an Honest Man / Hot Dogs and Hamburgers / Rooty Toot Toot

Big Daddy
May 9, 1989 (Mercury Records)
Big Daddy of Them All / To Live / Martha Say / Theo and Weird Henry / Jackie Brown / Pop Singer / Void in My Heart / Mansions in Heaven / Sometimes a Great Notion / Country Gentleman / J.M.'s Question / Let It Out (Let It All Hang Out)

Whenever We Wanted
October 8, 1991 (Mercury Records)
Love and Happiness / Now More Than Ever / I Ain't Ever Satisfied / Get a Leg Up / Crazy Ones / Last Chance / They're So Tough / Melting Pot / Whenever We Wanted / Again Tonight

Human Wheels
September 7, 1993 (Mercury Records)
When Jesus Left Birmingham / Junior / Human Wheels / Beige to Beige / Case 795 (The Family) / Suzanne & The Jewels / Sweet Evening Breeze / What If I Came Knocking / French Shoes / To the River

Dance Naked
June 21, 1994 (Mercury Records)
Dance Naked / Brothers / When Margaret Comes To Town / Wild Night / L.U.V. / Another Sunny Day 12/25 / Too Much to Think About / The Big Jack / The Breakout

Mr. Happy Go Lucky
September 10, 1996 (Mercury Records)
Overture / Jerry / Key West Intermezzo (I Saw You First) / Just Another Day / This May Not Be the End of the World / Emotional Love / Mr. Bellows / The Full Catastrophe / Circling Around the Moon / Large World Turning / Jackamo Road / Life Is Hard

The Best That I Could Do: 1978-1988
November 18, 1997 (Mercury Records)
I Need a Lover / Ain't Even Done With the Night / Hurts So Good / Jack and Diane / Crumblin' Down / Pink Houses / Authority Song / Lonely Ol' Night/ Small Town / R.O.C.K. in the U.S.A. / Paper in Fire / Cherry Bomb / Check It Out / Without Expression

John Mellencamp
October 6, 1998 (Columbia Records)
Fruit Trader / Your Life Is Now / Positively Crazy / I'm Not Running Anymore / It All Comes True / Eden Is Burning / Where the World Began / Miss Missy / Chance Meeting at the Tarantula / Break Me Off Some / Summer of Love / Days of Farewell

Rough Harvest
August 17, 1999 (Mercury Records)
Love and Happiness / In My Time of Dying / Between a Laugh and a Tear / Human Wheels / Rain on the Scarecrow / Farewell Angelina / Key West Intermezzo (I Saw You First) / Jackie Brown / When Jesus Left Birmingham / The Full Catastrophe / Minutes to Memories / Under the Boardwalk / Wild Night (live)

Skin It Back
March 21, 2000 (Snapper Music, Import)
Features tracks from *Chestnut Street Incident* and *The Kid Inside*

Cuttin' Heads
October 16, 2001 (Columbia Records)
Cuttin' Heads / Peaceful World / Deep Blue Heart / Crazy Island / Just Like You / The Same Way I Do / Women Seem / Worn Out Nervous Condition / Shy / In Our Lives

Trouble No More
June 3, 2003 (Columbia Records)
Stones in My Passway / Death Letter / Johnny Hart / Baltimore Oriole / Teardrops Will Fall / Diamond Joe / The End of the World / Down in the Bottom / Lafayette / Joliet Bound / John the Revelator / To Washington

Words and Music: John Mellencamp's Greatest Hits
October 19, 2004 (Island / UMe)
Walk Tall / Pink Houses / Lonely Ol' Night / Jackie Brown / Rain on the Scarecrow / Love and Happiness / Check It Out / Peaceful World / Paper in Fire / Your Life Is Now / Human Wheels / When Jesus Left Birmingham / Authority Song / What If I Came Knocking / Crumblin' Down / Small Town / R.O.C.K. in the U.S.A. / Cherry Bomb / Pop Singer / Thank You / Martha Say/ Key West Intermezzo (I Saw You First) / Hand To Hold On To / I Need a Lover / Hurts So Good / Get a Leg Up / Wild Night / Dance Naked / Teardrops Will Fall / Ain't Even Done With the Night / Just Another Day / Jack and Diane / Rumbleseat / I'm Not Running Anymore / Again Tonight / This Time / Now More Than Ever

Chronicles
June 21, 2005 (Island Records)
Three-CD box set contains reissues of *Scarecrow, The Lonesome Jubilee* and *Big Daddy,* presented in book-style long box format.

Freedom's Road
January 23, 2007 (Universal Republic)
Someday / Ghost Towns Along the Highway / The Americans / Forgiveness / Freedom's Road / Jim Crow / Our Country / Rural Route / My Aeroplane / Heaven Is a Lonely Place

Videos
I Need a Lover
Miami
Small Paradise
This Time
Ain't Even Done With the Night
Hurts So Good
Jack and Diane
Hand To Hold On To
Crumblin' Down
Authority Song
Pink Houses
Lonely Ol' Night
Small Town
Rain on the Scarecrow
R.O.C.K. in the U.S.A.
Rumbleseat
Paper in Fire
Check It Out
Cherry Bomb
Rooty Toot Toot
Hard Times for an Honest Man (unreleased)
I Saw Mommy Kissing Santa Claus
Pop Singer
Jackie Brown
Let It All Hang Out
Get a Leg Up
Now More Than Ever
Love and Happiness
Again Tonight
Human Wheels
When Jesus Left Birmingham
Baby Please Don't Go
Wild Night
Dance Naked

Another Sunny Day 12/25 (unreleased)
L.U.V. (unreleased)
Key West Intermezzo
Just Another Day
Your Life Is Now
I'm Not Running Anymore
Peaceful World
To Washington
Teardrops Will Fall
Walk Tall
Our Country

DVD / Videos
John Cougar Mellencamp: Ain't That America
1985 (RCA / Columbia Pictures Home Video, out of print)
Videos: Jack and Diane / Hand to Hold On To / Hurts So Good / This Time / Ain't Even Done With the Night / I Need a Lover / Miami / Small Paradise / Crumblin' Down / Authority Song / Pink Houses, as well as live footage from Southern Indiana

Trouble No More: The Making of a John Mellencamp Album
January 13, 2004 (Redline Entertainment)
A look inside the studio during the recording of the album *Trouble No More*.

John Mellencamp
January 2007 (Universal Music Enterprises)
CD/DVD two-pack includes the *Freedom's Road* CD, plus DVD with videos of Love and Happiness (From *MTV Unplugged*) / Jackie Brown (From *MTV Unplugged*) / Eden Is Burning (From *VH-1 Storytellers*) / Pink Houses (From *VH-1 Storytellers*) / Our Country (Video)

BIBLIOGRAPHY

Interviews

Kenny Aronoff, Dane Clark, Steve Cropper, Jenn Cristy, Tim Elsner, Don Gehman, Lisa Germano, John Gunnell, Ross Hogarth, Ray Kennedy, David Leonard, Rob Light, Paul Mahern, Elaine Mellencamp, Bob Merlis, Carolyn Mugar, Toby Myers, Pat Peterson, Mark Ripley, Mitch Ryder, Mirium Sturm, John Sykes, David Thoener, Mike Wanchic and Andy York.
Conducted between March 2006 and November 2006.

Books, Magaines, Newspapers and Websites

Torgoff, Martin. *American Fool: The Roots and Improbable Rise of John Cougar Mellencamp.* New York: St. Martin's Press, 1986.

Hoekstra, Dave; George-Warren, Holly, Ed. *Farm Aid: A Song For America, p. 109-113. New York: Rodale Inc.*, 2005.

Mellencamp, John. "Forget 'Trivial Matters' Plea." *Seymour Daily Tribune,* November 1, 1971.

Eds. "Cougar to Sing at Oktoberfest." *Seymour Daily Tribune,* September 24, 1976.

Cerf, Martin. "Johnny Cougar: Young, Gifted and Cocky." *Phonograph Record,* October 1976.

Swenson, John. "Chestnut Street Incident, Johnny Cougar." (Review) *Rolling Stone,* December 16, 1976.

McDowell, Mike. "John Cougar: Believing in Magic." *Blitz,* November / December 1979.

Naha, Ed. "Mucho Macho." *Village Voice*, 1980.

Pareles, Jon. "Mellencamp Aims at the Heartland." *New York Times*, September 1, 1985.

Rowland, Mark. "John Cougar Mellencamp Comes of Age (Sort Of)." p.41-44. *Musician*, October 1985.

Fricke, David. "Mellencamp: wildcat no more." *Rolling Stone*, February 2, 1986.

King, Wayne. "The Apprenticeship of John Cougar Mellencamp." *Backstreets*, Summer 1986.

Leonard, Mike. "John Cougar Mellencamp band looks forward to Saturday: 'The biggest concert ever' about to hit Bloomington." *The Herald-Times*, April 25, 1986.

Pearson, Mike. "Mellencamp concert caps Little 500 weekend." *The Herald-Times*, April 27, 1986.

Leonard, Mike. "Mellencamp comes home to 43,000 'small town' fans." *The Herald-Times*, April 27, 1986.

Holdship, Bill. "John Cougar Mellencamp: Working Class Hero In The Rumbleseat." *Creem*, February 1986.

Carroll, E. Jean. "John Mellencamp, Daddy's Boy: Even Rock -N- Roll Stars Have Parents." *Playboy*, February 1986.

Guccione, Jr., Bob. "Man on Fire: John Cougar Mellencamp was a wise guy once. He's older than that now." p. 32 - 39, 71 - 72. *SPIN*, September 1987.

Pareles, Jon. "Rock: John Cougar Mellencamp." (Concert Review) *New York Times*, November 28, 1987.

Holdship, Bill. "Growing Up In Public: John Cougar Mellencamp's Lonely Jubilee" p. 28 - 33. *Creem*, December 1987.

Perry, Steve. "John Mellencamp's Brutal Honesty." *Musician*, August 1989.

Sandow, Greg. "Mellencamp Takes Troubles to 'Daddy': Can the promise of rock & roll be fulfilled?" *Los Angeles Herald-Examiner*, May 14, 1989.

Guccione, Jr., Bob. "Mellencamp Melancholy." *SPIN*, June 1989.

Leonard, Mike. "The true scoop on that elusive Mellencamp movie." *The Herald-Times*, July 31, 1990.

Pareles, Jon. "Review/Pop; An Old-Fashioned Hip-Twitching Rock Concert." *New York Times*, September 18, 1991.

Forte, Dan. "David Grissom: Austin's Blazing Axe Slinger Goes Nationwide!" *Guitar Player*, December 1991.

Leonard, Mike. "Seymour to host premiere of John Mellencamp film." *The Herald-Times*, January 31, 1992.

Guccione, Jr., Bob. "Fanfare for the Common Man." *SPIN*, February 1992.

Christensen, Brent. "Details of Mellencamp wedding a private matter." *The Herald-Times*, September 5, 1992.

Gardner, Elysa. "Singer, Actor, Director: With a movie and a new album, John Mellencamp branches out." *Rolling Stone*, February 6, 1992.

Mills, Kathleen. "Mellencamp premiere draws odd mix of actors, devotees." *The Herald-Times*, February 19, 1992.

Leonard, Mike. "Editing of 'Jesus' video raises questions." *The Herald-Times*, January 16, 1994.

Steidenberg, Robert. "Modern Maturity: His wild nights over, John Mellencamp has mellowed, sort of, into rock's most irascible elder statesman." *Entertainment Weekly*, July 15, 1994.

DeCurtis, Anthony. "Bad to the Bone: John Mellencamp strips down to fighting trim on Dance Naked." *Rolling Stone*, September 8, 1994.

Eds. "Two of Hearts: Heartland roots-rocker John Mellencamp and maverick funk diva Me'Shell NdegeOcello go mano a mano to discuss their hit collaboration, "Wild Night," and the friction between art and commerce." *SPIN*, September 1994.

Rowland, Mark. "Frontman: John Mellencamp." *Musician*, January/February 1995.

Leonard, Mike. "Mellencamp finds new groove for new disc." *The Herald-Times*, August 28, 1996.

Rotter, Jeffrey. "Built To Last: John Mellencamp is still ornery after all these years." *SPIN*, October 1996.

Gajarsky, Bob. "John Mellencamp: Mr. Happy Go Lucky." Consumable Online, October 14, 1996.

Doerschuk, Robert L. "Frontman: John Mellencamp." *Musician*, November 1996.

Bessman, Jim. "Mellencamp's 1st 'Best of' heralds his Mercury exit." *Billboard*, October 25, 1997.

Eds. "John Mellencamp: The Theater at Madison Square Garden, New York, April 12, 1997." *Rolling Stone*, April 14, 1997.

DeMain, Bill. "The Roots Of An American Songwriter: John Mellencamp." *Performing Songwriter*, March/April 1997.

Langer, Andy. "A Piece of Their Souls." *The Austin Chronicle*, July 27, 1998.

Lindquist, David. "A band apart: After fateful rewards for a decade on top, the classic Mellencamp lineup began to crumble." p. 101. *The Indianapolis Star*, June 27, 1999.

Lindquist, David. "Despite old label, Mellencamp compilation's a winner." *The Indianapolis Star*, August 17, 1999.

Lindquist, David. "Mellencamp Outlines Future Plans: Mellencamp discusses future, New Year's concert." *The Indianapolis Star*, December 31, 1999.

Kenley, Casey. "She's a Model Hoosier: Elaine Irwin embraces the IRL, John Mellencamp and Indiana." *Indianapolis Woman*, May 2002.

Farley, Christopher John. "Rocking into Middle Age: John Mellencamp has a new album and a new outlook. But he's kept his old outspoken ways. *TIME*, November 30, 1998.

Johnson, Kevin C. "Making oldies new again." *St. Louis Post Dispatch*, September 30, 1999.

Mellencamp, John. "John Mellencamp's Style Diary: Wool, leather, sweat and tears on the road in Florida's gold coast." *Rolling Stone*, August 18, 1999.

Sorg, Lisa. "Moe-Z's road from rap to rock." www.moezmd.com.

Saraceno, Christina. "Mellencamp Talks Summer Tour." *Rolling Stone*, April 26, 2001.

Frank, Michael. "Midwestern Roots." *Architectural Digest*, June 2001.

White, Timothy. "John Mellencamp: A Portrait of the Artist." *Billboard*, December 8, 2001.

Lozovitsky, Dean. "An American Band: Remembering the John Mellencamp Band, one of America"s greatest. *NUVO*, November 27, 2002.

Scaggs, Austin. "Indiana's favorite son: Life Goes On." *Rolling Stone*, June 3, 2003.

Boehlert, Eric. "Ain't that America?" Salon.com, June 30, 2003.

Mellencamp, John and Elaine. "An Open Letter to America: It's Time to Take Back Our Country." CommonDreams.org, October 22, 2003.

Scaggs, Austin. "Kerry Campaign Rocks Radio City: Dave Matthews, John Mellencamp and Jon Bon Jovi raise the roof—and $7.5 million." *Rolling Stone*, August 5, 2004.

Fricke, David. "Taking It to the Streets: Artists unite for Kerry with historic Vote for Change Tour." *Rolling Stone*, August 11, 2004.

Edwards, Gavin. "John's Golden Years: Mellencamp releases a killer retrospective and avoids giving Dylan advice." *Rolling Stone*, November 4, 2004.

Daly, Sean. "The Blue In Blue-Collar: Despite Backlash, John Mellencamp Continues to Fight Authority." *Washington Post*, December 7, 2004.

Scaggs, Austin. "Mellencamp, Fogerty Unite: Veteran rockers bring the hits, and the kids, on the road." *Rolling Stone*, June 21, 2005.

Cohen, Jonathan. "Mellencamp, King Going Back To Work On Play." *Billboard*, September 30, 2005.

Willman, Chris. "Keith Urban 101: How Keith Urban became a star—EW examines the meteoric rise of country music's Entertainer of the Year." *Entertainment Weekly*, December 2, 2005.

Tully, Matthew. "You heard it here first: Mellencamp for governor." *Indianapolis Star*, April 5, 2006.

Carr, David. "The Media Equation; American Tragedies, To Sell Trucks." *New York Times*, October 30, 2006.

Farhi, Paul. "Chevy's new pickup ad carries extra baggage." *The Miami Herald*, November 6, 2006.

Skaggs, Austin. "Q&A: John Mellencamp." *Rolling Stone*, February 8, 2007.

Eds. "CMT Crossroads." CMT.com.

Moffittt, Julia. "The John Mellencamp Interview." WTHR, Eyewitness News, Published on WTHR.com, November 24, 2004.

Paulson, Ken. "John Mellencamp: 'Speaking Freely." Recorded May 13, 2003 for First Amendment Center, published www.firstamendmentcenter.org.

Interview between David Weiss and Kenny Aronoff, conducted in 2002.

ACKNOWLEDGEMENTS

It's hard to know where to start in the long list of individuals who helped bring this project to fruition. A huge thank you goes to everyone who gave their time to be interviewed for this book. Extra credit goes to webmaster Tony Buechler and Tim Elsner for fact-checking assistance, and especially to Bob Merlis, M.f.h., and Randy Hoffman and Miranda Hafford of Hoffman Entertainment for their hard work and generous cooperation.

On a personal note, I'd like to thank family and friends for their support and patience, especially those who cheered me on during the final countdown. Thanks to Andrea Rotondo at Omnibus Press for her faith in this writer and advice along the way; and to Tom Kenny at *Mix* magazine for encouraging me to pick up the phone.

I realized very early on that if anyone should write this book, it should be former *Billboard* editor-in-chief, bestselling author and friend to John, Timothy White, not me. Sadly, Mr. White left us before that opportunity came around. I never had the chance to meet him, but I feel that his eloquent writings as well as his high standards and integrity stayed with me through the entire process.

—Heather Johnson

About the Author

Photo by Steve Jennings

Heather Johnson is a San Francisco-based journalist. The Akron, Ohio native graduated from Middle Tennessee State University's Recording Industry Management program in 1994. After earning her B.S., Johnson went to work for historic Woodland Studios in Nashville, where she assumed the role of studio coordinator. She later started writing about the recording industry and published her first piece for *Audio Media* magazine in 1998.

In 1999, Johnson launched her own business, OutWord Bound Media, and gradually expanded her range as a writer to include contributions to professional audio magazines such as *Audio Media, Mix, EQ* and *Electronic Musician*, as well as music publications such as *No Depression, Performing Songwriter, Country Music* magazine and *Paste*, as well as regional publications such as the *Nashville Scene,* among others.

After moving to San Francisco in 2003, Johnson accepted a position with *Mix* magazine's editorial department. Her first book, *If These Halls Could Talk: A Historical Tour Through San Francisco Recording Studios* was published in May 2006. She currently serves as contributing editor for *Mix* and continues to write for a wide variety of publications. She also serves on the Board of Governors for the San Francisco Chapter of the Recording Academy. She spends much of her free time on the roads, trails and track as a long-distance runner, competing in numerous races each year from the 10K to the marathon.

INDEX

"30 Days in the Hole," 51

A

Abbott, Sam, 6
"ABC," 86
"Abilene," 6
Ackroyd, Dan, 39
After Image (film), 155
"Again Tonight," 114, 117
AIDS crisis, 106
"Ain't Even Done With the Night," 37, 38–39,
   49, 50, 84, 142
"Ain't Even Done With the Night" video, 39, 40
Air Studios (London), 27
Akins, Claude, 107–9, 118
Albert, Ron and Howard, 29–30
Album Network, 149
Alexander, Ross, 57
Allen, Ruthie, 34
Allman Brothers, the, 11
alternative rock, 115
AMA Awards (1980), 40
American Bandstand (TV show), 31, 40, 50
American Coming Together, 177
"American Dream," 21
American Fool (album), 43–49, 53–54, 61, 64,
   68, 75, 98
American Fool Tour, 84
American Talent International Ltd., 28
America's Heart and Soul (film), 176
Andrews, Jamie, 20

Animals, the, 7, 32, 67, 74
"Another Sunny Day 12/25," 125, 126
"Are There Any More Real Cowboys?" video,
   79
Arnold, P.P., 50
Aronoff, Kenny, vii
   aggressiveness of, 38
   audition for Mellencamp, 34–35
   baldness of, 127
   band bonus controversy and, 111
   Cropper and, 36
   firings and reconciliations, 37–41, 127
   Grissom and, 99, 113
   as Indiana University alumnus, 155
   joins band, 35
   leaves band, 133, 137
   on Lonesome Jubilee Tour, 93
   musical training of, 33
   preparedness of, 34–35
   side projects of, 80, 121–22, 127
   in Streamwinner, 33–34
   on Uh-Huh Tour, 67–68
   on Who tour, 55–56
   work on *American Fool,* 44–47
   work on *Dance Naked,* 124–29
   work on Hearts and Minds album, 104
   work on *Human Wheels,* 120–23
   work on *Lonesome Jubilee,* 87–90
   work on *Mr. Happy Go Lucky,* 133–37
   work on Ryder album, 57
   work on *Scarecrow,* 74–75

Asher, Dick, 124
"Authority Song," 64
Average House Band, 80

B

"Baby Please Don't Go," 123
Backyard Barbeque (VH-1 show), 138
Baez, Joan, 183
"Baggage Coach, The," 73
"Baltimore Oriole," 170
"Baltimore to Washington," 172–73
Basing Street Studios (London), 27
Baumann, Gus, 69
Baxter, Jeff "Skunk," 37
Beach Boys, the, 55–56, 74, 79
Beck, 132
Bee Gees, the, 45
Beginnings (Chicago club), 25–26
"Beige to Beige," 120, 121
Belmont Mall (recording studio), 69–71, 81,
    87, 89, 104–5, 109, 111, 117–18, 119, 123,
    156, 160
Belushi, John, 39
Benetar, Pat, 30, 31
Best That I Could Do (greatest hits collection),
    141–42, 178
Big Daddy (album), 99–104, 112–13
"Big Daddy of Them All," 100
"B.I.G.T.I.M.E.", 58, 59
Billboard magazine Century Award, 165
Biography, A (album), 27–28, 30
Bird, Larry, 123
BlackHawk, 132
Bladen, Rusty, 145
Blair, Dennis, 7
Blasters, the, 68, 69
Blige, Mary J., 176
Blue Chips (film), 123
blues, 161–62, 169–72
Blues Brothers Band, 35, 39, 47
Bob Costas Cancer Center (St. Louis), 176
Bobby Clark Band, the, 145
Boebinger, Gary, 2, 7, 9, 40
Bon Jovi, Jon, 176
Booker, Fred, 7
Booker T. and the MGs, 57
"Born in the U.S.A.", 66
Born in the U.S.A. (Springsteen album), 65, 77
Bottom Line (New York club), 31, 41
Bowery Ballroom (New York), 149
Bowie, David, 11, 13, 16, 21, 164
Boyd, Jimmy, 92
BR5-49, 149
Branch, Michelle, 180
Brando, Marlon, 13

Brandon's Way (L.A. studio), 178
"Break Me Off Some," 146
Breaking Away (film), 85
Brooks, Garth, 106, 150
Brown, Chris, 180
Brown, James, 6, 11, 68, 84
"Brown Sugar," 23
Buchanan, Roy, 113
"Bud's Theme", 109
Buechler, Tony, 145
Bunny Bread contest, 15
Burdon, Eric, 32
Burn, Malcom, 120–22, 126
Bush, 132
Bush, George W., vi, 158, 172–73, 181
Buskirk-Chumley Theater (Bloomington), 179
Buzzin' Cousins, the, 104, 109

C

"Candle in the Wind," 106
Candlebox, 132
Candy, John, 50
Capitol Records, 112, 122
Cardinal Clennon Children's Hospital
    (St. Louis), 176
Cardinal Stadium (Louisville), 132
Carey, Mariah, 144
Caribou Ranch (Colorado studio), 29, 69
Carmichael, Hoagy, 169–70
Carnegie Hall (New York), 116
Carter, Deana, 149
Carter Family, 172
Cascella, John
    death of, 122–23
    on Grissom, 113
    joins band, 81
    on Lonesome Jubilee Tour, 93
    work on *Human Wheels,* 120–23
    work on *Lonesome Jubilee,* 87–90
"Case 795 (The Family)", 120
Cash, Johnny, 79, 132
Cash, Rosanne, 80
Cataldo, Bill, 48
Catch, 19
CBS Sports, 180
Champion Entertainment Organization,
    83–84, 144
Chapman, Mike, 26, 30
Charles, Ray, 50
Chatterbox (Seymour bar), 12–13
Chavez, Rod, 7
"Cheap Shot," 39
Cheap Trick, 49
"Check It Out," 89, 92, 142
"Check It Out" video, 92, 178

Checker, Chubby, 6
Cherokee Studios (Los Angeles), 37, 39, 47
"Cherry Bomb," 89, 91, 92, 158
"Cherry Bomb" video, 92
"Cherry Cherry," 74
Chesney, Kenny, 175
"Chestnut Street Incident," 20, 22, 23–24
Chestnut Street Incident (album), 20–24, 162
Chevrolet, 181, 182, 183–84
Childers, Kenny, 160
Chirko, Roberta, 117–18, 119, 125, 132, 147
Christgau, Robert, 53
Christie, Lou, 74
Chuck D, 161
City of Hope hospital benefit, 140
Clapton, Eric, 132, 150, 164
Clark, Dane
    on *Crossroads* performance, 175
    on Cuttin' Heads Tour, 162
    Gunnell and, 148
    joins band, 137–38
    on Mr. Happy Go Lucky Tour, 139
    work on *Cuttin' Heads,* 156–58
    work on *Freedom's Road,* 182
    work on *John Mellencamp,* 145–46
    work on *Trouble No More,* 169–72
Clark, Dick, 31
Clarkson, Kelly, 180
Cleveland, Ashley, 104
Clinton, Bill, 150
Clinton, Hillary Rodham, 150
CMT Crossroads (TV show), 175
Cochran, Anita, 149
Coe, David Allen, 170
Cold Hard Truth (Eddie album), 99
"Cold Sweat," 84
Collective Soul, 132, 180
Collins, Phil, 45, 94
"Colored Lights," 68
Columbia Records, 144, 146–47, 148, 167,
    169, 172
Colvin, Shawn, 149
Concert for New York City, The (2001),
    163–64
Conlee, John, 132
Connelly, Chris, 53–54
Conseco Fieldhouse (Indianapolis), 150–51
Cool Hand Luke (film), 13
Costas, Bob, 176
Costello, Elvis, 149
country music, 169–72
Crabby Appleton, 142
Crane, Larry, vii
    as actor, 107–9, 118
    on Alberts, 29

band bonus controversy and, 111–12
    at "Johnny Cougar Day," 22
    joins band, 34, 35
    leaves band, 112
    on Lonesome Jubilee Tour, 93
    on Myers, 49
    side projects of, 80, 99
    in Streetheart, 25–30
    in Tiger Force Band, 18–20, 22–23, 24
    in Trash, 11–12, 18
    on Uh-Huh Tour, 67–68
    on Who tour, 55
    work on *American Fool,* 44–47
    work on *Lonesome Jubilee,* 87–90
    work on *Nothin' Matters,* 36, 37
    work on Ryder album, 57
    work on *Scarecrow,* 74–75
    work on *Uh-Huh,* 63
"Crazy Island," 157
Cream, 7, 86
Creative Artists Agency (CAA), 83–84, 108,
    144, 154
Creedence Clearwater Revival, 11
Crepe Soul, 7, 145
Crewe, Bob, 57
Cristy, Jenn, 160–61, 162, 164, 168–69
Criteria Studios (Miami), 29–30, 44–46, 50, 57,
    58, 69
Cropper, Steve, 35–39, 43, 47, 57
Crosby, Stills & Nash, 106
Crosby, Stills, Nash and Young, 11
Cross, Patricia, 85
Crow, Sheryl, 150, 168, 175, 180
"Crumblin' Down," 64–65
"Crumblin' Down" video, 65, 67, 178
"Cry Baby," 37, 39
Curfman, Shannon, 150
"Cuttin' Heads," 161–62
Cuttin' Heads (album), 156–58, 159–62, 164,
    167, 176
Cuttin' Heads Tour, 162–63

D

Daisy Chain, 140
Daly, Sean, 179
Dance Naked (album), 124–29, 133
"Dance Naked" remix, 127
Dance Naked Tour, 128–29, 133
"Dancing Days," 86
"Dancing in the Street," 132
Dashboard Confessional, 180
Dave Matthews Band, 176, 180
Davies, Ray and Dave, 41
Davis, Bob, 18, 25–26, 46
Davis, Skeeter, 170

Dean, James, 13
DeCurtis, Anthony, 125–26
"Deep Blue Heart," 161
DeFries, Tony, 16–18, 20–24, 56, 57
Denver, John, 80
Destiny's Child, 164
Detroit-Memphis Experiment, The (Ryder album), 57
Detroit Wheels, 56–57
Diamond, Neil, 74, 84
Dick Clark Productions, 59
Dickie Doo and the Don'ts, 170
Dilger, Fred, 153
Dio, 86
Dire Straits, 28
Dixie Chicks, the, 172, 177
"Do Re Mi," 90
"Do They Know It's Christmas?", 78
"Do You Believe in Magic," 20, 23
Donovan, 7–8, 32, 56, 179
Douglas-McRae, Jenny, 113
Dowd, Tom, 29
Dragon, Daryl, 69
Dreeson, Tom, 176
Drifters, the, 84, 143, 150–51
Dupke, Michael, 127
Dylan, Bob
    branding and, 184
    Farm Aid and, 78, 79
    Hall of Fame concert, 131–32
    as influence, 7, 8, 20
    Mellencamp's covers of, 13, 143, 158
Dylan, Jakob, 162

E

E Street Band, 86
Earle, Steve, 132, 170
"Early Bird Café," 145
Echo Park Studio, 142, 170
Eckstein, Ed, 128
Eclectricity, 134
Eddie, John, 99
Edmonds, Kenneth "Babyface," 177, 178, 179
Edward, Greg, 57, 69, 70, 74, 86, 87, 99
Edwards, John, 176, 177
Eldredge, Tim, 153
Elite Modeling Agency, 115, 119
Elsner, Tim, 6, 10–11, 54, 67, 70, 78, 83, 90, 95, 112
Ely, Joe, 99, 104, 109, 113, 124
Emotion (Streisand album), 68
"Emotional Love," 136, 146
"Empty Hands," 91
"End of the World, The," 170
Ernest, Donald H., 21

Esterline, Dennis, 11, 78
Esterline, Pricilla. *See* Mellencamp, Pricilla Esterline (first wife)
Esterline family, 9–10
Etheridge, Melissa, 150, 180

F

"Face the Nation," 74
Faithful, Marianne, 58
Falling from Grace (film), 104, 107–9, 114, 117, 118
Falling from Grace (soundtrack), 109, 137–38
Family Farm Disaster Fund, 180
"Farewell Angelina," 143
Farm Aid, 145, 159, 165, 180
    concerts for, v–vi, 78–79, 81, 106, 118, 132, 169
Farm Aid: A Song for America (book), 79, 118
farm crisis, 71–72, 82–83, 85
Fennelly, Michael, 142
Fettig, Rick, 90, 98, 103, 104
Fields, Simon, 40, 65–66
flag football games, 83–84
Flatt and Scruggs, 19
Fletcher, Louise, 155
Fletcher, Steve, 7
Florida Keys, 156–58
Flynn, Mike, 158
Fogerty, John, 79, 150, 176, 179
folk music, 7, 169–72, 176
Ford Field (Indianapolis), 179
Four Seasons, the, 74
Four Tops, the, 6
"Foxy," 30
Frampton, Peter, 49
Frank, Robert "Ferd," 25, 38, 44, 46
Franklin, Aretha, 132
Franklin, Jeff, 28, 35
Free, 11
"Full Catastrophe, The," 136–37

G

Gaff, Billy, 25–30, 36, 46, 48, 52, 56, 83
Galuten, Alby, 45
Gass, Jon, 178
Gehman, Don
    Belmont Mall projects, 86
    help on Belmont Mall's construction, 70
    help on Ryder album, 57
    Mellencamp's firing of, 98–99
    work on *American Fool,* 43–47
    work on Blasters album, 69
    work on *Cuttin' Heads,* 159–60
    work on *John Cougar,* 29–30, 35–36
    work on *Lonesome Jubilee,* 87–90

work on *Scarecrow,* 74
work on *Uh-Huh,* 62–64
Germain Amphitheater (Columbus), v–vi
Germano, Lisa
    Burn and, 120
    early career of, 80–81
    on *Falling from Grace* soundtrack, 109
    joins band, 81
    on Lonesome Jubilee Tour, 93
    solo career of, 112, 122, 127, 133
    work on *Dance Naked,* 124–29
    work on *Human Wheels,* 120–23
    work on *John Mellencamp,* 146
    work on *Lonesome Jubilee,* 87–90
    work on *Whenever We Wanted,* 113
"Get a Leg Up," 114, 117
"Get a Leg Up" video, 115, 116
Ghost Brothers of Darkland County, The (planned musical), 154
Gibb, Barry, 36
Gibson, Monique, 153
Gil, Mike, 25–26
Gilfoy, Jack, 19
Gilfoy Sound Studio (Bloomington), 19–20
Gill, Laura Mellencamp (sister), 1, 71–72
Gill, Mark (brother-in-law), 71–72
"glam" rock, 12
Glean, David, 149
Good Samaritan Tour, 158
Gooden, Harvey, 65–66
Gore, Tipper, 79–80
gospel music, 169–72
Gougeon, Mark, 57
Gowers, Bruce, 40
"Grandma's Theme," 73
Granucci, Vicky. *See* Mellencamp, Vicky Granucci (second wife)
Green, Al, 131–32
Green, George
    Bunny Bread contest and, 15
    eulogy for grandfather, 121
    heart attack of, 129
    in Mellencamp's photo, 16
    songwriting of, 12–13, 47, 64–65, 71–72, 136, 147, 156
    on *Storytellers* program, 148
    wife of, 77
Green Day, 180
Greene, Ed, 38, 39
Griff (dog), 71
Griffith, Nanci, 109
Grissom, David
    Aronoff and, 33
    at Carnegie Hall, 116
    joins band, 112–14

leaves band, 124
    work on *Big Daddy,* 99, 103
    work on *Human Wheels,* 120–23
Guccione, Bob, Jr., 73, 90, 108
Guilty (Streisand album), 36
Gulcher Records, 31
Gunnell, John, 147–48, 156–58, 159, 170, 182
Guns N Roses, 116
Guthrie, Woody
    as influence, 7, 20, 73, 91, 169, 178
    Mellencamp's covers of, 90, 158, 170, 172

H
Hackman, Melissa Ann, 118
Hall, Daryl, 79
Hall, Wayne, 19
Hamilton, Reggie, 178
Hammond B3 organ, 139
"Hand to Hold Onto," 46, 51
Handley, Randy, 28, 34
"Hang On Sloopy," 41
Happiness (Germano album), 112, 127
Hard Line (Blasters album), 69
"Hard Times for an Honest Man" video, 92
Harry P. Mellencamp Building & Construction Company, 4
Head East, 30
Healy, Jay, 109, 114
Heart tour, 51–54, 56
"Heartbreak Hotel," 67
Heartbreakers, the, 79, 80
Hearts and Minds, 104, 123
Helm, Levon, 35
Hemingway, Mariel, 107–9
Henderson, Bruce, 104
Hendrix, Jimi, 161
Henley, Don, 149, 168
Henrich, Dr. Carter, 139
Hill, Carol Sue, 67–68
Hit Factory (New York studio), 24
"Hit the Road Jack," 20
Hoffman, Randy, 144
Hoffman Entertainment, 144, 182
Hogarth, Ross, 69, 74, 86, 98, 99, 102–5, 109
Hohenberger, Frank, 69
"Honky Tonk Woman," 31
Hoosier Group, 69, 105
Hoosiers (film), 180
Hootie and the Blowfish, 132, 175
Horner, James, 156
"Hot Night in a Cold Town," 37
Hoyt, Janas, 143
Hubbard, Kin, 69
Hud (film), 73
"Human Wheels," 121, 142

Human Wheels (album), 119–23
Human Wheels Internet discussion list, 145
Humble Pie, 51
Hunter, Ian, 30
Hurricane Katrina, 180
"Hurts So Good," 47, 48–49, 50, 51, 52, 59, 114, 142, 165
"Hurts So Good" video, 52–53

I

"I Ain't Ever Satisfied," 114
"I Need a Lover," 26, 27–28, 30, 31, 34, 35, 51, 67, 84, 142, 178
"I Saw Mommy Kissing Santa Claus," 92
"I Wanna Be Your Dog," 11
Ian, Janis, 109
"If That's Your Boyfriend (He Wasn't Last Night)", 128
Iggy Pop and The Stooges, 11, 16, 31
Illegal Stills (Stills album), 29, 43
"I'm Not Running Anymore" video, 149
"In My Time of Dying," 143
"In the Air Tonight," 45
In the Heat of the Night (Benetar album), 30
India.Arie, 161
Ingram, Jack, 170
Internet, 132, 145, 183
Iovine, Jimmy and Vicky, 92
Iraq War, vi
Irwin, Elaine. *See* Mellencamp, Elaine Irwin
Islamorada, Florida, 156–58
"It's Just Another Day," 136
IU Student Foundation, 154

J

"Jack and Diane," 45–46, 50, 51, 53, 62, 139, 142, 148, 158, 165, 175
"Jackie Brown," 101–2, 142
Jackson, J.J., 85
Jackson, Michael, 77
Jackson Five, the, 86
Jaffe, Jerry, 26
"Jailhouse Rock," 20
Jam, the, 26
Jam Productions, 84
Jarvis, John, 37
Jason and The Scorchers, 104
Jean, Wyclef, 176
Jefferson Airplane, 182
"Jerry," 136
Jeter, Felicia, 53
Jezzard, Ralph, 127
"Jim Crow," 183
Joel, Billy, 164, 168
John, Elton, 106

John Cougar (album), 28–30, 34
John Mellencamp (album), 144, 145–46, 149, 160
Johnny Cougar Tour, 23
"Johnny Hart," 170
Johnson, Brother Louis, 63–64
Johnson, J. "Art," 7
Johnson, Robert, 161–62, 168, 169
Jones, Don, 55
Jones Beach concert, 128
Jordan, Steve, 157, 159, 161
Jostyn, Mindy, 128, 133
Journey, 132
Judas Priest, 30
"Just Another Day," 137

K

Kaiser, Courtney, 160–61, 162
Kennedy, Ray, 170–72
Kerry, John, 176–77
"Key West Intermezzo (I Saw You First)", 136, 137, 156, 164
"Key West Intermezzo (I Saw You First)" video, 178
Keys, Alicia, 180
"Kicks," 16, 31
Kid Inside, The (album), 24, 56
Kid Rock, 180
King, Albert, 113
King, B.B., 113, 150
King, Stephen, 154, 167, 175
Kinks, the, 40–41, 51, 52
Kinneson, Sam, 94
Kinnett, Troye, 182
Kiss, 12, 30, 31, 51
Knight, Bob, 123
Knopfler, Mark, 28
Knowles, Tom, 25, 34
Kovak, Alan, 134, 144
Kravitz, Lenny, 150

L

"Lafayette," 170
Lake Monroe (Indiana), 2, 31, 153–54, 184
Lanois, Daniel, 120
"Last Chance," 114
Late Show with David Letterman, The (TV show), 138, 148, 149
Lawson, Rick, 178
Leadbelly, 158
Lear, Merritt, 158
Led Zeppelin, 86
Left Bank Management, 134, 144
Lenner, Donny, 144
Lenz, Kay, 108
Leonard, David, 87, 89, 90, 121, 122

Let It Bleed (Rolling Stones album), 145

Levy, Alain, 124, 128

Lewis, Jerry Lee, 131–32

"Life Is Hard," 136

Life's Rich Pageant (R.E.M. album), 86

Light, Rob, 83, 109, 154

Like a Virgin (Madonna album), 77

LinnDrum, 45

Little b Pictures, 107

Little Big Town, 183

Little Nashville Opry, 80–81

Live Aid concert, 78–79

Live by Request (TV show), 179

"Living in Miami," 35

London, Julie, 1

London, Ontario, show, 55–56

"Lonely Ol' Night," 73, 77, 93, 116

"Lonely Ol' Night" video, 77

Lonesome Jubilee, The (album), vii, 86–92, 98, 100, 113

Lonesome Jubilee Tour, 93–94, 97

"Loser," 11, 13

"Louie, Louie," 41

"Love and Happiness," 114, 134

"Love and Happiness" remix, 127

Lowe, Joe (grandfather), 5

Lowe, Marilyn Joyce. *See* Mellencamp, Marilyn (mother)

Ludacris, 180

Ludwig, Bob, 146

M

Madison Square Garden (New York), 84, 93, 163–64, 168

Madonna, 77, 94

Mahern, Paul, 142, 143, 145–46, 160, 161, 178

MainMan Ltd., 16–18, 20–24, 56

Major Bill label, 112

"Make Me Feel," 37

Mamas and the Papas, the, 182

Mancini, Henry, 19

Manganelli, Bob, 155

Mar-Keys, the, 37

Marcus, Greil, 176

Marcussen, Stephen, 90

Market Square Arena (Indianapolis), 54

Marsh, Dave, 53

"Martha Say," 101, 103

Martin, George, 27

Mary Janes, the, 143

Mason Brothers, the, 18–19

Massey, Edith, 40

Matthews, Dave, 132, 176, 177, 180

Mattola, Tommy, 83, 144

Mayer, John, 180

MCA Records, 18–24

McCartney, Paul, 164, 180

McMurtry, James, 68, 104, 109

McMurtry, Larry, 73, 104, 107–9

McNally, Steve, 49

Medley, Sue, 104

Mellencamp, Carrie Mackey (great-grandmother), 5

Mellencamp, Elaine Irwin (wife)
  birth of first child, 127–28
  birth of second child, 131
  early life of, 119
  on husband's heart attack, 129
  marriage of, 118–19
  as Mellencamp's girlfriend, 117–18
  as model, 115, 116, 119
  new home of, 153–54
  political views and activism of, 173, 177
  positive presence of, 123, 127–28, 140, 162–63, 171, 179
  on *Storytellers* program, 148
  on White, 142
  on White's death, 168

Mellencamp, Harry Perry ("Speck"; grandfather), 3–4, 75–76, 85, 165

Mellencamp, Hud (son), 127–28, 137, 154, 162–63, 168, 171, 179

Mellencamp, James Archie (uncle), 4

Mellencamp, Janet (sister), 1

Mellencamp, Jerry (uncle), 4, 91

Mellencamp, Joe (brother), 1, 4, 6, 118

Mellencamp, Joe (uncle), 4, 6, 76, 85, 145

Mellencamp, John. *See also specific albums and songs*
  abstention from drugs and alcohol, 55
  as actor, 107–9, 155
  American Music Awards nominations, 59
  attitude problems of, 7–8, 23–24, 27, 28, 29, 43, 53
  audience for, 115–16, 125, 132–33
  in Australia, 28
  aversion to photographs, 171
  bad-boy image of, 17, 20–24, 27
  band bonus controversy, 111–12
  band named The Zone by, 30–31
  as basketball fan, 123
  birth of daughter Michelle, 9
  bullying behavior of, 2–3
  Bunker practice space, 44, 49
  cars of, 71
  Century Award presented to, 165
  charitable activities of, v–vi, 78–79, 81, 106–7, 117, 118, 132, 148–49, 154–55, 165, 176
  Chatterbox gig of, 12–13

church attended by, 1–2
club performances with Pearl Doggy, 131
as community college student, 10–11
corporate sponsorships and endorsements viewed by, 83, 180–81, 182, 183–84
"Cougar" erased from name, 115
cover songs viewed by, 19–20
credo of, 44, 47, 61
critics and, 23, 41, 53–54, 59, 65, 77, 91, 93, 116, 137, 142
demo deal, 14, 15–17, 31
determination of, vi–vii, 42
diet changes, 129, 139
directness of, 95, 164–65
divorces of, 41–42, 97–98, 99, 121
draft ineligibility of, 10
drug use of, 8, 9
early life of, 1–3, 5–9
early press views of, 23
elopement and first marriage of, 9–10
encores viewed by, 93
in England, 26–27
extramarital affairs of, 86, 95, 97
fans of, 52–53, 67–68, 144–45
first band of, 7
first manager of, 16–18
first record deal of, 18
first record of, 19–20
first royalty check of, 24
first song written by, 11, 13
as football team player, 6
as football team's mascot, 2
genre created by, vi–vii, 165
glam look for, 12, 24
goatee of, 149
Grammy Award nominations, 58–59, 117, 137, 164
Grammy Award win, 59
guitars of, 12
halftime show performance, 179
Hall of Fame concert, 131–32
on happiness, 114
health problems of, 40, 116, 128–29, 139
as hippie, 10
homes of, 9, 10–11, 13–14, 18, 31, 70, 151, 153–54, 184
honorary doctorate and commencement address, 154–55
Hurricane Katrina benefit concerts, 180
imperiousness of, 37, 51, 87–88, 102
lawsuit against Eldredge, 153
leaves Columbia, 167
leaves Mercury, 141–44
Los Angeles label-hunting trips, 25, 26
lyrics of, 39

management changes, 144
monthly stipend from DeFries, 18
in Montreal during terrorist attacks, 163
motorcycle accident of, 44
motorcycles of, 71
move to Bloomington, 24–25
move to Rockford, 5
musical censorship opposed by, 79–80
musical interests and influences of, 6–7, 11, 20, 32, 36, 62, 179
musical planned by, 154, 167, 175
New York label-hunting trips, 13–14, 16–17
as opening act, 30–31, 40–41, 51–53, 54–55
as painter, 103, 105–6, 115, 148–49, 167
personal life of, 71, 77–78, 85–86, 92, 94–95, 97–98, 114–15, 153–54, 162–63, 168
political views and activism of, vi, 66–67, 71–72, 82–83, 85, 92, 158–59, 172–73, 175–78, 181
as producer, 56–58
profanity used by, vi, 3, 11, 13, 22, 23, 24, 67, 150
promoted as "Johnny Cougar," 20–23, 26–28, 32, 162
as radio DJ, 11
recording studio built by, 68–71
relationship with father, 6, 8–9
remixes of, 127
restlessness of, 71
role models of, 13
sabbaticals taken by, 95, 129–30, 151
screenplay of, 104
second manager of, 25–30
second marriage of, 42
self-loathing of, 100–102
separation from Pricilla, 36–37
Shack studio of, 57–58, 62–64
showmanship of, 31, 41, 52, 54, 67, 82, 93
side projects of, 68
signs with Columbia, 144
smoking of, 90, 130, 179
songwriting of, 11, 12, 19–20, 24, 44–45, 46–47, 53, 61–62, 68, 71, 85, 91–92, 100, 120–21, 123, 147, 157–58, 178
spina bifida of, 10, 117
as telephone installer, 12–13
television appearances, 31, 40, 49–50, 148, 149, 150, 175, 179
temper of, 21, 23, 29, 30, 62–63, 78, 124, 130, 145
theater tours of, 138–39
third marriage of, 118–19

tour with Heart, 51–54, 56
tour with the Who, 54–55
Trash organized by, 11–12
video format embraced by, 66, 128
at White's funeral, 168
Mellencamp, John Henry (great-grandfather), 3, 5
Mellencamp, Justice (daughter), 77, 97, 114–15, 137
Mellencamp, Laura. *See* Gill, Laura Mellencamp
Mellencamp, Laura Noblitt (grandmother), 1–2, 3–4, 9, 73, 76
Mellencamp, Marilyn (mother), v–vi, 1
    as artist, 105, 145
    early life of, 4–5
    as parent, 8–9
Mellencamp, Mary (aunt), 4
Mellencamp, Michelle (daughter), 9, 71
    move to England, 26
    personality of, 51, 78
    pregnancy and marriage of, 97, 114–15
    relationship with step-mother, 36–37
Mellencamp: Paintings and Reflections (book), 148–49
Mellencamp, Pricilla Esterline (first wife)
    birth of daughter, 9
    as breadwinner, 9, 12, 16
    DeFries viewed by, 18
    divorce of, 42
    as Mellencamp's girlfriend, 8
    move to England, 26
    out-of-wedlock pregnancy of, 9
    post-divorce life of, 78
    separation of, 36–37
Mellencamp, Richard (father), v–vi, 1
    as associate film producer, 107
    career of, 3, 4–6
    as financial adviser, 70, 78, 83
    motto of, 6
    as parent, 5–6, 8–9, 14, 78
Mellencamp, Speck Wildhorse (son), 131, 154, 162–63, 168, 171, 179
Mellencamp, Ted (brother)
    early years of, 1, 5, 6, 13
    as road manager, 11, 23, 52, 67, 78
Mellencamp, Teddi Jo (daughter), 44, 71, 77, 91, 97, 114–15
Mellencamp, Toots (aunt), 4
Mellencamp, Tracy (cousin), 78
Mellencamp, Vicky Granucci (second wife)
    divorce of, 97–98, 121
    first child of, 44
    marriage of, 42
    "Martha Say" and, 101
    as Mellencamp's girlfriend, 36–37, 38, 41–42
    second child of, 77–78
    second pregnancy of, 71
Mellenfests, 144–45
Memorial Stadium (Bloomington), 84
Memphis Horns, the, 57
Mercury/PolyGram, 26, 28–30, 39, 43–48, 49, 53, 61, 65, 90–91, 92, 103, 109, 115–16, 121, 123, 124–25, 128, 132–33, 141–44, 150–51
Merlis, Bob, 26, 53, 168
Metheny, Pat, 113
"Miami," 30
"Mickey's Monkey," 84
Miles, Susan, 66
Miller, Jodi, 123
"Minutes to Memories," 72, 143
Minutes to Memories fan club, 145
"Miss Missy," 146
Missouri Rural Crisis Center (MRCC), 85
Moe Z
    band of, 147
    Cristy and, 162
    on Kaiser, 160–61
    on Mr. Happy Go Luck Tour, 139
    on *Storytellers* program, 148
    on Summer Work Tour, 169
    work on *Cutting' Heads,* 156–58
    work on *John Mellencamp,* 146
    work on *Mr. Happy Go Lucky,* 134–36
Mollencamp, Anna Marie (great-great-grandmother), 5
Mollencamp, Johann Heinrich (great-great-grandfather), 5
Mollencamp, Johann Herman. *See* Mellencamp, John Henry
Monument Circle (Indianapolis), 180
Moorings, The (Islamorada), 156–58
Mordente, Lisa, 51, 55
Morris, William, 144
Morrison, Van, 126
Motley Crüe, 86
Motown, 86
MP3s, 132
Mr. Happy Go Lucky (album), 132–40
Mr. Happy Go Lucky Tour, 138–40
MTV network, 52–53, 66, 84–85, 123, 149, 178
MuchMusic (Canadian show), 149
Mugar, Carolyn, 165
Music Machine, 74
musical censorship, 79–80
musical therapy, 117
My Honky Tonk History (Tritt album), 175

Myers, Toby, vii
    band bonus controversy and, 111
    on Bloomington gig, 84
    Clark and, 138
    death of father, 140
    excluded from *Uh-Huh*, 63–64
    joins band, 49–50
    leaves band, 147–48
    on London, Ontario, show, 55–56
    on management changes, 84
    marriage of, 132
    on Mr. Happy Go Lucky Tour, 139
    recording studio built by, 80
    relationship with Chirko, 117–18
    side projects of, 80
    social life of, 94
    songwriting of, 136, 146
    on Uh-Huh Tour, 67–68
    on Who tour reception, 54–55
    work on *Big Daddy,* 102–3
    work on *Dance Naked,* 124–29
    work on Hearts and Minds album, 104
    work on *Human Wheels,* 120–23
    work on *John Mellencamp,* 145–46
    work on *Lonesome Jubilee,* 87–90
    work on *Mr. Happy Go Lucky,* 133–37
    work on *Rough Harvest,* 143
    work on *Scarecrow,* 70, 74–75
    work on *Trouble No More,* 170–71

N

'N Sync, 150
Naha, Ed, 41
Nashville Network, 106
Nazarene Church, 1–2
NdegéOcello, Me'Shell, 126–27, 128
Nelson, Willie, 78–79, 132, 175
Never Kick a Sleeping Dog (Ryder album),
    57–58, 59
New York Dolls, the, 11
Newman, Paul, 13, 73
Nicks, Stevie, 149
Nightwatch (TV show), 53
Nile, Willy, 75
Noblitt, Laura. *See* Mellencamp, Laura Noblitt
    (grandmother)
Nolte, Nick, 123
Nordoff-Robbins Center, 117
Nothin' Matters and What If It Did (album),
    35–39, 41, 43, 75
Nothing Like We Planned (planned anthology),
    125
"Now More Than Ever," 157, 181
Nugent, Ted, 147

O

Odette, 1
"Oh, Pretty Woman," 20
Old Ways (Young album), 79
On the Way Down from the Moon Palace
    (Germano album), 112, 122
O'Neal, Shaquille, 123
Open Mike with Mike Bullard (Canadian TV
    show), 149
Orbison, Roy, 20
Orbit Room (Grand Rapids club), 131
Osgood, Ron, 171
"Our Country," 181, 183, 184
"Our Country, Our Truck" Chevy ad
    campaign, 183–84
Ovitz, Mike, 108, 144

P

"Paint the Mother Pink" MTV promotion, 66,
    126
"Paper in Fire," 88, 91, 92, 142
"Paper in Fire" video, 92
Pareles, Jon, 65, 93, 116, 137
Parents Music Resource Center (PMRC),
    79–80
Parman, Dave, 18–20
Paul Revere and The Raiders, 7, 16, 182
"Peaceful World," 157, 161, 163, 164, 167
Peach, Elexis Suzanne (granddaughter), 115
Pearl Doggy, 131
Pearl Jam, 177
Penn, Sean, 94
Perfect Storm, A (film), 155–56
Perry, George "Chocolate," 47
Peterson, Pat, 184
    "Cuttin' Heads" origin and, 161
    joins band, 50–51
    on Mellencamp's energy, 54
    on Mellencamp's heart attack, 130
    on Mr. Happy Go Lucky Tour, 139
    on Scarecrow Tour, 81–82
    stage acrobatics performed by, 52, 67
    on Uh-Huh Tour, 67–68
    on Who tour, 55
    work on *Cuttin' Heads,* 156–58
    work on *Dance Naked,* 124–29
    work on *Human Wheels,* 120–23
    work on *John Mellencamp,* 146
    work on *Lonesome Jubilee,* 87–90
    work on Ryder album, 57
Petty, Tom, 79, 184
"Philly Dog," 37
Pink Flamingos (film), 40
Pink Floyd, 50

"Pink Houses," 61–63, 63, 65, 66, 116, 126, 148, 158, 159, 161, 176, 178, 179
"Pink Houses" video, 65–66
Plantation Lullabyes (NdegéOcello album), 126–27
"Play Guitar," 68
"Please Don't Let Me Be Misunderstood," 67
PolyGram. *See* Mercury-PolyGram
Pomeroy, David, 104
"Pop Singer," 102, 103, 148
"Pop Singer" video, 103
"Pretty Ballerina," 67
Prince, 58
Prine, John, 104, 109
Punter, John, 27
Pure Funk, 49

Q

Quayle, Dan, 181

R

Radio City Music Hall (New York), 68, 176
Radiohead, 132
"Rain on the Scarecrow," 71–72, 74–75, 143, 179
"Rain on the Scarecrow" video, 77, 178
Rainbow, 30
Raitt, Bonnie, 106
Ramone, Phil, 29
Ramos, Mike, 170–71
Rascals, the, 86
RATT, 86
Rawls, Lou, 34
ReAct Now: Music and Relief (concert event), 180
Reagan, Ronald, 66, 102, 159
"Real Life, The," 91
Reed, Lou, 11, 13, 79, 132
Reeves, Martha, 132
Reid, Terry, 56, 142
R.E.M., 86, 177
REO Speedwagon, 30, 51
Reynolds, Burt, 46
Rhythm and Romance (Cash album), 80
Richards, Keith, 75
Richert, Bob, 31
Ridin' the Cage (Mellencamp screenplay), 104
Rink, Dr. Larry, 139
Ripley, Mark, 6, 7, 8–9, 16, 22, 71, 73, 94–95, 106
Riva Records, 25, 26–27, 56–58, 59
Roadmaster, 49
Robb, Bruce and Dee, 37, 39, 47
Robb, Susan, 47
Robbins Electric Company, 3, 5

"R.O.C.K. in the USA," 73, 74, 116, 158–59, 179, 180–81
"R.O.C.K. in the USA" video, 178
Rock and Roll Hall of Fame (Cleveland), 131–32
rock 'n' roll, 7, 74, 182
Rockford, Indiana, 5–6
Rodgers, Paul, 142
Rok-Sey Roller Rink (Seymour), 7, 76, 145
Rolling Stone (magazine), 23, 53–54
Rolling Stones, the, 13, 23, 31, 62, 145, 158, 180
Rollins, Larry, 109, 118
Ronson, Mick, 18, 20, 45–46
Room and Board (Nashville studio), 170
"Rooty Toot Toot," 88–89, 91
"Rooty Toot Toot" video, 92
Rose & the Briar, The: Death, Love and Liberty in the American Ballad (compilation CD), 176
Rosie O'Donnell Show (TV show), 149
Ross, Tom, 83
Rosser, Eric "Doc," 30, 38, 46
Rough Harvest (album), 142–44, 150–51
Rowland, Mark, 52
Roxy Music, 27
Rumbo Recorders (Canoga Park studio), 69, 70, 86
Rural Electrification Tour, 149–51
Rush, 49
Ryder, Mitch, 32, 46, 56–58, 59
Ryser, Jimmy, 125, 126, 133, 140, 145

S

Sam and Dave, 6
"Same Way I Do, The," 157
Sandler, Harry, 98, 107, 144, 150
Satriani, Joe, 113
Saturday Night Live (TV show), 49–50
Save the Music Foundation, 106, 148–49, 150
"Scarecrow," 70
Scarecrow (album), vii, 71–77, 98, 113
Scarecrow Tour, 81–84, 86
Schlosser, Rich, 38, 39
SCTV (TV show), 50
Sczymczyk, Bill, 29
"Search and Destroy," 31
Seger, Bob, 53, 133
September 11 terrorist attacks, 163
Serfs, the, 145
Setzer, Brian, 80
Sex Pistols, the, 27
Seymour, Indiana
    described, 1–2
    Falling from Grace filmed in, 107–9
    Falling from Grace premiere, 118

"Johnny Cougar Day" in, 21–23
Mellencamp's early life in, 1–3
"Shack" studio, 57–58, 62–64
Shaker, Kula, 132
Shannon, Del, 55–56
Shaver, Billy Joe, 170
Shaw, Russel, 52
Shore, Pauley, 94
Short, Martin, 50
Shulz, Adolph, 69
Silverchair, 132
Simon, Paul, 105
Slater, Andrew, 53–54
"Small Paradise," 30
"Small Town," 73, 77, 82, 84, 139, 148, 161, 169, 177, 179
"Small Town" video, 145
Snakepit Banana Barn, 7, 19
"Sock It to Me Baby!", 57
soul music, 6, 7, 36
Sounds of Blackness, 121
Southern Indiana Center for the Arts (SICA), 106–7, 118, 145
Special Olympics, 92
Spector, Phil, 28
spina bifida, 10, 117
Springsteen, Bruce
    Born in the U.S.A., 65, 77
    Hall of Fame concert, 131–32
    Mellencamp compared to, 32, 53, 82
    political activism of, 177
    theater tours of, 138
"Stand for Something," 73
Steele, Selma, 69
Steele, T.C., 69, 105
Steppenwolf, 37
Stewart, Rod, 25, 29, 46, 132
Stills, Stephen, 29, 43
Sting, 168
"Stones in My Passway," vi, 168, 169
Stooges, the, 182
Storytellers (VH-1 series), 148
Stradlin, Izzy, 146
Streamwinner, 33–34, 99
Streetheart, 25–30
Streisand, Barbra, 36, 68, 94
Sturm, Miriam
    on Cuttin' Heads Tour, 162
    as Indiana University alumnus, 155
    on Rural Electrification Tour, 150
    at White's funeral, 168
    work on Cuttin' Heads, 156–58
    work on Freedom's Road, 182
    work on John Mellencamp, 146
    work on Mr. Happy Go Lucky, 133–34, 139

work on Trouble No More, 170–71
"Suffragette Cry," 11
Summer Work Tour, 167, 168–69
Sun Devil Stadium (Tempe), 54
Sun Volt, 150
Sunshine Records, 14, 16
Supersuckers, 132
"Suzanne," 121
"Sweet Evening Breeze," 120–21
Sweet Music (Roadmaster album), 49
"Sweet Suzanne," 109
Swenson, John, 23
Sykes, John, 53, 66, 148–49, 177
Sykes, Keith, 58

T
Taliefero, Crystal, 81–82, 87–90, 93, 113
"Taxi Dancer," 25, 30
Taylor, James, 149, 164, 168
"Teardrops Will Fall," 170, 172
Tedeschi, Susan, 150
Temptations, the, 6
Terrylene, 155
"Texas Bandito, The," 176
"Thank You," 178
"This Land Is Your Land," 150, 176, 181
"This May Not Be the End of the World," 136
"This Time," 37, 38, 178
"This Time" video, 39, 40
"This Train Is Bound for Glory," 168
Thoener, David, 62, 63, 64, 146, 160
Thriller (Jackson album), 77
"Thrill's a Thrill, A," 58
"Thundering Hearts," 46, 51
"Tickets First" VH-1 promotion, 139, 140
Tiger Force Band, 19–20, 22–23
Tikis, the, 6
"Times They Are A-Changin', The", 8
"To Washington," 172
Todd, Joe, 65–66
Tom Petty and the Heartbreakers, 79
"Tonight," 39
Too Long the Wasteland (McMurtry album), 104
Torgoff, Martin, 12, 29, 37, 44, 54, 64
Toto, 59
Trash, 11–12, 18
Tritt, Travis, 175–76
Troggs, the, 74
Trouble No More (album), 169–72, 175
Trouble No More (DVD package), 171
"Turn on Your Love Light," 84
Tweeter Center (Boston), 163
"Twentieth Century Fox," 23
"Twist, The," 6

U

U2, 139
Uh-Huh (album), 61–66, 124
Uh-Huh Tour, 67–68, 84
UMe/Universal Republic, 183
"Under the Boardwalk," 84, 143, 150–51
Underwood, Carrie, 180
"Universal Soldier, The," 7–8
Urban, Keith, 93–94, 175
Uriah Heep, 37, 41
"U.S. Male," 31
USDA protest, 85
Use Your Illusions (Guns N Roses albums), 116
Usher, 180

V

Van Halen, 79
Vasquez, Junior, 127, 134–35
Vawter, Will, 69
Very Special Christmas, A (benefit album), 92
VH-1 network, 106, 128, 138–39, 148–49, 150, 178
Vincennes University, 10–11
Vision Shared, A: A Tribute to Woody Guthrie & Leadbelly (benefit album), 90
Vote for Change Tour, 176–78, 179

W

Wakefield Summit, 19
"Walk Tall," 178, 179, 181
"Walkin' My Shadow," 11
Wallflowers, the, 162
Wanchic, Mike, vi, vii
   on Aronoff's aggressiveness, 38
   on Aronoff's audition, 34, 35
   band bonus controversy and, 111
   on band's basketball games, 82
   on band's behavior, 82
   on band's musical prowess, 86
   on *Big Daddy*, 100
   on branding, 184
   as co-producer for "Your Forever," 156
   divorce of, 86
   on early band days, 30, 31
   early life and career of, 19
   on flag football games, 83–84
   on Gaff, 25, 27
   on Gehman's firing, 98
   on Grammy awards, 164
   Grissom and, 99
   joins band, 37
   on Lonesome Jubilee Tour, 93
   Mahern and, 142
   on making of *American Fool*, 43, 44, 48
   on making of *Uh-Huh*, 62
   on Market Square Arena show, 54
   on Mr. Happy Go Lucky Tour, 139
   on Myers, 49
   on Myers' marriage, 132
   personality of, 29
   on replacing Aronoff, 137–38
   on Rural Electrification Tour, 150
   on *Saturday Night Live* performance, 50
   side projects of, 80, 159
   talent of, 28
   in Tiger Force Band, 19–20
   tour responsibilities of, 55
   on Uh-Huh Tour, 67–68
   on Who tour, 55–56
   work on *American Fool*, 44–48
   work on *Cuttin' Heads*, 156–58
   work on *Dance Naked*, 124–29
   work on *Falling from Grace* soundtrack, 109
   work on *Freedom's Road*, 181–84
   work on *Human Wheels*, 120–23
   work on *John Mellencamp*, 145–46
   work on *Lonesome Jubilee*, 87–90
   work on McMurtry album, 104
   work on *Mr. Happy Go Lucky*, 133–37
   work on Ryder album, 57
   work on *Scarecrow*, 74–75
   work on *Trouble No More*, 169–72
   work on *Uh-Huh*, 63, 65
   York and, 123
Waters, John, 40
Waters, Roger, 168
"We Are the People," 88
Weeks, Willie, 63–64, 103, 157, 159
Weinstein, Harvey, 177
Weisner, Ron, 124
Welch, Kevin, 105
Wenner, Jann, 132, 177
Wessex Studios (London), 27
West, Kanye, 180
"What Say You," 175
"When Jesus Left Birmingham," 121, 122, 142
"When Jesus Left Birmingham" video, 123
"When Love Comes to Town," 150
"When You Were Mine," 58, 59
Whenever We Wanted (album), 111, 113–17
Whenever We Wanted Tour, 117–18
Whisky-A-Go-Go (Los Angeles club), 26, 30
White, Judy, 168
White, Ryan, 106
White, Timothy, 126, 142, 143, 148, 149, 165, 167–68
"White Room," 86
Whitted, Pharez, 114
Who, the, 54–55, 164

Why Store, the, 138
"Wild Angel," 37
"Wild Night," 126, 139, 150–51
"Wild Night" CD single, 127, 128
"Wild Night" video, 128
Wild One, The (film), 13
"Wild Thing," 74
Wilentz, Sean, 176
Williams, Big Joe, 123
Williams, Hank, 169
Williams, Hank, Jr., 127
Williams, Lucinda, 170
Williams, Tennessee, 156
Wilson, Ann and Nancy, 51
Wince, Tom "Bub," 19
Wissing, Kevin, 11
"Without Expression," 142, 145
"Women Seem," 157
Woodford, David, 37
Woodstock (film), 12
Words and Music (greatest hits collection), 178–79
Words and Music Tour, 179–80, 181
"World Don't Bother Me None, The," 176
World Trade Center (New York), 163
"Worn Out Nervous Condition," 157
"Wreck of the Old 97," 176
Wurlitzer organ, 139

X

X, 79

Y

Yearwood, Trisha, 161
Yoakam, Dwight, 104, 109
York, Andy, vi
    on Dance Naked Tour, 128
    with Hearts and Minds, 104
    on Indianapolis tornado, 180
    joins band, 123–24
    on Mr. Happy Go Lucky Tour, 139
    on Rural Electrification Tour, 150
    on Summer Work Tour, 169
    work on *Cuttin' Heads,* 156–58
    work on *Dance Naked,* 125
    work on *Freedom's Road,* 182
    work on *John Mellencamp,* 145–46
    work on *Trouble No More,* 169–72
Young, Neil, 79, 132, 180
"Your Life Is Now," 147, 177
"You're a Step in the Right Direction," 68, 94
"Yours Forever," 155–56

Z

Zappa, Frank, 80
"Ziggy," 11
Zimmerman, Duane, 7
Zippo-Evans, Tina Marie, 165
Zone, The, 30–31, 34–41, 51, 55
    basketball games of, 82
    flag football games of, 83–84
    name dropped, 86
ZZ Top, 49